Media Discours

Accession no.
6166245

D1335206

Media Topics

Series editor: Valerie Alia

Titles in the series include:

Media Discourse
Representation and Interaction

Mary Talbot

Edinburgh University Press

© Mary Talbot, 2007

Edinburgh University Press Ltd
22 George Square, Edinburgh

Typeset in Janson and Neue Helvetica
by Hewer Text UK Ltd, Edinburgh, and
printed and bound in Great Britain by
Antony Rowe Ltd, Chippenham, Wilts

A CIP record for this book is available from the British Library

ISBN 978 0 7486 2347 1 (hardback)
ISBN 978 0 7486 2348 8 (paperback)

The right of Mary Talbot
to be identified as author of this work
has been asserted in accordance with
the Copyright, Designs and Patents Act 1988.

Contents

Part Two: Representation and interaction

Acknowledgements

Thanks first of all to my husband, Bryan, for his support throughout. Thanks also to the anonymous readers of the initial book proposal for inspiring suggestions for interdisciplinary links. I would also like to acknowledge the invaluable support of the University of Sunderland School of Arts, Design, Media and Culture, since without a semester's research leave in late 2005 I could not have begun this book. Thanks too to colleagues past and present at the University of Sunderland for inspiration, interesting discussions and suggestions, comments on drafts and sometimes even data: Karen Atkinson, Richard Berry, Michael Higgins, Myra Macdonald, Shaun Moores, Michael Pearce, Angela Smith and John-Paul Stephenson. Thanks also to two students on our *Broadcast Talk* module for transcribed data: Emma Lawrence and Sarah Winter. In writing this book I have drawn on the support, inspiration, interesting discussions, suggestions, comments on drafts and data afforded by many people, all of whom I thank, and none of whom I have intentionally omitted to thank; if I have failed in this respect it is not through want of appreciation but memory. The primary sources I have used are all covered by the 'fair dealing' agreement. Sincere thanks, anyway, to the production teams whose prodigious efforts went into creating them.

Transcription conventions

CU	close-up
MCU	mid close-up
MLS	mid long shot
LS	long shot
v/o	voice over
[	Links simultaneous speech
::	vowel lengthening
(.)	pause
xx-	incomplete utterance
=	latching (immediate follow-on)
(xx)	indistinct utterance
.h	inhalation
h	exhalation
(h)	laughter in speech
?	rising intonation

>relative increase in rate of delivery shown by number of chevrons<
<relative decrease in rate of delivery shown by number of chevrons>
<u>heavy emphasis</u>
LOUDNESS
[gestures and other 'business']

Part One

Key issues in analysing media discourse

1 Introduction: media and discourse

Media discourse is a multidisciplinary field. In addition to extensive interest in media and cultural studies, it is the subject of scrutiny in linguistics – particularly conversation analysis, critical discourse analysis, ethnography of communication, linguistic anthropology, pragmatics and sociolinguistics – and also in cultural geography, psychology, sociology and tourism studies. This diversity and spread is both a strength and a weakness. There have been developments in parallel in a range of disciplines. One concern of this book is to explore some overlapping concerns, common origins and influences. The disciplinary diversity of media discourse as a field is reflected in its methodologies. However, discourse analysis is a method that cuts across many of them, and the conventions of discourse analysis are at the heart of this book.

What is media discourse and why study it?

Very few of us, if any, are unaffected by media discourse. The importance of the media in the modern world is incontrovertible. For some sections of society, at least, the media have largely replaced older institutions (such as the Church, or trade unions) as the primary source of understanding of the world. Since discourse plays a vital role in constituting people's realities, the implications for the power and influence of media discourse are clear. Moreover, in modern democracies the media serve a vital function as a public forum. In principle, journalists are committed to democratic principles in relation to the government, hence to provision of a diversity of sources of opinion about it – a function (highly) idealised as the provision of 'a robust, uninhibited, and wide-open marketplace of ideas, in which opposing views may meet, contend, and take each other's measure' (Gurevitch and Blumler 1990: 269). Everyday engagement with media, then, is hugely significant and a theoretical understanding of this engagement is crucial.

Underlying this book is a sustained interrogation of the concept of 'interaction', problematic in the context of mediated communication. There is a great deal of hype surrounding 'interactivity' in contemporary media, especially in broadcasting. In a televised lecture, Dawn Airey (Managing Director of Sky Networks) claimed that the best of contemporary television engages in a 'two-way conversation with the audience' (Airey 2005). In direct contrast with this view, however, it is well understood in media and cultural studies that – as viewers, readers and listeners – people 'merely' engage with representations. People in production communities interact with one another in their highly complex, joint production of texts; these texts, in turn, are consumed as spectacles by people in audience communities, in ways that are equally complex. It is axiomatic that mass-media practitioners and their audiences rarely engage in direct dialogue, though a quasi-interaction has been labelled 'para-social' and studied variously as 'broadcast sociability' and 'synthetic personalisation'.

In this book, I identify three distinct sites of interaction involving media discourse that I intend to explore: interactions in production communities, interactions in audience communities and 'interactivity' between producers and audiences. Producers of media texts interact with one another in production communities; they perceive audience in terms of demographics, not as interlocutors; for producers of media texts, audiences are commodities sold to advertisers. Some of this interaction is broadcast or appears in print, for consumption by audiences. Viewers, readers and listeners interact with one another in audience communities. People engage in practices of face-to-face interaction that involve media discourse as part of their daily lives. As Ron Scollon argues in his study of news discourse, while media practitioners 'carry on their social interaction as a spectacle for the consumption of the reader or viewer, those readers and viewers are using the spectacle as an active component of the construction of their own social environments and social interactions' (1998: ix). Interactivity of numerous kinds is possible between producers and individual audience members, however. Radio phone-ins, for example, are well established, letters pages even more so. New technologies of cable, satellite and the Internet have greatly enhanced the interactive potential of broadcast media: live webchat, user generated content and so-called interactive red buttons among them. The book will culminate with attention to such recent developments in TV and radio interactivity. These developments are primarily understood in terms of a rhetoric of dialogue, one which is equally relevant to print media.

The importance of attending to how the media 'provide inhabitable discourses that form the substance of culture and experience' (Spitulnik 2000: 149) is well understood within media studies and linguistic anthropology. For some linguists, on the other hand, interest in media discourse lies simply in the accessibility of language data, given the need to avoid, if possible, the observer's paradox that dogs any observation of naturally-occurring behaviour. In a brief overview of linguistic engagement with media language up to1990, Allan Bell points out its ready availability as data for the study of sociolinguistic phenomena: 'laboratory instances' of particular types of style shift, a proliferation of news stories for the study of narrative production, an abundant archive of material for investigating language change over time, a never-ending stream of broadcast talk for analysing the use of language in interaction among groups (Bell 1991: 3–4). In early sociolinguistics, media language was treated as second-best data for investigation of language patterning, because it was seen to fall short of the ideal of 'real', spontaneous conversation (e.g., Labov 1972). Fortunately, however, other language scholars have long had an interest in media language in its own right and, indeed, continue to do so. Media is a key public domain of language use for the sociology of language, along with Education and Government. Some of Erving Goffman's microsociological studies of the 'presentation of self' were based on scrutiny of radio presenters' talk that was extensive in scope and quite detailed (Goffman 1981). By no means least, Bell's own attention to media discourse – to the specifics of the joint production of copy in the news industries, to the dynamics of editing processes, to the structure of written news narratives and so on – testifies to his prolonged commitment to understanding the products and processes of the discourse of news media (Bell 1991, 1997). (For a fuller survey and assessment of work in the field, see the chapter on 'Approaches to media discourse' in Fairclough (1995a).)

But what do I mean by 'media discourse'? An initial broad understanding might be in terms of what it is not – direct, face-to-face communication – as Debra Spitulnik suggests (2000: 148). However, while this may serve as a starting point, it will turn out to be an inadequate definition, as I hope will become clear throughout the course of this book. Indeed, this whole book is an attempt to provide a more effective, even if still partial definition. Media discourse circulates in and across institutions and it is deeply embedded in the daily life and daily interaction of almost everyone. Attention to media and the circuit of culture and to the concept of discourse will flesh out this observation.

Media and the circuit of culture

In cultural studies, culture is broadly understood in terms of 'shared meanings' (Hall 1997: 1). In the modern world, the media are of paramount significance in the circulation of these 'meanings'. Stuart Hall presents them as being shared through language in its operation as a representational (signifying) system, and he presents the circuit of culture model as a way of understanding this process. We must bear in mind here that language is being understood broadly to include all systems of signification, as is common in cultural studies. Hall is introducing a volume whose chapters are offered to 'push forward and develop our understanding of how representation actually *works*' (ibid.: 2). The chapters deal with visual 'language' modalities, especially photography and painting, and do not focus on either speech or writing.

In the circuit of culture, meaning is produced at different sites, and circulated, in a continuous process (see Fig. 1.1).

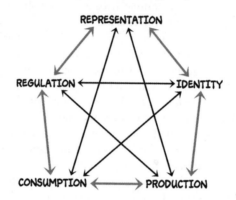

Figure 1.1   The Circuit of Culture (*Source*: Adapted from Hall 1997)

The model in Figure 1.1 is a refined version of Hall's original encoding/decoding model, first published in 1973. In its original form (Fig. 1.2), it was designed specifically to explore television discourse by identifying various sites where meanings are produced and establishing their relative independence from one another.[1]

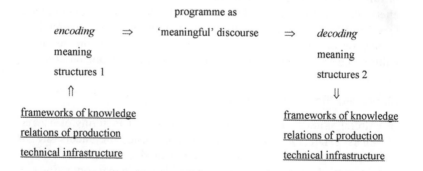

Figure 1.2   The Circuit of Culture (*Source*: Hall 1980)

Hall's article was a direct attack on the current, highly reductive 'sender–receiver' model of mass communication.[2] He was drawing upon semiotics to challenge the behaviourism in communication research of the period. He took issue with the simplistic notion of communication as a sender – message – receiver chain, in which the message being transmitted was assumed to have a transparently recognisable content. A semiotic understanding of language was central to his challenge to the notion of message transparency:

> Reality exists outside language, but it is constantly mediated by and through language; and what we can know or say has to be produced in and through discourse. Discursive 'knowledge' is the product not of the transparent representation of the 'real' in language but of the articulation of language on real relations and conditions.
>
> (Hall 1980: 131)

Utilising a notion of 'code' from semiology (Barthes 1967, 1973; Eco 1976) he introduced a concept of naturalisation:

> There is no intelligible discourse without the operation of a code. . . . Certain codes may, of course, be so widely distributed in a specific language community or culture, and be learned at so early an age, that they appear not to be constructed as the effect of an articulation between sign and referent – but to be 'naturally' given. . . . However, this does not mean that no codes have intervened; rather, that the codes have been profoundly *naturalised.*
>
> (ibid.: 131–2)

In his challenge to the sender–receiver model, Hall emphasised the importance of specific cultural conditions at every stage of any communication process. Creators of media texts produce them in particular institutional contexts, drawing on shared knowledge frameworks, professional norms etc; the same media texts are engaged with by audiences in different cultural contexts, where the resources drawn upon to understand them (or not, as the case may be) cannot be assumed to be the same. Hall is emphasising that the social processes involved in encoding the meanings of media texts are not the same as those involved in decoding them, to the extent that we simply cannot assume that the texts 'mean the same' to producers as to audiences.

The focus on both relations between production and consumption and on representation is particularly evident in the recent version of the model (Fig. 1.1) and marks the influence of Antonio Gramsci and Michel Foucault on cultural studies as an emerging discipline (Storey 2003: 5). The model is valuable for identifying appropriate sites for engagement with media discourse. It challenges assumptions about textual analysis, offering a corrective to unreflective assumptions that the text is the site of meaning and that the author is its originator. It also, of course, counteracts disregard for the reader's production of meaning. This is an issue explored in studies of audiences and popular culture (Fiske 1987; Morley 1980). Attention to audience reception was a corrective to the tendency to read off meaning from media texts and to assume their effects on audiences.

But losing sight of the text altogether is equally a problem, as linguists are quick to point out. As Norman Fairclough observes, for example, 'although readings may vary, any reading is a product of an interface between the properties of the text and the interpretative resources and practices which the interpreter brings to bear upon the text' (1995a: 16). Even when the textual point of the 'circuit' *is* engaged with within media and cultural studies, however, some of the resulting analysis can be frustratingly thin, from a language studies perspective, at least. There often seems to be a curious lack of attention *to* texts in discussion of them. For example, there is an interesting and detailed study of men's magazines that professes to engage with them in terms of production-text-consumption (Jackson et al. 2001). The authors include a chapter addressing 'Questions of content'. In it, they claim to focus on 'verbal content' (2001: 74) – with the aim of attending to sexual politics, personal relations, men's health and irony – but then go on to loosely describe it, without providing examples. While they claim to engage in narrative and stylistic analysis, what they actually present is rarely recognisable as either (ibid.: 76–7), though elsewhere in the same chapter they do provide some convincing sociological analysis (for example, p. 79), and, eventually, some interesting exploration of metaphor is brought into a section on men's health magazines (for example, body-as-machine on p. 98). In their coverage of irony, they reach similar conclusions to the more recently published work of Bethan Benwell, but without any of her theoretical or illustrative detail (Benwell 2004) (see Chapter 3 in this volume). Textual 'analysis' that bypasses language and merely describes its 'content' is seriously impoverished; the language in which meaning is articulated is *part of that meaning* and 'one cannot properly analyse content without simultaneously analysing form, because contents are always necessarily realized in forms . . . form is a part of content' (Fairclough 1995b: 188).

Linguistic anthropologists are also interested in the social circulation of media discourse; they focus closely on community and, of course, on language. As with cultural studies, linguistic anthropology views the social circulation of discourse as vital in the production of 'shared meanings' that constitute a society; it is this circulation that creates 'public accessibility' (Spitulnik 1997: 162 citing Urban 1991). In most accounts, this circulation seems to be construed as top-down, that is, with all the 'meanings' originating in the texts that are created by media professionals. Debra Spitulnik's own contribution to the field is particularly interesting because, as she puts it, it 'exhibits somewhat of a reverse direction – where the widespread availability of the communication form itself creates possibilities for social circulation' (ibid.). While her spatial metaphor is slightly awry (she refers to 'sideways' communication, not 'bottom-up', which would be the reverse of 'top-down') it is nevertheless a telling one. The point she is making is that pools of resources descend, as it were, from above, which makes them available for use 'sideways', by audience communities among themselves. She focuses on both the linguistic substance and availability of shared meanings in communities: 'because of the extensive accessibility and scope, mass media can serve as both reservoirs and reference points for the circulation of words, phrases, and discourse styles in popular culture' (ibid.). (I return to this issue in Chapter 7, in the section on 'Television talk and talking with the television'.) In linguistic anthropology, as in sociolinguistics, speech community is standardly defined in terms of shared language and density and frequency of interaction. Community is traditionally established and maintained by people in direct contact. In studying the circulation of media discourse, naturally, we are not often dealing with such direct, community-establishing contact. Community on such large scale needs to be understood as imagined, in Benedict Anderson's sense (Anderson 1983). Along these lines, Spitulnik offers a refinement of the sociolinguistic concept of speech community by the addition of criteria 'such as frequency of media consumption and large-scale exposure to a common media source' (1997: 181).

Texts, discourse and discourses

A distinction is often made in linguistics between *text* and *discourse*. This distinction can be useful in an exploration of media discourse and its circulation. We can use the term *text* to mean the observable product of interaction: a cultural object; and *discourse* to mean the process of interaction itself: a cultural activity. This distinction between *text* and *discourse* is an analytical one; it distinguishes between the observable material of a completed product and the ongoing process of making it (Brown and Yule 1983; Halliday 1985). This emphasises that text is the fabric in which discourse is manifested, whether spoken or written, whether produced by one person or several. The distinction, then, is between product and process, between object and activity. As I said, *text* here refers to an observable product. In terms of interaction, it often only comes into play as a category with an interest in interaction that is mediated. A text is something that is transportable from one context to another: a letter, a book, a DVD, an email message or some other artefact that is 'designed in one context with a view to its uptake in others' (Chouliaraki and Fairclough 1999: 45). From a broader cultural studies' perspective on signification, of course, *text* may involve other modes of representation in addition to language as is it understood within linguistics.[3] In fact, even in more linguistically-oriented approaches these days, *text* is also commonly understood to include images and other non-linguistic signifying elements, though actual attention to them is variable (Fairclough 1995a; Graddol and Boyd-Barrett 1994; Hodge and Kress 1988; Kress and van Leeuwen 2001).

Discourse is not a product; it is a process. To analyse it we need to look at both the text itself and the interaction and context that the text is embedded in. A text is part of the process of discourse and it is pointless to study it in isolation. It is the product of a meaning-producer (encoder) and a resource for a meaning-interpreter (decoder). We need to further unpack the term *discourse*, however. It has various meanings, two of which I will elaborate on as I intend to use them in combination.

In modern linguistics, discourse analysis is generally understood to involve the study of language in use. Discourse analysts investigate language as social interaction. In the early 1980s, one of the first books on discourse analysis characterised the emerging area as 'a **discourse-as-process** view . . . an approach which takes the communicative function of language as its primary area of investigation' (Brown and Yule 1983: 24). Much of the work in this tradition examines processes of discourse production and interpretation in close linguistic detail (see, for example, the journal *Discourse processes*). Underlying a lot of analyses of spoken discourse there is an assumption that, in looking at speech, the way something is said is as interesting and as significant as *what* is being said. Conventions of transcription – the practice of rendering spoken language in a written mode, as a text – have evolved in attempts to produce written representations of talk that do not indiscriminately erase the pauses and hesitations, the sighs and mumbles, the gasps, the laughter and the intakes of breath that are the reality of speech, at least of speech that is unscripted and unrehearsed. Linguists whose method is discourse analysis, then, are interested in the details of language in action in specific situations. In order to scrutinise spoken interaction, they painstakingly transcribe recordings of it to produce written texts that provide a representation of it that is sufficiently detailed for the purposes of their analysis. They may be investigating strategies in news interviews or doctor–patient dialogues, the function of casual conversation in workplace settings and so on. Of course, discourse analysts can equally engage with written or signed language, from the perspective of its use in interaction in specific contexts.

A contrasting use of discourse can be found in the work of Michel Foucault. Here the focus is not so much interaction, as what is spoken or written *about*: ideas, knowledge, opinions, beliefs. From this perspective, discourses are structures of possibility and constraint; they are historically-constituted social constructions in the organisation and circulation of knowledge. A particularly clear-cut, therefore useful, example is medicine: it is a body of knowledge, practices and social identities that has developed historically. Medical discourse defines health and sickness. A particular disease – as an object defined by the discourse – consists of all that has been said and written about it. Medical discourse also determines who has the power to define, in the social identities it bestows, that is to say, it positions people as experts or not. Crucially, Foucault does not present power as the property of powerful groups (such as the ruling class or capitalists) but as something circulated and deployed in discourse. He is engaging with the nature of the relationship between person and society and the part played by discourse in this relationship. Discourses *position* people as social subjects. When social changes bring about the intersection of a range of discourses, they may open up new subject positions for individuals; for example, in the 1980s the 'new man' emerged as a 'new subject-position opened up within the contemporary visual discourse of fashion, style and individual consumption' (Nixon 1997: 304).

In contrast with the analysis of discourse in linguistics, Foucault does not pay close attention to language at all (see Fairclough 1992a). What he does provide is a view of language as discursive, which avoids a false division between agency and structure. This artificial division is embodied in the distinction between *langue* and *parole* that is still used in semiotics. First coined by Ferdinand de Saussure (1916), the distinction separates the whole language system as an abstract set of rules (*langue*) from the act of speaking (*parole*). What Foucault does is to examine the social constitution in language of accumulated conventions (that is, structure) related to bodies of knowledge, by investigating how power is exercised through them (that is, agency), including how they define social identities.

Some brief observations he makes about the 'unity' or discreteness of texts and discourses are interesting as they challenge the easy notion of a 'solid' self-contained text by highlighting its intertextuality or inter-discursivity. He points out that 'the materiality of the book' (picture it bounded by its front and back cover) is only one kind of 'unity' and by no means the most significant. For example, a camcorder instruction manual and an anthology of poems are both concrete texts, but it is the unity that each derives from *discourse* that constitutes them as instruction manual and anthology. Discourses may not be as obviously tangible as individual texts, but in an important sense they are far more durable. Foucault maintains, plausibly, that the physical unity a single actual text has (inside that front and back cover) is weaker than the 'discursive unity of which it is the support' (2002: 25). This 'discursive unity' itself is not homogeneous. To illustrate this point we could contrast the relation between the novels that compose Dan Brown's output as a novelist with the relation between, say, *The da Vinci code* and *Holy blood, holy grail*, which was a 1960s treatment of the same quasi-historical material. The point Foucault is making is that there is more to a text than its concrete, physical form. It only exists in relation with other texts, as 'a node within a network' in a mesh of intertextual relations:

> The frontiers of a book are never clear-cut . . . it is caught up in a system of references to other books, other texts, other sentences: it is a node within a network. . . . It indicates itself, constructs itself, only on the basis of a complex field of discourse.
>
> (ibid.: 25–6)

What comes through clearly here is the constitutive, productive character of discourse: he is, as he says, not 'treating discourse as groups of signs . . . but as practices that systematically form the objects of which they speak.' (ibid.: 54) What he is articulating is a break from structuralist semiotics. He goes on to concede that

> Of course, discourses are composed of signs; but what they do is more than use these signs to designate things. It is this more that renders them irreducible to language [*langue*] and to speech. It is this 'more' that we must reveal and describe'.
>
> (ibid.)

Discourse as social practice in critical discourse analysis

Since its emergence as a field, critical discourse analysis (henceforth CDA) has, like cultural studies, been influenced by Gramsci and Foucault. An early influence on CDA that is perhaps less apparent is cultural studies itself, especially Hall's seminal work on encoding/ decoding and ideological positioning (e.g., Fairclough 1992b). CDA engages directly with the circuit-of-culture model, given its 'political aim of putting the forms of texts, the processes of production of texts, and the process of reading, together with the structures of power that have given rise to them, into crisis' (Kress 1990: 85). Common to both are a Marxist stance, the pivotal importance of language and the 'struggle over

meaning' (Voloshinov 1973: 23) and, in relation to media, an understanding of its active role in the formation of consensus in modern
democracies (e.g., Clark and Ivanič 1997: 27).

The two senses of discourse outlined in the previous section come from
different analytical traditions. Understanding them as complementary, the
CDA formulation of discourse as social practice combines them. Discourses are bodies of knowledge and practice that shape people. They give
positions of power to some but not others. But they can only come into
existence by taking place in social interaction in specific situations. Each
being entirely dependent on the other, they exist in a dialectical relationship. Consider an example: reading about 'bogus asylum seekers' in a
newspaper. That particular discursive event (reading the paper) does not
happen in a social vacuum; it is shaped by situational, institutional and
social structures. But it also shapes them, in the sense that it helps either to
sustain the (racist) status quo or, perhaps, to contribute to transforming it.
As social practice, then, discourse is highly influential, since, as Fairclough
and Wodak (1997) put it, it is 'socially *constitutive* as well as socially shaped:
it constitutes situations, objects of knowledge, and the social identities of
and relationships between people and groups of people' (p. 258).

Figure 1.3 represents this dual view of discourse, encapsulating the
CDA conception of discourse as social practice as formulated in Fairclough (1992a and 1995a).

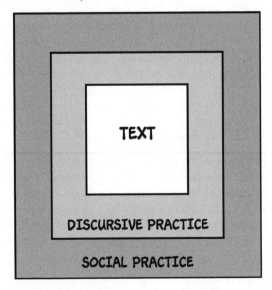

Figure 1.3 A framework for critical discourse analysis of a communicative
event

The text is in the centre, embedded within discourse practice, which is itself embedded in sociocultural practice. As a product, the text consists of traces of production processes (Hall's 'encoding'). From the position of the person decoding it, it is a resource, consisting of cues for interpretation processes (Hall's 'decoding'). It has 'meaning potential' only (Halliday 1978). Writing about television news broadcasts, Ulrike Meinhof observes that

> no audience is just a receptacle for a given set of messages. . . . there are multiple realisations of the meaning of a text, which in turn depend on the viewers' motivation and ability to rapidly and intuitively draw inferences across visual and oral channels. Viewers must actively create their own texts by responding to a sophisticated interplay of visual and oral stimuli, they must be willing and able to activate their previous knowledge and engage with the broadcast.
>
> (Meinhof 1994: 221)

Focusing solely on the verbal component of this text, we can take this point further, in a fuller and more technical way, as follows. As a resource for the interpreter, a verbal text consists of lexico-grammatical realisations and *nothing else*. These realisations relate to three basic language functions that are inherent in any text (the ideational, interpersonal and textual meta-functions of systemic functional linguistics). The ideational function is perhaps easiest to come to grips with, since it refers to the function of language to communicate ideas, to language as representation. The interpersonal function refers to the function of language of establishing and maintaining social identities and relationships. Note that texts embody ideational and interpersonal meanings simultaneously; they are always both representation and social interaction. The third, textual function, refers to the text-creating function of language – put simply, how a text hangs together. This three-way distinction offers a useful way of thinking about language

> because it allows us to distinguish between the way in which the writer/speaker relates to the world of ideas, or the propositional content of texts [ideational], how s/he relates to the receiver(s) of those ideas [interpersonal], and the way in which the writer/speaker organises these into a cohesive stretch of discourse [textual].
>
> (Clark and Ivanič 1997: 162)

These lexico-grammatical cues to ideational, interpersonal and textual meanings are interpreted with the help of other resources *beyond* the text. A text only has meaning when it is engaged with, but its formal features impose constraints on what it can mean, on how it can be interpreted.

In CDA, textual analysis involves both linguistic and intertextual analysis. The latter requires focus on the genres and discourses that are drawn upon. As it is understood in CDA, intertextual analysis is influenced by Foucault's work on discourse and also by Bakhtin's theory of dialogism (see Chapter 4 of this volume on 'Dialogism and voice'). Texts are understood as enactments of particular text-types, or genres. Genre expectations about a particular text that viewers, listeners and readers may have will influence their interpretation of it (see Chapter 2 of this volume on 'Reconfigurations' for some detailed attention to media genres). The media order of discourse is a domain of cultural power and hegemony (Fairclough 1995a: 67) that has complex configurations of discourses and genres which intersect public and private spheres (Chapter 2 also engages with the blurring of the domains of public and private).

About this book

To examine media discourse we need a model that facilitates attention to more than representations. As forthcoming chapters will argue, aspects of the interpersonal are crucial in understanding it. Martin Montgomery observed in the mid-1980s that

'If we are to have a comprehensive account of the role of media discourse in the reproduction of social life, then it must be one that includes the interpersonal dimension of talk as well as its ideational aspects – the social relational as well as the ideological.

(Montgomery 1986: 88)

In any case, as CDA has since argued strongly, the social relational is full of ideological significance. This book picks up the argument and takes it further (see especially Chapter 6 on 'Interpersonal meaning in broadcast texts: representing social identities and relationships'). It is not a matter of choosing between either one or the other, but of giving due and proper attention to both.

What I set about to do in this book is, in a sense, to insert discourse-as-interaction into the circuit of culture model presented in Figure 1.1. In this opening chapter, I have begun to establish the book's model of media discourse in the following way: I have brought together the notions of the cultural circuit from cultural studies and of discourse as social practice from CDA; I have identified three distinct sites of interaction involving media discourse that I will go on the explore in Part Two – production communities, audience communities and producer-audience interaction; I complete the picture by adding three modes of interaction (Thompson 1995) in Chapter 5, which introduces into the model an extended exploration of media simulations of interaction. Meanwhile, three chapters present a further range of issues and concepts that are necessary for an exploration of contemporary media discourse. Chapter 2 is entitled 'Reconfigurations' and deals with issues of modernity. Chapter 3, on 'Texts and positioning', explores some influences on CDA, particularly from cultural studies, and then exemplifies the kind of text-focused critical investigation characteristic of its approach. Chapter 4 takes up issues of 'Dialogism and voice'.

This volume examines (and is relevant to) media discourse generally, but there is more coverage of broadcast talk than print, especially in Part Two 'Representation and Interaction.' I have tried to attend as much to radio as to television and where possible to draw out parallels in print media. Much is applicable to all. The overall organisation of the book is not by genre or case study but, as the title says, by issues of representation and interaction. It is within that remit that the case studies fall into place. In examining interaction from a range of perspectives, there is some inevitable overlap, particularly across case studies attending to simulations, representations and participation frameworks in production communities. However, the analytical distinction that I make should be abundantly clear. A glossary of discourse analytic terms used is provided as an appendix.

Finally, given the potential scope of the subject, I should acknowledge that there are clearly limitations in what anyone can hope to cover in a single volume. It is for this reason only that I focus on non-fiction genres. Moreover, in this book the mass media is at the centre, to the exclusion of a proliferation of other fascinating forms of modern media discourse. For example, I simply do not have space to begin to explore the formation of online communities in special interest groups, such as soap fandom (Baym 2000) or to do any justice to the Internet as an 'alternative' medium (Atton 2004).

I hope you enjoy reading this book as much as I enjoyed writing it.

Notes

1. I have included both because in some respects the earlier one is more informative but, as Hall says, he

    made a mistake by drawing that bloody diagram with only the top half. You see, if you're doing a circuit, you must draw a circuit; so I must show how decoding enters practice and discourse which a reporter is picking up on. (Cruz and Lewis 1994: 260)

2. In a critical engagement with the Centre for Contemporary Cultural Studies' ideological approach to media analysis, Paddy Scannell oddly confuses it

with their object of criticism; he attributes to the encoding/decoding model the very reductiveness that the model was designed to challenge (Scannell 1991: 11).

3. Broader still: as everything can signify, everything can be 'read' as a text. But this is too all-encompassing to be helpful for media discourse.

Activities

Make a list of as many names for the social activity of talk as you can think of. How many of your examples are found in the media? Now do the same for the social activity of writing.

Keep a diary of one day's engagement with media, giving details of what, when, who with, why, how. How many other things were you doing at the same time? What were they?

Further reading

Bell, Allan and Garrett, Paul (eds) (1998), *Approaches to media discourse*, Oxford: Blackwell.

Cameron, Deborah (2001), *Working with spoken discourse*, London: Sage.

Fairclough, Norman (1992), *Discourse and social change*, Cambridge: Polity.

Fairclough, Norman (1995), *Media discourse*, London: Arnold.

Fairclough, Norman (2001), *Language and power* (2nd edn), London: Longman.

Graddol, David (1994), 'What is a text?' in Graddol, David and Boyd-Barrett, Oliver (eds), *Media texts: Authors and readers*, Clarendon: Multilingual Matters pp. 40–50.

Hall, Stuart (1980), 'Encoding/decoding', in Hall, Stuart, Hobson, Dorothy, Howe, Andrew and Willis, Paul (eds) *Culture, media, language*, London: Routledge pp. 128–38.

Macdonald, Myra (2003), *Exploring media discourse*, London: Arnold.

Richardson, John (2007), 'Analysing newspapers: context, text and consequence', in Richardson John, *Analysing newspapers: an approach from critical discourse analysis*, Basingstoke: Palgrave Macmillan, pp. 15–45.

Scannell, Paddy (1991), 'The relevance of talk', in Scannell, Paddy (ed.), *Broadcast talk*, London: Sage, pp. 1–13.

Talbot, Mary, Atkinson, Karen and Atkinson, David (2003), 'Language in the media', in Talbot, Mary et al., *Language and power in the modern world*, Edinburgh: Edinburgh University Press, pp. 9–71.

2 Reconfigurations

There is a range of concerns common to both media and cultural studies and critical discourse analysis, relating to shifts and reconfigurations that can be said to characterise the modern world. These concerns are the subject of this chapter.

I begin with issues relating to time, place and their compression in the modern media. I then go on to outline two tensions or dichotomies that will be familiar to anyone working in the field of media discourse. These are public and private, information and entertainment. Fairclough relates them to two tendencies, which he identifies (in characteristically abstract nominalisations) as the conversationalisation of public affairs media and marketisation in the shift towards entertainment (Fairclough 1995a: 10). The chapter concludes with attention to other hybrid media genres, including pastiche and parody.

Time and place

Discursive events always involve some form of addresser and addressee. If we take the example of a live theatre performance, both the actors (the addressers) and the audience (the addressees) are physically co-present, so that production (at least, its end result in a rehearsed performance) and consumption are taking place at the same time. Discourse in the media tends to be rather different; there is typically a considerable distance, in space and often in time, between the production of a media text and its consumption. In itself, of course, this disjunction between production and consumption is by no means a modern phenomenon. In fact, it is as old as writing itself.

Media texts have multiple producers; media text production involves highly complex chains of communication. For example, not only is news produced syntagmatically on an 'assembly line' (Bell 1991: 44), it is assembled paradigmatically in, and out of, a highly diverse range of communicative events in different genres, including interviews over the phone, press releases, briefings from the chief editor and so on and so forth. The complexity of this assembly can be seen in terms of inter-textual chains of texts in production. Consider, for instance, the sources for 'copy' that go on to become 'the news'. There is a tight timescale for the production of news copy that leads to an understandable preference among journalists for prefabricated sources that are already in news format (ibid.: 58). A single news broadcast on the radio has a complicated history, both in terms of its production and its consumption. The complex intertextuality of its production tends to be erased in the text that is made available for consumption. The timescale for production varies greatly according to genre and medium. A TV documentary may take many years and involve multiple locations, though there may be little evidence of the time elapsed in the eventual text that is available for transmission. We could perhaps simply liken this to the rehearsal and other pre-production preceding a polished stage performance, or to the messiness of written text production which is invisible in the version that is finally published. However, this has to be balanced with another consideration: for the subject matter of a documentary, information about timescale may be quite crucial.

In an observation specific to live broadcasting, Paddy Scannell remarks on the 'doubling' of place of broadcast events: 'Public events now occur, simultaneously, in two different places: the place of the event itself and that in which it is watched and heard. Broadcasting mediates between these two sites' (Scannell 1996: 76). Mulling over this observation, Shaun Moores reflects:

> Of course, it is only ever possible for any individual to be in one place at a time physically, but broadcasting nevertheless permits a live 'witnessing' of remote happenings that can bring these happenings experientially close or 'within range', thereby removing the 'farness'. In such circumstances, listeners and viewers may come to feel they are simultaneously 'here-and-there'.
>
> (Moores 2005: 63)

In a later chapter, he reflects on the phenomenon of international mourning following the death of Diana Princess of Wales in 1998 (ibid.: 78–81). An international audience was 'present' at her funeral. Scannell also remarks on the 'doubleness' of communicative interaction of all broadcast talk. As he points out, it has at least a 'double articulation' (Scannell 1991: 1), in that it is designed to be heard by more than one audience.

In a global economy in which North American and European con-glomerates dominate the media industries, the physical distance between the producers and consumers of media texts may be great indeed.

Predominantly, it is media texts produced in the industrialised 'West' that circulate globally, so that for the most part 'first-world' texts are consumed by 'third-world' audiences, but not vice versa.

In their bridging of geographical distance, the modern media contribute to the impression that the world we inhabit is getting smaller. There were enormous changes in the production, circulation and consumption of news media throughout the course of the last century. An illustration of the extent of these changes is provided by contrasting the coverage of two Antarctic expeditions, in 1913 and in 1999, as Allan Bell has done (Bell 2003).

Antarctica is the remotest continent on the globe and its most hostile environment. In January 1912, the Terra Nova expedition – a British team of explorers led by Captain Robert Falcon Scott – reached the South Pole. They had hauled their sledges themselves one-and-a-half-thousand miles to the Pole, having had to abandon their ponies at their base camp on the coast in McMurdo Sound. On arrival, they discovered that a rival Norwegian expedition, led by Roald Amundsen and more suitably equipped with dogs, had reached the Pole a month earlier. None of Scott's team survived the return journey; by March 1912, every member of the expedition was dead. A search party could not be sent out until November when the long Antarctic winter had passed, so that it was eight months before the bodies were found, along with Scott's diary containing a detailed account of the expedition's daily progress until its fatal end.

Once they were back in New Zealand, the relief party telegraphed the news secretly to London in February 1913. It was circulated to the world (including New Zealand) from there, in accordance with the 'imperial geography of news' (ibid.: 9) of the period. The events at the South Pole did not become news until a year after they took place. Tragic as they were, they formed an 'archetypal late-imperial story of heroism for Britain and Empire' (ibid.: 8).

In the Antarctic summer of 1998–99, a three-person team led by Peter Hillary undertook to complete, eighty-six years later, Scott's attempted sledge-haul from McMurdo Sound to the Pole and back. The technology at their disposal, however, made the undertaking somewhat different. They kept a video diary. They had a daily satellite phone-link keeping the media up to date with their progress, as well as satellite navigation. As weather conditions were deteriorating they flew back, rather than undertaking the hazardous return journey on foot. And, naturally, their arrival at the Pole was eagerly awaited by the media:

The expedition arrived at the Pole at 5.17 p.m., and the world heard of their arrival within minutes. An hour after they got there, Peter Hillary was sitting on a sledge at the South Pole doing a live audio interview on television and talking to his wife back home in New Zealand.

(ibid.: 14)

Bell speculates that the timing of the expedition's arrival (just in time for the prime evening slot) was orchestrated; indeed the whole sponsored trek can be seen as a 'pseudo-event' (Boorstin 1963: 59), an event organised specifically to generate media coverage. In New Zealand, Judy Bailey, an anchor on *One Network News*, presented the news item. Part of the coverage was a short phone interview with Hillary:

JB: Judy Bailey
PH: Peter Hillary

1. **JB:** And joining us now live by phone from the
2.   South Pole is Peter Hillary: Peter,
3.   congratulations to you all. Has it been
4.   worth it?
5. **PH:** Oh look it's – I must say having got
6.   here- ah- to the South Pole- everything
7.   seems worth it, Judy. I'm sitting on my
8.   sled at exactly ninety degrees south, it's
9.   nearly thirty degrees below zero, but I
10.   wouldn't- I wouldn't want to be anywhere
11.   else. It's just fantastic.
12. **JB:** Peter, how are you going to celebrate this
13.   wonderful achievement down there?
14. **PH:** Well I must say I think under different
15.   circumstances it could be very difficult
16.   but the Americans at the South Pole
17.   station have been most hospitable. About a
18.   hundred of them came out and cheered us as
19.   we arrived at the Pole and they've given
20.   us a wonderful meal. They're making us
21.   feel very very much at home. Look it's um-
22.   I don't think it's going to be any
23.   difficulty whatsoever. It's just wonderful
24.   to be here.
25. **JB:** Wonderful.

(adapted from Bell 2003: 14–15)

The interviewer and interviewee index the distance between them using the deictics 'here' (lines 6 and 24) and 'down there' (line 13). Hillary renders his first 'here' explicit, after a pause, with 'at the South Pole'. His details of grid reference and temperature also focus on his remote location, the key to the newsworthiness of his 'story'. At the same time, the informality of their social engagement closes up this distance, as does the detail about the hospitality of the Americans stationed at the Pole. Particularly striking things about this exchange are its 'liveness' (to which the false start and hesitation in 5 and 6 contribute), its informality and the domestication of the Antarctic wilderness. As a geographical location, the South Pole is extremely remote and inhospitable, yet in the news coverage it is represented as a domestic space: the Americans inhabiting the South Pole station provide the New Zealand team with 'a wonderful meal' and make them 'feel very very much at home' (lines 20–1). I return to the issue of informality in the expedition coverage later. In the following evening's TV coverage, the expedition team, back at McMurdo Sound, engaged in conversation with Hillary's wife Yvonne Oomen, their son and his father, Edmund Hillary, in New Zealand – with the help of TV cameras (Bell 2002: 62). This further intensified the domestication of Antarctica.

Public and private

In this section, I want to consider the claim that, in terms of social engagement in the modern world, the domains of public and private have in a significant sense become permeable and 'blurred'. Gunther Kress, a CDA practitioner, argues that the media define these domains: 'the media do not so much perform the function of regulating access to either domain, as to ensure the constant reproduction of both domains' (1986: 397). As he says, the media constantly assert the existence of public and private as distinct domains and assign events and activities to each. So, for example, domestic violence is private whereas football hooliganism is public (and the gendering of these activities is very evident: domestic violence is overwhelmingly a crime against women, but it is perceived as a private matter, not a public one and therefore not one of public concern) (see Talbot, Atkinson and Atkinson 2003). Kress makes it clear that this is a power issue:

> To assign an event to the sphere of the private is at once to declare it devoid of power, and to assign responsibility to individuals. . . . To classify an event as belonging to the public domain is to assert that it is

beyond individual responsibility and within the domain of social control.

(Kress 1986: 400)

The public–private division is sustained in newspaper genres: the front page is public; the letters pages (especially the 'agony columns') are private.

However, with something of a contradictory tendency, even while the boundary between the domains of public and private is constantly asserted, it seems to blur and intermingle. As Macdonald observes, in

the world of media representations, women seem to have taken occupation of public space, men are allowed to cry in public, actors pose as 'real' guests on talk shows and 'real' people become overnight celebrities on shows that we curiously describe as 'reality TV'.

(2003: 79)

Public events are made accessible for private consumption. Mass media texts are frequently produced from public domain source materials (such as political statements and speeches, press releases and interview transcripts), and then consumed in the private domain of people's homes. They *mediate* between public and private. On the other hand, private events may acquire public status as news. For instance, the anguish of bereaved parents may be presented as a newsworthy event, with cameras dwelling on their private behaviour (crying and otherwise expressing emotion) for the public's consumption. Part of the coverage of the Antarctic expedition in 1999 involved eavesdropping on a husband and wife's 'private' phone conversation. John Hawkesby, a second news-anchor covering the story on New Zealand television, conducted a live interview with Hillary and his wife Oomen. Hillary was linked by phone from the South Pole, Oomen on camera at their home in New Zealand:

```
JH:  John Hawkesby
YO:  Yvonne Oomen

1. JH: Peter's able to listen to you at the
2.     moment. Would you like- do you mind us
3.     eavesdropping if you just like to say to
4.     him-
5. YO: Oh no, that's fine. Darling,
6.     congratulations, I'm so proud of you.
7.     It's just so wonderful.
8. PH: Oh look, I'm delighted to be here and
```

```
 9.        I'm- I'm- ah- just glad to be talking to
10.        you- in fact I've- I partially did it for
11.        you too darling.
12. YO:    I know, I know.
```
(adapted from Bell 2003: 15)

Interpersonal rather than ideational meanings are being exchanged here. We hear terms of endearment ('darling' in lines 5 and 11), congratulations and other expressive speech acts. Bell comments on the mix of public and private in the broadcast and the sense of voyeurism in watching it:

> Publicly-oriented clichés – *delighted to be here* echoes Hillary's repeated phrasings throughout the interview – mix with the very private: *I partially did it for you too darling – I know, I know.* There are catches in the couple's voices as they address each other direct. The sense of voyeurism becomes acute, and during the interview Hawkesby himself refers three times to this embarrassment.

(Bell 2003: 15)

The numerous examples of disfluency contribute to the impression of unplanned private talk (hesitations and false starts in lines 2–4, 9–10). This is especially the case with Hillary's faltering expressions of love for his wife.

These days, of course, a new generation of programming is doing some very strange things with the domains of public and private; for example, by engineering personal daily engagements among 'ordinary' people in front of TV cameras, *Big brother* transforms them into hyper-public events. In his treatment of communication and new technologies, Moores remarks on the permeability of the boundaries of public and private in the other direction too, with the introduction of such personal media as mobile phones, walkmans and iPods: 'personal sound systems such as the Sony "Walkman" make public spaces private' (Meyrowitz 1985; cited in Moores 2005: 63). Macdonald, on the other hand, reminds us that we need to exercise caution in drawing conclusions about any accompanying socio-political change, since, as she says,

> the evidence that media discourses are redrafting our concepts of public and private is, at best, mixed. Despite the inclusion of ordinary people in the public space of the television screen, and the exposure of intimate details about politicians or celebrities, the hierarchical supremacy and power of the public world remains remarkably untouched.

(Macdonald 2003: 101)

Throughout the course of the twentieth century, the mass media attempted to bridge the gulf between the domains of public and private (Fairclough 1995a: 37). In the process they have restructured the boundaries between them. A key aspect of this restructuring is the subject of the next section.

Informalisation and infotainment

The restructuring of public and private domains is visible in the development of a distinct style of communication in the media, a 'public colloquial' language (Leech 1966, Fairclough 1995a). Broadcasters, in particular, have to be aware of the communicative dynamics of radio and television broadcasting. Scannell remarks on a 'communicative ethos' in emergent broadcasting (Scannell 1992: 334). He notes that they have had to learn how to address their audiences. While the context of broadcasting production is the public domain, most people listen or watch in the private domain, where they do not necessarily want to be lectured, patronised or otherwise 'got at':

> The voices of radio and television . . . are heard in the context of household activities and other household voices . . . It is this that powerfully drives the communicative style and manner of broadcasting to approximate to the norms not of public forms of talk but to those of ordinary, informal conversation.
>
> (Scannell 1991: 3)

There are striking differences between the styling of contemporary broadcasting and early recordings of British radio broadcasts. Perhaps the most striking change is in the range of accents used these days. In the early years of British broadcasting, received pronunciation (RP) was chosen as the appropriate voice of authority to address the nation. We now frequently hear other accents, though RP is still used by newsreaders for the most 'serious' genre: the national news. In post-devolution Britain there are now one or two exceptions here; two news anchors have a modified RP with faintly discernable national characteristics (Huw Edwards: Welsh; James Naughtie: Scottish). Another change is towards 'chattiness', the simulation of a private kind of talk in broadcast media genres. In contrast with the stiff formality of early BBC broadcasting, a huge amount of effort goes into giving an impression of informality and spontaneity in a lot of contemporary programming. People who may look as though they are having an 'ordinary' conversation on a television 'chat show' are in fact, of course, performing in front of the cameras and as much in the public domain as you could possibly imagine. 'Sociability' and the creation of 'ordinariness' in broadcast talk (and indeed media discourse generally) are big issues; I return them in Chapter 5 on 'Simulated interaction'.

The New Zealand coverage of Hillary's polar expedition illustrates my point about informalisation. Interviewers and interviewees use first names throughout. The focus is on the interpersonal, with very little attention to information content (ideational meanings). In the first extract quoted above, Hillary does provide some information about the conditions at the Pole, but even these details (its remoteness, the intensity of cold (line 9)) are linked to the emotional experience they generate. Bell remarks on how the informality of this extract contributes to the articulation of national in-group identity. The news anchor is a woman attributed with a 'mother-of-the-nation role' (Bell 2002: 61). Articulating her excitement about the achievement of a fellow New Zealander, she 'enthuses over Hillary's achievement, lets her hands fall to the desk in delighted emphasis, over-smiles, and exhausts the lexicon of in-group self-congratulation' (ibid.).

Andrew Tolson identifies the informal style of talk in on television talk shows as a broadcast speech genre that pervades programming: 'Chat is a form of studio talk, which can be found in all types of interviews, panel discussions, game shows and human interest programmes (for example, *That's Life!*) – wherever in fact there is a studio' (Tolson 1991: 179). He characterises talk shows in terms of ambivalence in the balance between being informative and providing entertainment. They display 'a certain ambivalence between forms of talk which are designed both to inform and to entertain; to appear serious and sincere, but also sometimes playful and even flippant' (Tolson 1991: 178). There is tension between information and entertainment in other media genres too, including the 'tabloidisation' of current affairs and other factual programming. It is especially prevalent in the 'happy talk' of US network news (Richardson and Meinhof 1999: 58). The emphasis on entertainment rather than factual detail in news is clear in the extracts from the Antarctic expedition coverage above (see also *Rock 'n' roll years* below).

The general shift towards entertainment across the media is often attributed to commercial pressures in the competitive marketplace of the media industries.[1] Fairclough identifies this trend as part of wider economic and cultural change towards consumer culture (Fairclough 1994, 1995a). The shift towards market forces is not only impacting on the media domain; education and the health service are also increasingly 'marketised'. In Britain and other European countries, public service broadcasting continues to have a commitment to public involvement in political processes. As Richardson and Meinhof argue,

TV may not always live up to its best civic goals, but it has embraced them: to give citizens some access to their political leaders, to make representatives accountable for their actions and decisions, to involve us all in the political process.

(1999: 9)

Critics have argued that the shift towards entertainment undermines this role claimed for the media as a democratic space for public debate. It is claimed that as public discourse has increasingly become media discourse, in the context of consumer culture, modern populations have effectively undergone a kind of 're-feudalisation' (Habermas 1989, cited in Scannell et al. 1992: 5). Consumers have displaced citizens. Citizens are positioned as consumers of spectacle – for example, listening to televised political debates – rather than as fully enfranchised participants in democratic processes. Livingstone and Lunt (1994) have outlined the limitations of 'empowerment' and democratic space provided by contemporary media discourse in the context of the public debating spaces of audience-participation programmes. According to Fairclough, this leaves a vacuum: 'if the media is not sustaining a political public sphere, where else can it be constructed in our mediatized society?' (1995a: 11). If there is a public domain that is not under the control of either state or conglomerate it is located in the 'small media' of email, chatrooms, leaflets, graffiti and so on. These non-state-controlled media spaces may be sites of public democratic and potential emancipatory space; 'small genres' like email and leafleting can function 'as participatory, public phenomena, controlled neither by big states nor big corporations' (Sreberny-Mohammadi and Mohammadi 1994; cited in Spitulnik 2002: 180).

However, so-called infotainment can be viewed more positively. Some critics take issue with the bipolar contrast between information and entertainment. For instance, Myra Macdonald points to the Enlightenment principles underlying such a contrast, with its implicit appeal to objectivity. She observes that the so-called tabloidisation of news involves its personalisation, a mode likely to 'encourage dialogic interaction and multivocality' thereby providing a 'sharper sense of discursive contest, and of the blinkered nature of our own vision, than can be achieved through the frequently closed discourse of "objective" analysis' (Macdonald 2003: 78). However, there is more to it than the simple presence of voices. Alignment to those voices is crucial too (as argued in Chapter 4 on 'Dialogism and voice').

Another potentially positive use of infotainment is in mediatised political activism. An example of such use is a campaign by the 'celebrity chef' Jamie Oliver to improve the quality of food in British schools and impose constraints on the junk food industry, with the aim of 'a cooler, cleverer, healthier nation'. The website of his *Feed me better* campaign explains: 'Jamie's School Dinners is all about making radical changes to the school meals system and challenging the junk food culture by showing schools can serve fresh nutritious meals that kids enjoy eating' (*Feed me better* website). This politically motivated use of popular media not only attempts to influence public opinion in order to bring about social change, it also engages directly with government. A key part of Oliver's campaigning is the four-part Channel 4 series *Jamie's school dinners*. In the introduction to the first episode he explains:

> I've decided that >I'm gonna devote the next year of my life< at <u>least</u> (.) to (.) try an' make some big change in (.) not just er (.) one (.) school (.) but y'know my dream (.) is (.) to take over (.) a <u>bo</u>rough or at least a >huge part of a< borough and actually get a whole handful of schools (.) <u>un</u>der our control (.) doing <u>wic</u>ked things that we're all proud of so we can actually *[v-sign]* go right <u>we</u> know what we're talking about (.) *[pointing]* <u>li</u>sten to us now (.) *[pointing]* <u>this</u> is what you gotta do and if you <u>don't</u> do it it's because you don't give a <u>shit</u> about it

It has been instrumental in a substantial increase in funding and the publication of nutrition guidelines for school meals by the Department for Education and Skills, though one columnist suspects 'a typically gimmicky reaction from Downing Street to the media storm created by Jamie Oliver's television series on school dinners' (Macleod 2006). The political activism of the series is set in heroic terms ('his quest to change British school dinners') and has been highly acclaimed by the media industry, winning Oliver a string of awards.[2] The majority of media coverage tends to give credit for the agenda to Oliver, a single media celebrity, as Jonathan Freedland does here:

> Well I think (.) <u>credit</u> to Jamie Oliver for showing that you can <u>do</u> politics even if you're not a politician (.) >I mean< one of the most effective campaigns of recent memory (.) led by a chef with <u>no</u> history in politics and yet it's <u>changed</u> the way things are done it's a credit to him

(*Any questions?* BBC R4 18 May 2006)

In fact, there have been campaigns for improvements in food provision for children for years (notably Sustain's Children's Food Bill Campaign and the Soil Association's 'Food for life' school meals initiative). A prominent individual is Jeanette Orrey, an actual dinner lady who has been a grassroots activist and campaigner for several years (see, for example, Orrey 2005) and who provided the initial impetus for Oliver's campaigning. In respect of the London borough transformation featured in the series (see Chapter 6), Greenwich Borough Council's website presents the story very differently. Oliver has also been actively contributing to the Soil Association's initiative.[3] While clearly far more than a figurehead, then, the media depiction of the campaign as Oliver's single-handed mission is an exaggeration. However, his high media visibility and TV persona are clearly contributing to driving government policy: 'Jamie Oliver condenses both the impact of heroic images from the worlds of commerce and celebrity on the public sector, and the importance of the media in shaping and reshaping ideas of what is and is not a public matter' (Newman 2005: 5).

The blending of information and entertainment involves hybridisation of genre formats. *Jamie's school dinners* is a combination of docu-soap, celebrity biopic and makeover programme. This general tendency of media genres is the subject of the next section.

Hybridisation

The traditional genres of politics – parliamentary debates, party conferences and international conferences – are now also media genres:

> they are represented within the formats and genres of the media – news, documentary, and so forth – so that their representation is always a selective recontextualization . . . according to the requirements of these formats and genres. At the same time, genres for political discourse that the media themselves generate are increasingly important for politicians – most notably the political interview, but also, for instance, phone-in programmes. (Fairclough 1995a: 188)

Fairclough goes on to consider the blurring of categories and identities across genres brought about by the appearance of politicians as guests on talk shows and even, on occasion, as programme hosts themselves. There are some particularly gruesome examples, such as when a politician hosts a quiz show (for example, William Hague, former leader of the Conservative shadow cabinet, hosting BBC 1's *Have I got news for you*), or when two politicians in opposing political parties engage in a weekly 'love-in' on a current affairs programme (Diane Abbott and Michael Portillo on *This week*, as characterised by Radio 4's *Any questions?* host). The appearance of a politician on 'reality TV' has a similar effect of blurring categories and identities across genres (for instance 'Respect' MP George Galloway's stay in the *Celebrity big brother* house in early 2006). Linking back to the public-private issue, in making such informal public appearances these political figures are exploiting opportunities for displays of the 'private' person. At the same time, it also renders them vulnerable. There is 'a new and distinctive kind of fragility' (Thompson 1995; cited in Moores 2005: 78) in exposure of the 'private' person in public. As the host of *This week* observed, 'If you want the good publicity about your personal life, if it goes sour you take that as well' (his subject was David Cameron who, as a contender for Conservative party leadership, fielded allegations about past use of cocaine in BBC1's *Question time*, on 13 October 2005).

One particular hybrid media genre in which political discourses are articulated is the party political broadcast. It is a genre hybrid, in the sense that such broadcasts may be a mixture of political speech, current affairs programming, advertising, soap opera, documentary and diverse other media genres. One detailed study (of a Conservative broadcast in 1992) argues that the salient genre in this hybrid is advertising:

> They rest upon a more or less direct injunction to vote for the party which figures in the broadcast. It is this feature which marks their resemblance most clearly to the televisual commercial with its injunction to buy. Indeed, party election broadcasts are often referred to dismissively as political advertising. This label usually implies criticism on the grounds, first, that they are not as good as 'real' commercials . . . and, second, political parties should in any case not be presented to the public like commodities for consumption.
>
> (Allan, Atkinson and Montgomery 1995: 372)

Another study points to the tensions between propaganda and biography in Labour's 1997 election broadcast (Pearce 2001). As a hybrid media genre, party political broadcasts are flexible and responsive to media trends, making them 'sensitive registers of social, political and cultural change':

> In 1959, for example, the Labour broadcasts were consciously designed (by Tony Benn) to resemble the BBC's *Tonight* – a fast-moving news and current affairs programme. In 1997, the Labour party adopted the techniques of 'celebrity-documentary' in its 'biopic' of Tony Blair.
>
> (Pearce 2005: 69)

Hybrid genres combining advertising with other genres are endemic in the modern 'marketised' media. In advertorials, a well-established genre hybrid in magazines, the division between advertising and editorial material is eroded. In some publications, there continues to be some effort to signal the boundaries between ads and other genres of the magazine, such as feature articles (for example, with a banner headline announcing a *Marie Claire Advertising Promotion*). In others, the distinction between advertising and other material seems to have virtually disap-

peared (in teen and pre-teen publications, in particular). Similar phenomena can also be seen in broadcasting, especially on television in
Britain since around the mid-1990s, as the advertising genre intrudes into
other broadcast genres. Highly conventional broadcast forms such as
feature film and weather broadcast have now been infiltrated by advertising on commercial television. For example, at the beginning and end of
every ad break to a film, we are informed that it is sponsored by *Stella
Artois* or *Cobra*. The regional weather, we are told, is brought to us by the
electricity suppliers, *Powergen*, or by *Swinton* car insurance. On occasion,
ideational content is continuous across genres, such as when a programme on UFO sightings is flanked by ads with flying saucer images
requiring (for me, at least) some effort in distinguishing them. By
contrast, in parts of Europe more resistant to accommodating commercial
production, advertising genres are marked off very clearly. Until about
2000 in Denmark, for example, the commercial channel announced every
ad break with a warning: *Reklamer* (adverts). This explicit announcement
signalled the genre shift, presumably so that viewers would alter their
expectations accordingly.

Before going on to my last set of issues in this chapter, which deal
specifically with mimicry in media genres, I want to make one last
general observation about genre hybridity in the modern media. As
consumers of media forms we have expectations about particular genres.
On encountering a particular text, we will engage with it according to
those expectations. So, for example, if I switch on the radio to listen to the
news and think I am picking up a commercial, I will interpret it as such,
and not as the news bulletin I was looking for. As a reasonably competent
listener, I can interpret the range of linguistic cues to ideational,
interpersonal and textual meanings along with the other aural cues
(such as jingle-like music, perhaps) that manifest it as an advert.

Hybrid forms can stretch this kind of genre identification. For
example, the clothing company, *Diesel*, appropriates youthful 'guerrilla'
genres, such as graffiti, pirate radio broadcast and fanzine, using hybridisation and pastiche as marketing strategies (Osgerby 2004: 4–5). The
multimodal texts that characterise modern television sometimes defy
genre identification. A particularly extreme example of a hybrid is a TV
series called *Rock 'n' roll years*. The series consisted of thirty half-hour
episodes, each covering a single year. Each of them was made up of
newsreel and music footage from that year, in the manner of compilation
documentary. However, the film footage was only minimally 'fixed' by
informative subtitles into its historical context and the way it combined
vision and sound made extensive use of elements more frequently
encountered in pop videos and advertising. A study of the complex

blends of image and music in one of these programmes is worth examining in some detail. The episode in question covered the year 1968, a year that has 'achieved mythic status in that it is often quoted as representative of the entire decade of the 1960s, arousing connotations of energy and youthfulness, revolt against tradition' (Meinhof and van Leeuwen 1995: 64). Coverage of two rock songs featured in the programme is examined closely by Meinhof and van Leeuwen. One of these numbers is the Rolling Stones' *Jumpin' Jack Flash*: for the first two verses, 'we see, in big sweaty close-ups, Mick Jagger and the other Rolling Stones . . . The music is dominated by an energetic back-beat and by Jagger's hard, tense, raw and rasping voice' (ibid.: 68). As a short instrumental break begins, the screen cuts to newsreel footage of the Paris streets in May 1968. Rapid, violent images of police batoning demonstrators, smoke-filled streets, burning cars and so on are 'rhythmacized by driving guitar riffs, the raw energy of a loud drumming, and occasional vocalizations such as "Yeah!", "Oooh"' (ibid.). The instrumental break makes way for the third verse:

10. MLS two policemen in front of
    banner ('The bank is closed')
    Subtitle: Prime Minister   *3rd stanza starts:*
    Pompidou claims there has   *'I was drowned . . .'*
    been an attempt . . .

11. Banner in red paint: 'I was washed up'
    unlimited strike

12. LS shopping street with garbage   'Left for . . .'
    piling up

13. LS church with piles of garbage   '. . . dead'
    in front of it
    Subtitle: . . . to start a civil war

14. CU BBC interviewer   *music fades out*
         (sync) 'Just how
         far is France
    Subtitle: Michael Blekey   from civil war
         At the moment'

[continues]

(adapted from Meinhof and van Leeuwen 1995: 69)

The violent images of upheaval are re-signified by the music. The music attaches cues to interpersonal meanings, imbuing them with 'optimistic and energetic feeling' (ibid.: 70); it makes them exciting. The lyrics link the demonstration, a political event, with 'the personal and emotive rebellion against the older generation' (ibid.). For the full account, see Meinhof and van Leeuwen (1995), which also discusses a combination of music and newsreel footage that is even more elaborate: Mannfed Mann's version of 'Mighty Quinn' coupled with snapshot visual accounts of the 'Prague Spring' and Vietcong offensive in 1968.

Parody and pastiche

Mimicry of one genre in another is a feature of contemporary media. Much of it is pastiche, rather than parody, since the imitation is simply that and not especially hostile or mocking. Pastiche is a mainstay of contemporary advertising, especially in broadcasting, where leakage between genres is very common (for instance, in a pastiche of *Star trek*'s 'captain's log' on Galaxy radio, someone speaking with Captain Kirk's stilted delivery records making 'contact with a mutated monkey species with music on their *Three* mobiles' who offer him a download of Madonna's latest single). Such mimicry indulges in a playful knowingness, requiring an audience that is proficient enough to understand the references being made and can derive pleasure from recognising them.

I want to turn now to a particular hybrid television genre: a hugely popular and somewhat controversial programme on British television in the 1980s and 90s that has been identified as 'TV pastiche' (Meinhof and Smith 1995b: 44). *Spitting image* was a comedy sketch show using grotesque puppet caricatures of public figures, ranging from quiz show hosts, comedians, actors and rock stars to prominent politicians and members of the royal family. In a sketch involving George Bush senior, the then US president appeared as a contestant on a British quiz show called *Mastermind*. This long-running programme had the rigid question–answer format characteristic of the quiz-show genre, with distinctive opening and closing sequences recognisable to anyone familiar with the programme. The host, Magnus Magnusson, asked questions on the contestants' chosen specialist subjects. The *Spitting image* episode containing the Bush *Mastermind* sketch was broadcast in late 1991 (earlier in the year, United States forces had liberated Kuwait from Iraqi occupation; the base of operations was in the adjacent country of Saudi Arabia). In the sketch, Bush senior's specialist subject is democracy:

(Dramatic *Mastermind* theme music and visual opening sequence revealing the contestants' chair occupied by a latex puppet of George Bush Sr)

MM   Your name?

 GB   George Bush.

MM   And your specialist subject?

 GB   Democracy!

MM   Which country allows only seven per cent of its population to vote?

 GB   Iraq!

MM   No, Kuwait!

MM   Which country was condemned by Amnesty International in November of this year for the systematic torture of a minority population?

 GB   Iraq!

MM   No, Saudi Arabia!

MM   Which country's invasion of an independent state was condemned by the UN General Assembly resolution no. 44/240?

 GB   Iraq!

MM   No, America's invasion of Panama!

MM   Ten other countries have been invaded in the last two decades. Why were no American troops sent to assist?

 GB   Ehm, pass!

MM   President Bush, you scored no points. You passed on only one, why were no American troops sent to assist the ten other countries, and the answer is because they don't produce lots of cheap oil!

 GB   Damn, I knew that one!

The opening and closing dialogue sequences 'replicate Magnusson's formal, somewhat ritualistic manner, which was a hallmark of the BBC programme' (Meinhof and Smith 1995b: 53). Bush's ignorance of his own 'specialist subject' satirically exposes the motivations behind US foreign policy as economic (*lots of cheap oil!*) rather than emancipatory (*democracy!*). However, Meinhof and Smith argue that *Spitting image* is not predominantly political satire but pastiche of TV genres (ibid.: 54). It is not politics that is central to the programme, but television itself. The political discourse is mediatised and presented as entertainment: 'In the context of *Spitting image*'s general tendency to TV pastiche, news and current affairs formats are assimilated to light entertainment' (ibid.: 57).

Spitting image also drew attention – through mocking imitation – to the way broadcasting formats shape news events; for example, a sketch about a politician trying to engineer a disaster in the Channel Tunnel to win media attention (recall the timing of the Antarctic expedition to coincide with main evening news slot in New Zealand). *Spitting image* was notable in the extent to which it made explicit 'a certain kind of otherwise largely unformalized knowledge of the ways in which meanings are produced and exchanged, by programme makers and by their audiences' (ibid.: 46). More recent renderings of the TV pastiche genre have used actors rather than puppets, sometimes allegedly misrecognised as the 'real thing'. However, in the case of *Ali G* and *Brasseye*, it appears to be invited participants who misread genre cues – the hoax is at the guests' expense, not the viewers.

Comedy central: *Harlan McCraney*

To finish this chapter, I look at a 'mockumentary' about Bush Jr's PR. MTV comedian, Andy Dick plays an imaginary presidential speechwriter who carefully cultivates halting delivery in the President's speeches. Extracts from recordings of actual speeches by Bush are embedded into a spoof interview with his 'speechalist'. This documentary-short was initially placed on a fake whitehouse.gov website. Contributions from a familiar real-life political analyst, Arianna Huffington, add to the illusion. It was made and distributed in 2004 and, at the time of writing, it is still widely available. It can be viewed at crossroadsfilms.com, or on the comedian's own website (andydick.com) among others; there are countless links to it in weblogs. Drawing attention to Bush's inarticulacy and extreme disfluency in the inappropriate contexts of televised election debate and other formal public speaking, it opens as follows:

```
B:   Bush
H:   Arianna Huffington, Political Analyst
M:   Harlan McCraney, 'Presidential Speechalist'
A:   A 'real American'
K:   Kerry
C:   pre-election debate chair
```

```
1. B at rally      B:  [Audience cheering] Families is
                       where our nation finds hope(.)
                       where wings take dream [fade]
2. H in study      H:  I think that when people hear the
                       President speak (.) frankly they
                       think he's really stupid
3. B at rally      B:  If you don't stand for anything
                       you don't stand for anything if you
```

```
                          don't stand for something you don't
                          stand for anything [Audience cheers]
                          H:   (v/o) But what
4. H in study             people don't realise is that there is
                          a genius behind this stupidity
5. B on stage             B:   (fool me) once (. . .) shame on- (. . .)
                          shame on you (. . . .) (x fool me) can't
                          get fooled again
                          [Applause]
6. MCU M in wings         M:   yyess!
                          H:   (v/o) and that genius is Harlan
                          McCraney
7. CU M in wings          M:   [to colleagues in wings] >>foo
                          can't get fooled again<< (.) I
                          wrote that! [Applause]
8. M in wings             [thumbs up sign to B]
9. B on stage             [smile and nod]
```

Bush frequently garbles his delivery of formulaic expressions (in 1, 3 and
5 above), his speech is peppered with grammatical flaws (the number-
concord error in 1), long hesitations and false starts (in 5). The 'expert'
explains:

```
                          M:   (v/o) you have to understand one
                          thing about the American people
10. M in office           <<They are not interested in a
                          politician that speaks smoothly or .h
                          who er insists on using [scare quote
                          gesture] real words or>> (.) who er
                          can actually talk
11. B on stage            B:   In my state o' the- in my state of
                          the union- er state- my speech to the
                          (.) nation (. .) whatever you wanna
                          call it
12. M in office           M:   The American people of today's
                          Americas (.) <<want a politician who
                          can speak (.) their language .h
                          and speak it badly>> [nodding]
13. B on stage            B:   and then you wake up at the high
                          school level and find out that the
                          illiter - literacy level of our
                          children are appalling
```

McCraney speaks with the slow, measured delivery of the expert in interview, in 10 and 12. These interview shots are intercut with further illustrations of Bush's inarticulacy. In 11, his fumbled formulaic expression, hesitations and false starts are dismissed with an informal hedge: 'whatever you wanna call it'. In 13, he has difficulty with number concord again, and also with the word 'literacy'. As the presidential speechwriter explains his craft, we are informed that Bush's stumbling inarticulacy in addressing the nation is cultivated with great skill and care. The electorate love him because he speaks 'their language ... badly'. His verbal clumsiness is researched and scripted:

```
25. M interviewing    M:   (v/o) >>I find that the best
                           speeches are
26. M in office           the ones that er come<< straight out
                           of the mouth of a real American
27. M and A           A:   [in Hispanic accent] I'm (.)
                           working hard (.) to putting food on my
                           family [shakes head] hhh
                      M:   [points to A, nods approvingly,
                           closes notebook] (. .) perfect
28. B on TV           B:   you're working hard to put food
                           on your family (.)
29. M and A in            which is the toughest job in America
bar watching TV           [M and A clink glasses and drink]
```

This fictitious interview provides an explanation for Bush's factual misrendering of another formulaic expression ('putting food on the table') by framing it as the outcome of research into the speech of 'real Americans'. Ironically, the informant, unlike Bush, is a non-native speaker of English. McCraney's perception of his own power and importance becomes clear as, one media person to another, he explains his craft. In his 2004 election debate with Kerry, Bush sustained a silence lasting approximately 60 seconds, an extraordinary period of silence in this key political TV genre. The mockumentary provides an elaborate (and almost convincing) explanation that reduces the president to puppet-like status:

```
                      M:   (v/o) <<I'm (.) always looking for
                           new ways (.)
30. M in office           to speak to the people (.) and what
                           speaks (.) louder than words (. . . . .)
```

	<u>no</u> words>> *[triumphant expression,*
	open hand gesture]
31. **B** and **K**	**C:** 90-second response Mr President
	at podiums;
	Backshot of **Chair**
32. CU **B**	**M:** (v/o) Mr President (.) can you
	hear me (.) testing
33. **M** in booth	**M:** one-two (.) Mr President (.) can
34. CU **B**	you hear me (. .)
35. Back shot	
of **B** at podium,	
Chair at desk	
M's reflection.	**M:** *[knocks on glass]* (.) hello-o
36. CU **B**	**M:** can you hear me <u>now</u>? *[B turns]*
37. **M** in booth	**M:** *[adjusting ariel]* that better?
38. CU **B**	**M:** Better *[B shakes head]*
39. **M** in booth	**M:** *[adjusting ariel]* better better
	(.) good (.) <<is that good?>>
40. CU **B**	**M:** ok >>don't say anything (.) don't
	say anything<< (.)

Here we see the 'expert' in operation. In contrast with the interview sequences, his delivery is rapid and intense as he takes charge of Bush's performance.

41. Back shot	
of **B** at podium,	
Chair at desk	
M's reflection.	**M:** just hold it (.) just ho:ld it (.)
42. CU **B**	**M:** don't don't don't
43. MLS **B** and **K**	**M:** don't >>don't don't don't<<
	at podiums
Backshot of **Chair**	
44. CU **C** *[frowning]*	**M:** just hold it hold it
45. **M** in booth	**M:** hold it hold it hold it ho:ld it

His control over Bush's turntaking is absolute. Bush's opponent waits, patient but bemused, for him to embark on his response in the 90 seconds allocated, but McCraney continues to restrain him:

46. CU **B**	**M:** ho:::ld (.)
47. CU **K** *[quizzical]*	**M:** ho:::ld

```
48. CU B          B:  erm—
49. CU M in booth M:  >>don't say anything just hold
                     it<< (.) hold it
50. CU B          M:  hold it (.) now (.) start blinking
51. M in booth    a lot (.) just start blinking
52. CU B          M:  (.) that's it (.) holy
53. Back shot
of B at podium,
Chair at desk
M's reflection.      crap that's a lotta blinkin'
54. CU B          M:  ok that's good that's it now ho- hold it
                     (.)
55. Back shot
of B at podium,
Chair at desk
M's reflection.   M:  >>hold it one more time now hold
                     it<<
                     hold it
```

It becomes apparent that, in terms of genre, this performance is more like a dog trial than a presidential election debate. McCraney is employing the craft of the dog-trainer. The humour of the mockumentary derives largely from the absurdity of the presence of this dog-trial genre of activity. As the trials go on, the trainer displays his subject's obedience (and of course his own skill) by releasing and restraining again:

```
56. M in booth    ho:::ld
57. CU B          M:  ho:::ld it
57. M in booth    one more time one more second (.)
59. CU B          M:  hold it and talk
                  B:  the only thing consistent about my-
                  M:  >>no no no no<< stop stop stop (.)
```

before finally letting him off the leash, allowing him to complete his final absurdity:

```
60. M in booth    >>hold it one more second hold it<< (.)
                  and talk talk (.)
61. CU B          M:  talk
                  B:  my opponent's position (.) is that he's
                  been inconsistent
```

| 62. **M** in booth | **M:** *[national anthem in b/g]* (v/o) >>My hope is (.) |
| 63. **M** in office | that my work stands the test of time (.) that <u>years</u> from now (.) people will look back <u>on</u> President Bush and think (. .) >>I have no friggin' idea what that guy was talkin' about *[musical crescendo]*<< but he talked <u>exact</u>ly what I wanted to hear *[closing bars of anthem] [puzzled expression, but nodding]* |

(Russell Bates 2004, 'Harlan McCraney, presidential speechialist', *Comedy Central*)

On one level, this documentary-short is a highly conventional mix of genres. The interview responses to off-camera questions by the McCraney character, the inserted extracts of authentic footage of Bush's public appearances, the pretence of insight into the backstage machinery of presidential PR in the performed inserts of backstage excitement, as well as backstage work in the booth: combined, these all add up to a video text that is readily recognisable as a documentary. So, in that sense, it is an effective TV pastiche.

In terms of its subject matter, however, it clearly parodies the coaching practices of PR advisors and, specifically, Bush's performance as a presidential candidate. This key element seems to hinge on the improbable inclusion of another genre: the dog trial. The parody rests in the contrast of what we don't get (presidential debate) with what we do (dog trial). Our expectations of a presidential debate include long extended turns by the two presidential candidates, with a third participant, the chair, in charge of highly formal turn-taking, nominating speakers and designating length of turns. All of this is present, apart from Bush's contribution to the proceedings. The imposition of a PR coaching frame (or dog trial) adds a fourth participant, McCraney, filling in Bush's long silences with frenzied backstage activity. From his place in the booth, McCraney produces repeated short, single-syllable directives, often with a long, sustained vowel characteristic of vocal control of animals. His rapid delivery of longer commands is urgent and intense. The fourth participant's engaged concentration contrasts with Bush's apparent lack of engagement as the Bush footage is intercut with shots of his speech-making coach. The McCraney sequences are spliced in with a combination of verbal and non-verbal communication; for example, the illusion of collaborative teamwork in 8–9, and the channel-checking sequence in 32–40, scripted around Bush's facial expressions and head movements.

The mockumentary claims that Bush's popularity lies precisely in his inability to perform his role as a public speaker effectively. It culminates in the final shot with triumph of the interpersonal over the ideational: 'I have no frigging' idea what that guy was talkin' about, but he talked <u>exactly</u> what I wanted to hear.' The PR advisor's coaching practices facilitate the President's projection of ordinariness.

The occurrence of ordinary talk, spoken by ordinary people (understood to include even the rich and powerful) in media discourse contributes to its apparent seamlessness with domestic life. Developing these themes, Chapter 5 looks more closely at attempts to close the gap between media producers and audiences and the pervasiveness of 'chat' as a broadcast genre.

Notes

1. But see Jensen's chapter in Scannell et al. (1992): why should politics be more appealing than fun?
2. Most recently, a Channel 4 political award in February 2006 ('most inspiring political figure') and a Bafta in May 2006 (Richard Dimbleby Award for Outstanding Presenter of a Factual Programme). Also in 2006 a Bafta for Best Factual Series and Webby for 'best activism' website for *Feed me better*.
3. He is both a campaigner and a valuable figurehead. For example, their 'Food For Life' campaign has a School Food Award for 'School Food Hero of the Year', which Jamie Oliver presents (whyorganic.org).

Activity

Examine the erosion of the division between advertising and other genres. What genre hybrids can you find in magazines and in broadcasting?

Further reading

Bell, Allan (2003), 'Poles apart: globalisation and the development of news discourse in the twentieth century', in Aitchison, Jean and Lewis, Diana (eds) *New media language*, London: Routledge, pp. 7–17.

Fairclough, Norman (2006), 'The media, mediation and globalization', in Fairclough, Norman, *Language and globalization*, London: Routledge, pp. 97–120.

Meinhof, Ulrike and van Leeuwen, Theo (1995), 'Viewers' worlds: image, music, text and *The rock 'n' roll years*', in Meinhof, Ulrike and Smith, Jonathan (eds) *Intertextuality and the media: From genre to everyday life*, Manchester: Manchester University Press, pp. 62–75.

Moores, Shaun (2005), *Media/theory: Thinking about media and communications*, London: Routledge.

Scannell, Paddy (ed.) (1991), *Broadcast talk*, London: Sage, pp. 1–13.

Scannell, Paddy (1992), 'Public service broadcasting and modern life', in Scannell, Paddy, Schlesinger, Philip and Sparks, Colin (eds), *Culture and power: A media, culture & society reader*, London: Sage, pp. 317–48.

Scannell, Paddy (1996), *Radio, television and modern life*, Oxford: Blackwell.

3 Texts and positioning

In this chapter I focus on the meaning potential of texts and conceptualisations of the reader/listener/viewer who engages with it. There have been theoretical shifts in perceptions of a text and its reception. In an article on news analysis, Meinhof points to early text-based studies that work with 'closed text models', according to which meaning is assumed to originate in the text and interpreters of it are mere 'reading subjects constructed by the text' (1994: 213). If considered at all, the addressee is treated as 'a fiction embodied in the writer's rhetorical choices' (Hyland 2005: 12). Meinhof's subject is news analysis; as examples, she cites the Glasgow University Media Group (1976, 1980), early critical linguistics (Fowler et al. 1979) and screen theory (Heath and Skirrow 1977). However, her observation applies equally to analyses of other textual forms. Names for this fiction include the 'inscribed' reader (Volosinov [1923] 1973) of Marxist philosophy of language, the 'postulated reader' (Booth 1961) of literary theory, the 'model reader' (Eco 1979) of semiotics, the 'implied reader' (Leech and Short 1981) of stylistics and the 'ideal spectator' (Brunsdon 1982) of screen theory.

In contrast with text-based studies, research using reader-based models operates 'with a more open version of what the text means' (Meinhof 1994: 213). Meinhof cites as examples reception studies, where actual viewers are consulted (e.g. Morley 1980), and approaches that attend to the circulation of meanings and specifically to potential discrepancies between inscribed and actual addressees (e.g., Hall et al. 1980). In the latter case, the addressee remains hypothetical, but as conceptualised a distinction is being attempted between an 'inscribed reader' and the closed-text model. Explorations of texts and positioning working towards reader-based models are the focus of this chapter. This will involve returning to the 'circuit of culture' discussed in Chapter 1, then coming back to work in CDA and, finally, connecting textual analysis with audience research.

Circuit of culture and reading positions

Recall that, in devising the circuit of culture model, Hall was taking issue with a simplistic notion of communication as a sender – message – receiver chain in which the message being transmitted was assumed to have a transparently recognisable content (see Chapter 1). When 'mis-understandings' of media producers' intended meanings take place, it is not just that their message has become distorted. Hall distinguishes between literal misunderstanding (the result of ignorance of technical terms or other unfamiliar language, perhaps, or difficulty with complex logic of exposition) and non-literal, where the meaning perceived by the viewing audience is not the meaning that broadcasters intended. Drawing on Parkin (1972), he establishes three hypothetical positions for decod-ings of television discourse, stressing that they are not empirical and certainly do not correlate with sociological groups (Cruz and Lewis 1994: 256). As already outlined in Chapter 1, the argument is that creators of media texts produce them in particular institutional contexts, drawing on shared knowledge frameworks, professional norms etc; the same media texts are engaged with by audiences in different cultural contexts, where the resources drawn upon to understand them cannot be assumed to be the same. The social processes involved in encoding the meanings of media texts are not the same as those involved in decoding them, so we cannot assume that the texts 'mean the same' to producers as to audiences.

If the resources *are* the same (when one broadcast journalist views a text produced by close colleagues, perhaps), then, and only then, can there be an exact match. In this case, the reader is likely to take up the first hypothetical position fully and produce a *dominant-hegemonic* or *preferred* reading. Preferred reading is, as Hall puts it

> simply a way of saying if you have control of the apparatus of signifying the world, if you're in control of the media, you own it, you write the texts ... Your decodings are going to take place somewhere within the universe of encoding. . . . a preferred reading is never fully successful, but it is the exercise of power in the attempt to hegemonize the audience reading.
>
> (Cruz and Lewis 1994: 261–2)

Outside the domain of professional practice, the second hypothetical position is much more likely, leading to a *negotiated* reading. In this case, a viewer operates with the dominant code with local exceptions, leading to contradiction between 'logics'. As an example, Hall considers a worker agreeing with arguments for a wage freeze at the level of 'the "national interest" economic debate' (thereby adopting a hegemonic position) but 'this having little or no relation to his/her willingness to go on strike for better pay and conditions' (Hall 1980: 137). A viewer who takes up the third hypothetical position makes an *oppositional* reading. It involves perception of the dominant code in operation, then a contrary interpretation of it: 'the case of the viewer who listens to a debate on the need to limit wages but "reads" every mention of the "national interest" as "class interest" ' (ibid.: 138).

In a pioneering reception research study, David Morley conducted a modest attempt to test out these three decoding positions on actual viewers (Morley 1980). He looked at how twenty-nine groups of viewers varied in their responses to one broadcast of a British news magazine *Nationwide*. He anticipated differences in decoding on class lines and selected his respondents accordingly. Some of his findings fitted with his expectations; for instance, he found that shop stewards produced the most oppositional readings, whereas student teachers moved between negotiated and dominant readings. But, contrary to his expectations, working-class apprentices and middle-class bank managers both produced predominantly dominant readings, leading him to realise that his viewers produced specific readings as a result of discourse position, as well as class position (ibid.: 134). This enabled him to highlight the significance of discourse:

> 'The meaning of the text will be constructed differently according to the discourse (knowledge, prejudices, resistances etc) brought to bear upon the text by the reader and the crucial factor in the encounter of audience/subject and text will be the range of discourses at the disposal of the audience'.
>
> (ibid.: 18)

In subsequent research, Morley shifts focus to the 'domestic viewing context itself – as the framework within which "readings" of programs are (ordinarily) made' and suggests the family, rather than the isolated individual, as the 'dynamic unit of consumption' (Morley 1986: 13–14). As he realised (Morley 1981), his early study had dislocated viewing from its institutional context of the household, where people usually watch TV. Moreover, in focusing on a single programme, it was isolated from the context of the day's scheduling and from viewers' range of interests across genres (Moores 1992: 146). Morley's subsequent study examined viewing embedded in context, as a set of social relations in households involving accommodation to other family members' preferences.

I take up audience issues again in the final section of this chapter (and develop them in terms of community interaction in Chapter 7). The next sections take further the textual aspect of reader positioning. In order to examine 'preferred readings' we need to engage with the text offered for the reader's consumption.

Text and positioning in critical discourse analysis

A prominent theme of CDA is looking for ways to explore how discourse constructs commonsense attitudes and opinions, observing that what we take to be matters of common sense are largely ideological. Since 'ideological common sense' contributes to maintaining the status quo, we can view it as *'common sense in the service of sustaining unequal relations of power'* (Fairclough 2001: 70). A particular perception of the world comes to be accepted as simply the way things are; that is, it becomes naturalised. An important early phase of CDA developed as a response to Language Awareness work in British educational linguistics, aimed at schools. It was concerned with diverse issues, including the social context of literacy and minority language education. Known as Critical Language Awareness, and referred to as 'the pedagogical wing of critical discourse analysis' (Pennycook 2001: 94), it purported to engage in denaturalisation and advocated explicit attention to unequal relations of power, particularly when they are covert, as 'a prerequisite for effective democratic citizenship' (Fairclough 1992b: 3):

> People cannot be effective citizens in a democratic society if their education cuts them off from critical consciousness of key elements within their physical or social environment. If we are committed to education establishing resources for citizenship, critical awareness of the language practices of one's speech community is an entitlement.
>
> (ibid.: 6)

In the search for points of focus, analysts look for fruitful textual sites for investigating how 'ideological common sense' might be articulated. It means examining the texture of texts, not just their propositional content, with close attention to specific textual properties, for example, features of lexis, grammar and cohesion, presuppositions, implicatures and other implicit propositional content, metaphors, politeness strategies, turn-taking systems and other aspects of genre structure. Looking at how a text hangs together – for instance, at the textual resources available for connecting clause with clause and sentence with sentence – is one way of bringing attention to the reading positions 'inscribed' in texts. It also highlights the active reader's 'complicity' in producing meaning, by drawing attention to the resources that a reader needs to bring to a text in order to make sense of it (see below, especially the section on 'Guilt over games boys play'). This kind of analytical objective is sometimes explicitly articulated in terms of the construction of an implied reader as the potential entry point for ideology in interpretation (Stephens 1992, Talbot 1995b).

In attending to the producer-audience relations constructed in texts, unequal power relations are always of prime significance. When we talk to one another face to face, we can take into account who we are speaking to and design our talk accordingly. However, the distance built into mass communication means that addressers do not know who their addressees actually are. Addressing a distant, unknown audience imposes on media producers the need to construct an imaginary addressee. Any text can be said to have an implied reader, an imaginary addressee with particular values, preoccupations and commonsense understandings. In having to construct an imaginary person to speak to, media producers are placed in a powerful situation. They are in a position to attribute values and attitudes to their addressees, presenting them in a taken-for-granted way. For example, these are headlines from two advertisements:

Are you doing enough for your underarms?
You too can stop biting your nails!

The first is from an advertisement for hair-removing cream that appeared in a magazine for young teenage girls. Since *enough* entails *some*, the headline expects you to be doing something *for your underarms*. In fact, it is likely that it introduced the target audience to the notion of removing underarm hair, before they had even grown any. The second was targeted at a similar audience and presupposes, rather obviously, that its addressee is a habitual nail biter. Taken for granted elements can often be less easy to perceive. An actual reader who has a great deal in common with the imaginary addressee inscribed in a text is likely to take up the positions it offers unconsciously and uncritically.

Presuppositions, and assumptions more generally, may tend to go unnoticed, unless they are totally misdirected. Conversely, of course, distance enables a reader to be more aware of the positioning and perhaps more critical of it. However, even if misdirected, such background assumptions still create or reinforce ideas. For example, in a language workshop with undergraduate students, I had a selection of advertisements that I was using in a session on, among other things, presupposition. One of them was taken from an environmental magazine and engaged the reader with the question: 'Are your savings as green as you are?' Students' reactions to this particular ad were deeply hostile. It was no surprise that they poured scorn on the depicted couple's dress sense, hairstyle and activity (earnestly constructing something out of chicken wire). They were clearly not in the target readership (I had chosen this particular ad for that reason). One student volunteered that the ad was intended to provoke envy. He had seemingly processed the language to the extent that he retrieved at least one of the presupposed ideas embedded in it (that *you have savings*), and he deeply resented it. The other presupposition triggered (that *you are green*) seems to have underlain his green-with-envy interpretation. Incidentally he did not oblige me by identifying either of the two textual cues to presupposition (an attributive and a comparative: what reception researchers would call the textual anchorage for his interpretation) to which he had so ably responded.

At the same time as constructing an imaginary addressee, a media addresser must create a persona for themselves. With regard to the informalisation of modern media (discussed in Chapter 2), this very often involves concerted attempts to minimise the distance between addresser and addressee. It is easy to point to traces of such strategic efforts in both broadcast and print texts. Fairclough has called the strategy 'synthetic personalisation' (2001: 52), referring to the manipulation of interpersonal meanings and forms for instrumental purposes. This strategy may involve

> constructing fictitious individual persons, for instance as the addresser and addressee in an advertisement, or of manipulating the subject position of, or the relationship between, actual individual persons (in the direction of equality, solidarity, intimacy or whatever), as in interviews.

> (ibid.: 179)

In the context of the media, it is 'a compensatory tendency' that sets out to 'give the impression of treating each of the people "handled" *en masse* as an individual' (ibid.: 52).[1] This view forms part of his exploration of 'discourse technologies' in late capitalism.

Operating within this general framework, I have applied this concept to popular culture catering for women. As part of a study of a magazine for young teenage girls, I examine the addresser-persona of friendly older sister (Talbot 1995a). Building on early speculations about the publication offering its readers a 'false sisterhood' (McRobbie 1978: 3), I take up the notion of synthetic personalisation to examine the way a lipstick advertorial sets up a friendly relationship between magazine producers and readers. I detail the linguistic means by which this close relationship is simulated: the construction of a 'synthetic sisterhood' on the printed page. The advertorial text is modern, but the strategy is not, since the 'roots of synthetic personalization as a gendered capitalist strategy lie in the history of women's magazines ... developed in the context of patriarchal and capitalist social relations' (Talbot 1995a: 148–9). The aim of achieving an active and 'intimate' relationship is by no means new; indeed, it was explicit editorial policy in the first issue of *Women's weekly*, which came out in 1910 (Talbot 1995a, White 1970).

Media producers are also placed in a powerful position in that they can postulate imaginary groups for their audiences. These are communities based on patterns of consumption: *Tango* drinkers, *Sainsbury's* shoppers, *Guardian* readers and so on. To belong to the consumer group of *Tango* drinkers, all we have to do is buy and consume the commodity. Being a certain kind of consumer does not in itself form relationships, although at times it may have a perceivable spatial dimension (for example, at a football ground). In the lipstick advertorial, the consumption community offered to readers is based on cosmetics. I framed my dialogic approach to analysis as scrutiny of the 'text population' (Talbot 1992, 1995a) that the reader associates with in reading the advertorial text. Part of that 'population' is the reader herself. (See Chapter 4 for discussion of dialogism.)

The next two sections focus on studies of masculinity, each illustrating an approach to analysis of printed texts and reader positioning. The first is a demonstration of coherence as a focus for examining identity construction in discourse. It is taken from a case study on heteronormativity in the press (the original study was also a theoretical engagement with models of coherence, challenging the narrow understanding of context in linguistic pragmatics and discourse analysis). In the second I present a study of contemporary men's magazines, drawing on the approach developed to examine the 'synthetic sisterhood' of a now defunct girls' teen magazine. Accordingly, that section looks at British 'lad mags' as a 'phallacious fraternity'.

'Guilt over games boys play': heteronormativity in a problem page

What follows is an exploration of the construction of heterosexual masculinity. It arose from two distinct interests: homophobia in the press, on the one hand, and CDA on the other – specifically, the use of CDA for focusing on the reader's complicity in the production of meaning and its implications for constructions of identity in the act of reading (Gough and Talbot 1996).

Val Gough and I looked at a single letter and reply from a problem page in a British tabloid newspaper, which had been given the heading: 'Guilt over games boys play'. The letter itself is from an adult man who is anxious about some homoerotic experiences that he shared with his best friend when they were both still schoolchildren. As adults, he and his friend are both actively heterosexual (he is married, his friend has a girlfriend) but, he says, he still experiences a confusing combination of guilt and curiosity. The letter, in other words, is a sighting of the 'dread spectre of homosexuality' (Cameron 1997: 51) that hovers around male friendships. The reply to it, which Gough and I concentrated on, banishes that spectre. This exorcism is performed by Marje Proops (the doyenne of British 'agony columns' until her death in 1996). Proops' reply reassures him that he is 'normal'. Her overall message is that homosexual experiences like his are legitimate, as long as they occur in the context of a development towards confirmed heterosexual, 'normal' relations:

> Many heterosexual men have a passing curiosity about homosexuality, and that isn't a bad thing. It compels you to make choices.
> (*Sunday Mirror*, 17 January 1993)

In encountering these contiguous sentences, a reader needs to find some way of connecting them together. As Gough and I observe in our analysis, in order to make coherent sense of them – to fit them together – a reader has to entertain all sorts of background assumptions. There are two explicit cohesive links which help to join them together. The first is straightforward enough: *It* links back to *passing curiosity*. The second cohesive connection is between *you* and *Many heterosexual men; you* therefore functions as a generic pronoun referring to a heterosexual male subject. Since the pronoun *you* also refers specifically to the letter writer, it has a dual function: as both a generic and a specific pronoun. But there is also an implicit *because*, a causal link, between the two sentences, which is not cued textually. A reader has to bridge the gap by inferring two things. Firstly the reader needs to infer that heterosexuality and homosexuality are separate sexualities. This inference is easy enough to make since, as I have already indicated, the *you* addressed is constructed as heterosexual. Secondly the reader needs to infer that interest in homosexuality is valid in so far as it reinforces this separate heterosexual identity (Gough and Talbot 1996: 220–1). These inferences, contentious as they are, are needed to make coherent sense of the two sentences. If they were stated they would be much more noticeable, hence much more likely to be challenged. As they stand, they are unlikely to be contested by a reader, especially an unreflective heterosexual one, even though – or precisely because – s/he is complicit in its creation.

Inferences and presupposed ideas are part of the 'commonsense' that a reader needs to draw upon in order to read a text as coherent. They are assumptions about the social world that are set up in such a way that they are not asserted, but readers still need to supply them to make sense of texts. Whether they are noticeable or not depends on the reader. They may be very visible for some readers, as the assumption about the predatory nature of male heterosexuality is for me in this extract from Proops' reassuring reply – 'You made [your choice] many years ago when you began to pursue women' (*Sunday Mirror*, 17 January 1993).

Here it is presupposed that the letter writer *began to pursue women* (cued by the temporal connective *when* beginning the second clause). This presupposed bit of 'commonsense' rests on an assumption that the male sexual drive is naturally predatory, which is, to say the least, debatable (Hollway 1984). Proops was outspoken in defence of homosexuals for decades before the legal reforms of the sixties. There is nothing reformist about her reply to this letter, however. In this instance she is reassuring the letter writer that his masculinity is unambiguously heterosexual. In the process, she is reinforcing some very conventional notions about sexuality. Though she deplored the oppression of gay men, she was evidently aware of the importance of being hetero.

The claim of the theory is that, in the act of reading, readers must construct coherence. As readers, we do this on the basis of the cues manifested in the text and our own knowledge and expectations that we bring to that text. Textual cues are a useful starting point when exploring the resources that a reader employs. These, in turn, provide a focus for attending to all the other resources a reader brings in, thus allowing us to look at the construction of social subjects in the act of reading. As the above example of heteronormativity illustrates, sometimes coherence has to be constructed with very few textual cues indeed.

Men's magazines: a phallacious fraternity?

It is argued that contemporary masculinity is a response both to feminism (e.g. Gough 2001) and to consumerism (e.g. Mort 1988). But it does not necessarily follow that dominant forms of masculinity have been seriously undermined. The broadening out of media representations (domesticated men, men concerned with relationships etc) is not necessarily an indication of change. It could just be serving to sustain hegemonic masculinity, if the older, dominating, authoritative kind of masculinity is still in place. Its resilience may lie in its very flexibility (as argued by Gough 2001, and myself elsewhere (Talbot 1997)). In Britain, there is a new, lucrative kind of publication that is reasserting a youthful form of hegemonic masculinity – the 'new lad' – as an imaginary community identity. To put it another way, these magazines for young men are offering their readers a highly reductive 'phallacious fraternity' (cf. Talbot 1995a). In this section, I explore the building of solidarity in lad mags through the signalling of friendship: the assertion of shared values including, importantly, ways of simultaneously performing friendship and transgression in the form of ritual abuse and other humour, offensiveness and taboo breaking.

So how do we signal friendship? In part, by communicating 'I know what you're like and I'm the same'. Friendly behaviour like this, the signalling of interest in others and closeness to them, is known as positive politeness (Brown and Levinson 1987). It involves attention to 'positive face': a person's need to be liked, approved of or thought of as interesting. 'Positive' here is not meant in an evaluative sense; it distinguishes this friendship-building form of politeness from another, predominantly used among strangers and to superiors, that involves attention to 'negative face' needs: people's need to maintain social distance.

Simulations of a close relationship between the writers and their readership are very common in magazines, including ones targeting a male readership. While, at first glance, men's magazines seem far from 'polite', this simulation can be highlighted by identifying two forms of synthesised positive politeness, as in the girls' magazine pages I have considered elsewhere (Talbot 1992, 1995a). These two forms are the simulation of friendship and the simulation of reciprocal discourse. We can spotlight the simulation of friendship by focusing on relational and expressive elements – that is, aspects of interpersonal meaning relating to the construction of social relations and social identities respectively. This can be done by attending to relational and expressive meanings cued in the use of the pronouns *you* and *we* and other lexis and in punctuation, and in the setting up of shared presuppositions and other signals of like-mindedness. A rather obvious way of signalling like-mindedness is by matching the supposed lexical choices of the target audience, such as a writer projecting a 'laddish' identity by peppering an article with 'laddish' vocabulary, as in the 'Handbag corner' text below.[2] We can identify the simulation of reciprocal discourse on the printed page by attending to response-demanding utterances (especially commands and questions), to adjacency pairs and interpolations. In one issue of *FHM* (January 2004), for instance, a friendly, bantering editorial voice in the Contents page introduces the readers' letters section as 'Three pages of your frankly alarming rubbish', and in outlining another section interjects with a self-congratulatory 'Well done us!' Editorial enthusiasm for the 'Cover story' is conveyed with the help of punctuation:

Baywatch!
COVER STORY
Lined up here for your delectation. Every. Single. *Baywatch*. Honey.
Ever. Need you know more?

Setting up the consumption of pin-up images as a shared preoccupation,
this entry is punctuated to indicate slow, heavily emphatic delivery
(deviant punctuation of a similar kind is fairly common in advertisements
targeting men – for example, *Clinique* products (Myers 1994)).

The establishment of like-mindedness and sharing of common ground
is notable in the Contents page entry above, and also in the numerous
reader-contribution sections in *FHM*. For example, there are regular
readers' letter columns devoted to sharing scorn at the ignorance of out-
groups: such as female *faux pas* ('Out of the mouths of babes') and the
linguistic ignorance of foreigners ('Funny foreigners'). Common strategies for positive politeness in recent men's magazines are friendly banter
and other humour, as well as the establishment of like-mindedness.
Joking is relentless. A reader's letter and editorial reply from the same
issue of *FHM* provides an example:

Handbag corner
I have to disagree with you. On November's cover it says, 'For one
month only . . . rugby is interesting!' When is it not? Thirty men
bashing seven bells of shite out of each other, big tackles, fights, more
point scoring and heavy drinking! And the players aren't overpaid,
undereducated, flashy gits pretty boys . . .
CHRIS OFFREDI, VIA E-MAIL
**You've had your month-and-a-bit of fame – now it's back to
pissing in pint pots and communal baths**.

The letter involves an argument over the relative merits of football and
rugby. I presume it mimics locker-room talk: aggressive, sexualising banter
among men. There are numerous accounts the exchange of abuse and insult
as friendly strategies among men (e.g., Curry 1991; Kuiper 1991, in the
context of sport activities). Labelling it 'Handbag corner' belittles the letter
writer, though why this odd use of 'handbag' is belittling, or indeed why it's
supposed to be funny, is not entirely clear (to me, that is). Mystifyingly, men
hitting one another with handbags crops up in British television comedy:
Monty Python sketches, and more recently Reeves and Mortimer. In the
1980s, a verb *to handbag* came into British usage, initially to describe then-
prime minister Margaret Thatcher and her belligerent behaviour as a
politician, as in: 'she handbagged her European counterparts'. *To handbag*
became a term for verbal attack, with pejorative female connotations.

The establishment of reciprocity contributes to the friendliness generated in magazines. *FHM* and *Loaded* are both highly interactive, with features centred on email and other correspondence, the submission of photos etc. The interactivity is both foregrounded and simulated, as in this letter:

He said it . . .
FHM discusses political, racial, social and ethical issues. It's not all chicks and how-many-people-you-can-squeeze-in-a-Mini kind of stuff – there's a fashion section, film, book and music reviews. But there's one area of modern popular culture I think you've missed out on: theatre. Wait! No! don't delete this yet! Hear me . . .
DANIEL PRIESTLEY, VIA E-MAIL
Unless it's a fat sweaty comedian on the boards or a trendy-for-five-minutes indie band, no one at *FHM* sets foot in a live venue. Like the rest of the country. Next!

Response-demanding utterances are common in other genres than letters. For example, a consumer feature called 'Double vision!' uses an interactive style in the question and command in the sub-heading: 'Watching telly from a chair too strenuous? Try this!' This feature (about a bed with its own built-in wide-screen TV) also supplies examples of the establishment of common ground: shared preoccupations and traits (in this case: idleness, squalor, TV watching, porn and gadgets).

I have already touched on the projection of a youthful masculine community in attending to the establishment of common ground. It is clear in the distancing from women and from foreigners, but also in the overall catalogue of things-worth-knowing-about. Gossip – or, to be more specific, 'bitching': pejorative talk about an absent other (Guendouzi 2001) – contributes to the establishment of a community with shared values. Gossip reinforces the values of a group. Here is one of Bethan Benwell's examples:

MANY a funny bone was tickled recently when it came out that two strapping Welsh guardsmen had been well and truly hung out to dry by three slightly built women during a late night brawl in a West London 7-Eleven. In the course of what appears to have been a merry old dust-up, Private Dean Morgan suffered a gashed head, while Private Vincent Jones was reduced to seeking refuge in a nearby bakery after suffering a broken nose and bruised jaw. Conclusive proof, some might say, that all Welshmen are as soft as a limp chip.
(*Loaded* 1997, cited in Benwell 2002: 22)

As a piece of gossip, it displays third-person focus, involving polarisation of 'us' and 'them', and negative evaluation, here in terms of national identity. The guardsmen's departure from normality (perceived cowardice, vulnerability) is used as a 'hook to hang the pejorative evaluation on' (ibid.: 23). The two Welsh army privates simply don't 'fit'.

Ritual insult, taboo and transgression function in the projection of a masculine community identity in the magazines. We have already seen an example of friendly insulting behaviour in looking at the establishment of a friendly relationship. Swearing is a key element: it implies both aggression and the breaking of taboo (which itself has connotations of strength. See de Klerk 1997 on men and swearing). Deliberate grossness, as transgressive behaviour, also implies aggression and strength.

Irony: to recognise it, we need to be familiar with assumptions. It is heavily dependent on shared culture, beliefs and values. As Benwell (2004) argues in an article on ironic discourse in magazines, it involves evasiveness of authorial intention. 'Water for men', another of Benwell's examples, is taken from a humorous piece in *GQ* on imaginary household products providing 'gender reinforcement' for men (other imaginary products include a 'trouser-fitted apron suit' and a 'five pointed ninja pastry cutter'):

> **Water for men** This isn't some fancy foreign water, full of poncy minerals. This extra-butch bottled water contains just one mineral: salt, and plenty of it. And because it's oestrogen-free it won't turn you into a eunuch like tap water does.
>
> (Dowling 1997: 29; cited in Benwell 2004: 13)

The target of the humour is a traditional form of masculinity. Is the humour based on mimicry of views not shared? For this to be so, the ironist would presumably have to be writing from a feminist position. Or is it, rather, voicing homophobia, misogyny and xenophobia while appearing to ironise traditional masculinity? Benwell argues for the latter view: 'by way of this ostensible ironization of traditional heterosexual masculinity, the concomitant values of homophobia, misogyny and xenophobia are given voice and status' (ibid.).

Irony is deniable. It subverts political critique and is linked with the emergence of the 'new lad'. Irony is used to distance the user from the difficulties in reinventing heterosexual identities; 'strategically employed in the constitution (and evasion) of a specific textual masculine identity [it] serves to continually destabilize the notion of a coherent and visible masculinity' (Benwell 2004: 4). As Jackson, Stephenson and Brooks observe, offering a political critique of it places you outside the community altogether – it 'misses the point'. Arguably this alleged 'irony' is not ironic at all, but available as a retreat position when placed under threat; in other words, it is a cynical and hypocritical position. This, indeed, is Benwell's conclusion.

When I first engaged with this study on men's magazines in summer 2004, I anticipated a decline in the resort to irony, assuming increasing confidence in reassertions of traditional hegemonic masculinity and having struggled to find anything I could confidently call irony in the January 2004 issues of *Loaded* and *FHM* that I have discussed briefly above. When I turned to the December 2004 issue of *Arena*, however, I found plenty. For example, a feature accompanying a booklet called *Movie Trivia* seems heavily self-ironic about masculine preoccupations:

> When we set about putting together a movie trivia guide we didn't just want to shove a load of facts in there at random – particularly about movies that we didn't give a shit about. Hence no lengthy thesis on the socio-psychological impact of *Fried Green Tomatoes at the Whistle Stop Café* or a Lacanian re-reading of *One Of Our Dinosaurs Is Missing*. Instead we artfully cherry-picked 84 'man' movies we felt the *Arena* reader wouldn't mind watching again and again, and in some cases, already knew word for word. The best bits of nerdy trivia (or as we like to call it, 'the building blocks of life itself'), the most memorable scenes or the convoluted back stories were all expertly sourced and compacted into a handy sized 100-page book.
>
> (*Arena*, December 2004)

Irony is visible in its double-voicing (see Chapter 4 on 'Dialogism and Voice'), with 'nerdy trivia' reworded as 'the building blocks of life itself', and perhaps in the parodic titles of films and stated rejection of mock-feminist readings of them. The writer seems very self-conscious of conflicting discourses on cinema available to him. The article seems to assume a university education and resist it. By contrast, it seems to me that to call the aggressive banter of *Handbag corner* 'ironic' would be stretching the term to implausible extremes.

I began this section on men's magazines with speculation about hegemonic masculinity, feminism and consumerism. I am not convinced that the younger end of the market (*Loaded, FHM* etc) is 'responding to feminism' at all. The response to consumerism, on the other hand, is phenomenal. This should come as no surprise at all, since modern magazines are predicated on consumption. Magazine masculinity is constrained by the political economy of journalism. As the fight for the market share grows fiercer, with magazines dependent on big circulation figures to secure advertising revenue, available representations of masculinity in magazines get narrower and narrower.

The last two sections have offered some detail in textual analysis of 'inscribed' readers of different texts dealing with articulations of masculinity. This is all they set out to do. Actual readers, whoever they may be, are assumed to negotiate with the hypothetical reader supposedly 'inscribed'. Any consideration of how readers might actually engage with or consume these texts is of course purely hypothetical and speculative. Text-and-positioning work of this kind in CDA makes no claims about 'media effects' at all, though it may be that there is a tendency to take the analyst's interpretation as canonical and (despite explicit claims to the contrary) to set up a notion of reader-as-dupe. In the other corner, criticism from linguistic pragmatics argues that this approach does not go far enough in theorising the text–reader interface (Christie 2000: 94–7).

Texts and audiences

In Joke Hermes' study of the readers of women's magazines she concludes with a warning against doing only textual analysis (by implication, of textual forms with low status that are likely to be subjects of scorn):

> it simply is not possible to read characteristics of an audience from the surface of a text: there is no single text that has the required monopoly position to exert such influence. All texts are used in the context of other media texts and genres; all readers bring their social and cultural backgrounds to texts; reading can be a fleeting, transient pastime that does not leave much of a trace.
>
> (Hermes 1995: 147)

Reception-research practitioners have rightly complained that media criticism focusing solely on media texts disregards 'what readers *do* with texts' (Radway 1984: 8). Reception research – of which Morley (1980) is an early example – seeks to augment textual analysis with the empirical study of actual audience practices. However, research that combines *close* attention to both text and reception is actually not that easy to find. A study of a British documentary called *A hard day's fiddle*, however, provides an early example, in which 'detailed study of textual form is undertaken within the terms of a broader investigation into the contingencies of text–reader relations and the very elements and practices constitutive of reading, hearing or viewing' (Richardson and Corner ([1986] 1992: 159). In doing this, they positioned their study in relation to Morley's initial research on the *Nationwide* audience, avoiding what they saw as two major shortcomings: a tendency to 'cream off' responses, with insufficient regard for the signifying surface of the text, and lack of opportunities for clarification and follow-up in a discussion-group situation. Accordingly, they undertook a preliminary study of the documentary text and conducted one-to-one interviews with respondents immediately after viewing. What is notable about this study is the close attention both to features of the text generating viewers' understandings and also to features of respondents' talk in articulating those understandings. By beginning with preliminary textual analysis, they established 'some specific, though tentative, hypotheses about aspects of the programme's meaning and organization' which would facilitate an investigation of 'the extent to which, and the terms upon which, those aspects featured in respondents' accounts' (ibid.: 165). The result was explicit focus on interpretive processes in the transcripts of the respondents' talk in the post-viewing interviews, what they term a 'discourse of interpretation'. They found two basic kinds of tendency in interpretation: 'transparency reading' and 'mediation reading' (ibid.: 163). One respondent's reflection on the documentary's positioning of the viewer provides a simple illustration of the latter: 'you're led into that argument by the camera'. The study, preliminary as it is, is illuminating in its exploration of ambivalence and displacement. They focus on whether viewers perceive a representation of events as a 'transparent' account or as 'mediated' and suggest that either of these positions may be 'displaced' on to another viewer (for example, 'my mother would think . . .'). (I return to issues of ambivalence and attribution in Chapter 4.)

Unfortunately, close reading is rare in reception research. Often we have to be content with 'audiences' loosely 'talking about it' and we are left to wonder wherever the texts have gone. Sometimes they may be omitted for reasons of space, or acknowledgement of them may be cursory and simply there to facilitate presentation of reception-research findings. There is an example of the latter (supplied in an endnote) in some interesting discussion group work with teenage girls (Frazer ([1986] 1992). This study is interesting in its examination of the girls' contradictory responses to a range of material from a teenage girls' magazine, including a photo-romance; however, the texts to which they respond are invisible (some implied-reader analysis of the photo-romance does exist, however, and can be found in Talbot 1986, 1995b).

Some reception-research practitioners question the wisdom of detailed preliminary analysis of text, arguing that, if clumsily used, it can run the risk of turning the interviews into a test of whether the respondents can match the expert reader's cleverness (Schrøder et al. 2003: 126). An interesting alternative is to do the textual analysis *afterwards*, tracing back responses to what stimulated them, as in some research on news reception.[3] In a study based on fifty viewing/interview sessions, Justin Lewis produced some rather intriguing findings about recall of news items, pointing to striking divergences from what he took to be the texts' preferred meanings. TV news is not presented in narrative format but largely follows the established conventions of print journalism. The broadcast 'news headlines' and 'main points' function very much like headlines and lead paragraphs in newspapers, so that first elements deal with outcomes. The story-resolution-in-headline format seems to be attended to less closely than more standard narrative format, with curious consequences. Lewis observes a 'failure of the news narrative to use narrative codes to forge links between the "history" and the "event". Because the history is invariably presented after the event, the narrative is thrown out of sequence and the hermeneutic [suspense] code completely subverted' (Lewis 1991: 148–9). This, quite simply, makes it hard to follow as a story. He maintains that it is not so much that TV news omits historical details as that 'it simply fails to persuade the viewer to fit these details together' (ibid.: 144). In some illuminating detail on responses to specific news items, he traces viewers' accounts of their readings back to their textual anchorage. For example, the respondents recalled a news item on trouble between Israelis and Palestinians as an account of apparently unmotivated rioting on the West Bank, even though, as far as Lewis could see, the piece was structured around that motivation (ibid.: 133). The first action sequence – in this case, film footage of street combat – seems to have overridden the spoken elements, including the headline. Lewis's recognition of distinctive properties of news, as inside-out narratives, came about as a consequence of struggling to make sense of the audience responses that his interviews had elicited (ibid.: 131). However, in an interesting coincidence, in the same year his study was published, a close linguistic study of the same inside-out structure of news narratives also appeared in print (Bell 1991).

A recent combination of attention to texts and their audiences explicitly engages with interview talk with readers not just as a resource for understanding reception but as a topic of analysis in its own right (Benwell 2005). The study examined two unstructured interviews with altogether six readers of men's magazines: two 17-year-olds in one interview and four 21-year-olds in the other. Benwell identifies implicit categories of kinds of reader that emerge – 'invested' and 'uninvested' readers – and notes that the older group have frequent recollections of the activities of their 'former invested reading self' (ibid.: 157). Interestingly, the distance of these 'uninvested' readers is contradicted by the way they ventriloquise magazine discourse and by the shared commonsense cultural knowledge referenced throughout interviews (ibid.: 161). Benwell points to the readers' articulation of discourses that she had previously identified in the magazines; for instance, observing that the interview talk among the 21-year-olds 'mirrors the teasing, joshing register of the magazines themselves' (Benwell 2005: 160). This observation produces a rather intriguing mirror image of my own, above, about the magazines approximating their readers' language habits. It would be a mistake, however, to try to prioritise one site of articulation over another. The 'ventriloquism' goes both ways. As one of the interviewees remarks about the magazines' style of humour:

> **M**:   It's the same kind of humour as when you're out with your pals and one of your pals falls over and you laugh at him (.) it's laughing at rather than with (1.0) asking the kinds of questions likely to embarrass them (.) looking for a rise
>
> (ibid.)

This 'joshing' manner circulates across different communicative contexts.

As data, the interviews with readers are not treated as transparent records of their views. Instead, Benwell investigates them as emergent accounts with the potential to reveal attitudes and opinions indirectly and even in contradiction to explicitly stated views. For instance, among the topics of discussion were 'grooming' products; the discussion generated is interesting for norms of masculinity that are implied rather than outright statements. A question about attention to product advertising elicits the following:

> **M**:   I don't (.) at all but that's because I'm a bit of a scab
> **G**:   You moisturize!
> *[laughter]*
> (ibid.)

Mike's self-disparagement positions him at a distance from the feminised identity potentially attributable to users of grooming products. Gordon mockingly challenges this position: 'Mike *is* invested in his appearance after all – a familiar put-down in masculine culture, and one invoking the spectre of femininity' (ibid.). Benwell argues that drawing inferences from such sequences of interview talk is more revealing about attitudes than direct questioning would have been. Both in this extract and the one below, the general laughter suggests group policing of others' accounts and hints at implicit norms. In this next extract, Jonathan 'confesses' his former self as an 'invested' reader:

> **J**:   I remember doing a Nivea thing that I bought Nivea after reading it (.) years ago like y'know how they have like articles
>
> [

I: An article rather than an
    advert
    [
J: Yeah it was like a sponsored article
M: L(h)ucky this is anonymous
     [laughter]
(ibid.: 163)

In terms of understanding reception, the study indicates, as other audience research has, that the interviewee-readers are both critically distant and complicit: 'The concomitant critical distance and complicity via a "lived" or ventriloquized internalization of the magazine values points to a complexity and sophistication of reading practices and an easy ability to accommodate contradiction in the reading experience' (ibid.: 167).

In conclusion, for fruitful engagement with media discourse it is not particularly helpful to isolate either text or audience as the object of study, since clearly we need to focus on both. New media are eroding the distinction in any case, as viewers/listeners/readers begin to enter the textual fabric themselves (an issue that I consider in Chapter 8 on 'Interactivity').

Notes

1. Similarly, Erving Goffman notes that broadcast talk is addressed to 'imagined recipients', leading to a simulated mode of conversational address: 'broadcasters are under pressure to style their talk as though it were addressed to a single listener' (1981: 138).
2. Such demotic address is hardly new. Indeed, it is probably as old as print itself. A study of British tabloid newspapers investigates the systematic employment of language 'to build a composite version of the vocabulary and style of their ideal average reader; a sort of vernacular ventriloquism' (Conboy 2006: 14).
3. This does not free the inquirer of the charge of putting respondents to the test. The feats of memory required here are considerable – a challenge for any volunteer audience.

Activities

Select a newspaper article and investigate its articulation of 'ideological common sense'.

Critically analyse a sample of men's magazine articles, focusing on (1) irony and other humour, (2) gossip, in-groups and out-groups.

Further reading

Benwell, Bethan (2001), 'Male gossip and language play in the letters pages of men's lifestyle magazines', *Journal of popular culture*, 34(4): 19–33.

Benwell, Bethan (2004), 'Ironic discourse: evasive masculinity in men's lifestyle magazines', *Men and masculinities*, 7(1): 3–21.

Benwell, Bethan and Stokoe, Elizabeth (2006), 'Commodified identities', *Discourse and identity*, Edinburgh: Edinburgh University Press, pp. 165–203.

Clark, Romy and Ivanič, Roz (1997), *The politics of writing*, London: Routledge.

Moores, Shaun (1992), 'Texts, readers and contexts of reading', in Scannell, Paddy, Schlesinger, Philip and Sparks, Colin (eds), *Culture and power: a media, culture & society reader*, London: Sage, pp. 137–57.

Talbot, Mary (1995), *Fictions at work: language and social practice in fiction*, London: Longman.

Talbot, Mary (1995), 'Synthetic sisterhood: false friends in a teenage magazine', in Hall, Kira and Bucholtz, Mary (eds), *Gender articulated: language and the socially constructed self*, New York/London: Routledge, pp. 143–65.

4 Dialogism and voice

This chapter explores media discourse using the concept of dialogism, or intertextuality. This means conceiving of a media text as a tissue of voices and traces of other texts; when we engage with it we go into dialogue with them. In studying media texts, we need to be aware that they are dialogic, or embedded in a mesh of intertextuality:

> When we look at the communications that emanate from mass media, we see that, like most other forms of speaking, they are preceded and succeeded by numerous other dialogues and pieces of language that both implicate them and render them interpretable. Such is the social life of language . . . indexically linked to past and future speech events.
>
> (Spitulnik 1997: 161–2)

Part of its appeal as a conceptual framework 'is that it enables us to think of media discourse as being qualitatively continuous with the experience of everyday life' (Meinhof and Smith 1995a: 3).

Intertextuality is about interconnections. Starting with its most obvious examples, a *Desperate housewives* instalment that begins 'Previously on Desperate Housewives . . .' is connecting back to the previous episode alluded to. Similarly, speech reportage (for example, indirect speech: 'Zac said you kidnapped his father so you could kill him') involves explicit signalling of one utterance inserted into another (in this case, the voice of Zac into another's). There are also intertextual connections of less obvious, foregrounded kinds. The reported 'voice' may be a collective, anonymous 'common sense', as in 'It was an accepted fact on Wisteria Lane that Ida Greenburg liked her liquor.' Also, a single episode is produced in highly complex intertextual chains of interaction among scriptwriters, designers, producers, directors, actors, camera operators, sound technicians and so on; only a fraction of the voices involved ever appear in the broadcast text, yet all of them are part of the dialogic environment in which it comes into existence. Yet another form of intertextuality – linkage by genre – connects the broadcast serial *Desperate housewives* with others with the same genre format (beginning with the same kind of framing device, setting up the same kinds of audience expectation etc).

Intertextuality and the dialogic word

The term 'intertextuality' was coined by Julia Kristeva in her introduction of Soviet writing on dialogism to the French-speaking world in the 1960s. The work of the 'Bakhtin Circle' started to become available in English, via Yale French Studies, soon after. At the heart of this body of work lie both an interactive and reciprocal, and fundamentally social, view of language and a challenge to a transmission model of communication. In Mikhail Bakhtin's writing on dialogism, he argues that we need to study language as discourse, as a fundamentally social phenomenon. Discourse is not detachable from its uses by people interacting in social life and any utterance 'cannot fail to brush up against thousands of living dialogic threads, woven by socio-ideological consciousness around the given object of an utterance; it cannot fail to become an active participant in social dialogue' (1981: 276). This necessarily means viewing language as a site of struggle.

In his treatment of dialogism in novelistic prose, Bakhtin anthropomorphises the 'dialogic word'. By metaphorically 'animating' utterances (as words that 'cringe in anticipation' of criticism etc.), his description highlights the omnipresence of multiple voices in the writing of a single novelist and, more generally, the fundamentally interpersonal, responsive nature of language. In attending to the novel's interior, he observes that, in some cases, neither the direct authorial word nor direct speech representation contains any sign of struggle; there is no intrusive external voice with an agenda that is 'foreign' to the author's own (because of this absence of conflict, this is often referred to as 'monologic'). In other cases, the author introduces a signification that is opposed to the other's word; as in parody, which Bakhtin sees as a form of conflict between two voices:

> The author speaks through another person's word . . . he introduces a semantic direction into that word which is diametrically opposed to its original direction. The second voice, which has made its home in the other person's word, collides in a hostile fashion with the original owner and forces him [sic] to serve purposes diametrically opposed to his own. The word becomes the arena of conflict between two voices.
>
> (1973: 160)

For example, in the mockumentary I looked at in Chapter 2, George W. Bush's utterances are being used 'against their will'. A media anthropologist provides other, rather striking examples from a different socio-political context, where official discourses are critically reworked:

> In Zambia the World Bank's Structural Adjustment Program (SAP) is reinterpreted in ChiBemba and ChiNyanja as 'Satana Ali Paano' ('Satan is here'). This is an extremely straightforward comment on what Zambians perceive to be the disastrous effects of economic restructuring. Along similar lines, the name of the large Zambian government trucks manufactured by the IFA company (of the former East Germany) has been rendered in new ways to reflect their dangerous effects. Because these vehicles are involved in so many fatal road accidents, the acronym is interpreted as designating 'International Funeral Association', 'International Funeral Ambassadors', or a very closely related word in ChiBemba, *imfwa* 'death'.
>
> (Spitulnik 2002: 195)

Similarly, in ironic or mocking repetition of someone's speech, 'the other person's word is being used to communicate aspirations which are hostile to it' (Bakhtin 1973: 161). In Chapter 3 I looked at examples of ironic double-voicing in men's magazines (for example, the apparently self-ironising rewording of 'nerdy trivia' as 'the building blocks of life itself'). Bakhtin observes that this type of word is very common in everyday speech. In such cases, the external voice (real or imagined) is 'passive'. It is being used against its will, as it were, and is at the mercy of the author. For Bakhtin, another kind of double-voiced word is more active. In this category he includes aggressive 'cutting remarks' and defensive 'self-deprecating, florid speeches' (ibid.: 163). Again, examples can be found in the men's magazine coverage in the previous chapter, most strikingly in the readers' letters and responses ('Wait! No! don't delete this yet! Hear me . . .' etc). These inner polemical words are acutely aware of the words of another and cast a 'sideward glance' at them:

> In practical everyday speech all cutting remarks – 'jabs' and 'needles' – belong to this category. But all self-deprecating, florid speeches which repudiate themselves in advance and have a thousand reservations, concessions, loopholes, etc. belong to this category, too. Such a speech as it were cringes in the presence or in the anticipation of another person's word, answer, or objection.
>
> (ibid.)

Similar to the 'sideward glance' is the dialogic word that responds to the voice of another by answering it in anticipation: 'Such a word envelops and draws into itself the speeches of the other people and intensely reworks them' (ibid.: 163).

The 'sphere of the genuine life of the word' is interaction. Yet again, it is best to quote Bakhtin himself:

> The word is not a thing, but rather the eternally mobile, eternally changing medium of dialogical intercourse. It never coincides with a single consciousness or a single voice. The life of the word is in its transferral from one mouth to another, one context to another, one social collective to another, and one generation to another. In the process the word does not forget where it has been and can never wholly free itself from the dominion of the contexts of which it has been a part.
>
> (ibid.: 167)

All words are intertextual, but this intertextuality is not always recognised. Or, to use Bakhtin's anthropomorphic metaphor again: people forget where words have been, but words do not.[1]

In this attention to interaction and positioning, there are parallels with the later work of microsociologist Erving Goffman. Bakhtin's novelistic prose is populated with highly sociable and self-conscious words, while Goffman's theatre or stage motif generates discussion of roles, fancy footwork and audience. Yet beneath their different motifs of novel and theatre respectively lie interesting similarities. To my knowledge, there is little evidence of direct influence, except when Goffman quotes from a member of the Bakhtin circle, Voloshinov, in a discussion of speech representation (Goffman 1974: 529 n. 26). The likely influence is discussed briefly in Scollon (1998: 85).

Goffman is interested in social interaction, in the minutiae of people's participation in everyday life. He takes issue with the notion of 'speaker' as an interactional role. In critiquing it, he distinguishes between a range of speaker roles. In his essay on 'footing' these are: *Author*, the person who selects the wording; *Animator*, 'the talking machine' (1981: 167); and *Principal*, the person whose position is expressed, who stands behind what is said.[2] This range of social roles enables us to discuss the possible merging of numerous 'voices', as in the case of an actor in a stage role, who 'animates' a character that has been imagined and written by someone else, or, more elaborately, a news anchor who makes a Cabinet policy announcement, thus animating a report composed by a journalist on the basis of a press release compiled by a PR team.

Footing and 'neutrality' in broadcast journalism

Goffman's concept of 'footing' has been used in conversation analysis of news interviews to examine broadcast journalists' 'neutralism' in operation (Clayman 1992, 2002). In broadcast discussions of 'hard news', journalists have a mediating role; in this role, interviewers work at maintaining distance from the views that they are charged with recycling. The position of 'neutrality' requires them to actively refrain from aligning themselves with the opinions that they report. This involves tactical self-presentation as mere animators of the views 'authored' by others. For example, this opening topic initiation by an interviewer immediately follows a recorded 'soundbite' from Bishop Desmond Tutu:

> .hhhhh We hear fir:st from thuh top South African official in thuh United States, the ambassador designate, Herbert Beukes. .hhhh Mister Ambassador, (.)
> Bishop Tutu jus' said you cannot get peace at the end of a gun. Why is the state of emergency so necessary
>
> (Clayman 1992: 175)

This kind of shift in footing can be seen as a shift in voice. In practice, the views thus animated tend to be contentious ones, involving considerable face-threat. Such shifts in footing are defensive tactics functioning to deflect responsibility for what is often a provocative comment or question, pushing it back on to the speaker designated as its author and principal.

Consider a more detailed example below, from BBC Radio 4's *Any questions?* in October 2005. The format of this programme differs from the 'standard' news interview genre. Jonathan Dimbleby, the anchor, is chair as well as interviewer. Questions are submitted in advance by members of the studio audience and addressed to a panel of public figures. The presence of the audience affects the stance of the interviewer. As the questioners are there to animate their own views, the interviewer has less need to 'ventriloquise' for them. There are other voices to animate, however, as in the following example. In the broadcast under discussion, one of the panellists is a government minister, Tessa Jowell, Secretary of State for Culture, Media and Sport. One question from the audience is: 'Are the government's proposals on smoking in public places an unworkable shambles or a sensible compromise?' As the only government representative on the panel, it is Jowell, rather than the other three panellists, whom Dimbleby challenges and interrogates for almost every question. In lines 392–6, he makes reference to his encounter with another Cabinet minister a week earlier, Patricia Hewitt, Secretary of State for Health. This ITV1 interview took place the day after a lengthy Cabinet discussion around the details of proposed restrictions to smoking in public places. In the interview, the Health Secretary expressed some frustration at the 'smoking compartment compromise' that was reached (a reference to the former practice on UK trains of designating one carriage as a smoking compartment). In the *Any questions?* broadcast, Dimbleby has elicited lengthy responses from each of the other panellists before turning to the Culture Secretary herself. In the opening lines, his characterisation of Cabinet debate as 'productive discussion' is almost certainly sarcastic (the extract is taken from a BBC transcript):

> DIMBLEBY Just get it clear as a sort of starting point, Secretary of State, you were very clearly in favour of a total ban before this productive discussion took place in the Cabinet, is that right?

370. JOWELL Jonathan, I was the first public health minister, I have always been in favour of a ban on smoking in public places because I think if you're going to be serious about reducing the number of people who die or who become ill from breathing other people's smoke then you have to do that. And let me say I think those of you who feel confused
375. about what the outcome of these negotiations this week actually is, I mean I think you can be forgiven for that. So I would like to focus on the – I'd like . . .

> DIMBLEBY I expect you'd like to focus on all sorts of other issues.

> JOWELL No, no, no . . .

380. DIMBLEBY Let's stick with this one.

> JOWELL No, I'm focusing on the second part of the excellent question, which is that . . .

> DIMBLEBY Compromise.

385. JOWELL . . . that where we did get to was a sensible compromise, which is entirely in line with our manifesto, which means that the only place in public now that people will be able to smoke if they're not members of private members clubs is in those – that small number of pubs who choose not to serve food but only to offer smoking. So . . .

390. DIMBLEBY You said – sorry – Secretary, you said it was a sensible compromise, the manifesto commitment, but it was precisely that

manifesto commitment that the present health secretary said last Sunday, as it happens to me in another place as they say, that it was unworkable and that is what is now going into the House of Commons
395. – do you think it's unworkable, as she thought it was unworkable last Sunday?

JOWELL No, no, no I don't – I don't think it's unworkable, I think there will be . . .

DIMBLEBY Do you think she was wrong in believing it was unworkable?

400. JOWELL Look shall we actually focus on the policy and a policy which is actually . . .

DIMBLEBY Well I would have thought – I would have thought – forgive me Secretary of State – I would have thought that it was a very direct focusing on the policy to ask whether it's workable or not.

405. JOWELL But this is exactly the problem isn't it, everybody is confused as to where we've ended up. We've actually ended up much closer to a complete ban on smoking and a complete ban – a position that was supported by people who voted for us in the election and we will make it work, it is complicated to make it work, I mean Patricia was
410. absolutely right in reflecting the difficulty . . .

DIMBLEBY In saying that I don't think that the proposal will work.

JOWELL In saying that she doesn't think the proposal will work, well now we've had a process of Cabinet decision, we have to make it work. And you know let me just pick up the point that Tim made
415. because there's a choice here isn't there. People complain when – they claim we have a presidential prime minister and there's no Cabinet government but then they also complain about disarray when there is Cabinet government as I've been part of for the last four and a half years and you have people who have strong views, in many cases held
420. for a very long period of time, discussing . . .

DIMBLEBY So there's going to be a lot more of this is there – despite John Prescott kicking you all upstairs and downstairs for leaking it around?

(Transcript: *Any questions?* BBC Radio 4, 28 October 2005)

Dimbleby challenges Jowell's claim that the policy on smoking in public places is 'a sensible compromise' (line 385) with the claim that 'the present health secretary said last Sunday ... that it was unworkable' (lines 392–4). In line 411, he reiterates this claim, completing Jowell's utterance with a supposed first-person quotation:

> JOWELL Patricia was absolutely right in reflecting the difficulty . . .
> DIMBLEBY In saying that I don't think that the proposal will work.

His animation of Patricia Hewitt's words here is clearly tactical. He presents disagreement with the outcome of the Cabinet discussion (the details of which we never actually get to hear) as Hewitt's rather than his own, so that it is ambiguous as to whether he is behind the view of merely reporting it. This tactic allows him to reduce a presumably complex process of negotiation and debate to two agonistic individuals. Jowell seems to be trying to supply the outcome of the discussion. While, if permitted, her account would probably not have contained any account of the number of voices in the debate, its reduction to two people falling out totally erases such intertextual complexity. (There is further discussion of this transcript in Chapter 7, in the section on 'Frontstage in production-community interaction'.)

Rather than recycling the words of a specific individual, an interviewer may evoke the studio audience, viewer at home or the general public. For example, Jonathan Dimbleby speaks on behalf of 'a lot of people' in a follow-up question to Harriett Harman MP:

> HARMAN there's a regulation issue all those things that used to be decried as the nanny state, like making sure that there's labelling on food so you can actually, when you are informed and you know what you need to be avoiding by way of fat or salt or sugar, that you actually are able to have that information. So I know that . . .
> DIMBLEBY Do you think that's gone far enough? 'Cos a lot of people say that it's all very well but they're still pretty incomprehensible, a lot of the labelling and a lot of the detail is incomprehensible.
> (Transcript *Any questions?* BBC Radio 4, 13 October 2006)

In this way, the concerns expressed are attributed to the public, on whose behalf the interviewer speaks, as 'tribune of the people' (Clayman 2002). A recent study of media celebrity argues that this identity 'has extended beyond the role of the interviewer towards a form of celebrity that can be usefully described as the "public inquisitor"' (Higgins 2007: 19). This role refers to the discursive position bestowed upon a media figure who is empowered to engage in particular forms of aggressive, inquisatorial dialogue. Higgins considers Jeremy Paxman and John Humphreys, two prominent figures in British broadcasting who have extended the remit of this elite discursive role to media genres other than 'hard news' interview. (I turn to the inquisatorial dialogue of Jeremy Paxman in current affairs interviews as a topic in Chapter 6.)

Randy fish boss branded a stinker: feminism on the *Sun*'s page three?

A dialogic perspective is useful in exploring issues of erasure and ambivalence around attribution. This section is a study of masculinity's accommodation to (and undermining of) feminism, based on an article from a traditional tabloid newspaper with the following headline: '£6,000 BILL PUTS RANDY FISH BOSS IN HIS PLAICE!' Like the problem page study in Chapter 3, it engages with reader positioning. It demonstrates how, in order to read a text as coherent, readers must draw on a number of resources, some of which are contained in the text itself, but some of which must be taken from outside it. In contrast with the problem page study, this one examines the constitution of subjectivity from a more explicitly dialogic, or intertextual, perspective.

Sexual harassment of working women is an expression of dominant heterosexual masculinity that is now liable to prosecution. In 1989, a news feature in *The Sun* reported on an industrial tribunal's successful conviction of a male employer for sexual harassment of two female employees. The article was a surprise to me because the newspaper is politically conservative yet, superficially at least, it appeared to support the conviction. Legislation against workplace sexual harassment has come about as a consequence of feminist intervention and *The Sun* is not at all where I would have expected to read a favourable account of feminism in practice, least of all on its 'page three', the site customarily dominated by a topless pin-up. What this analysis sought to show, however, is that while the text seems to disapprove of the defendant's behaviour, it leaves intact traditional assumptions about masculinity and male–female sexual relations. In order to show how these contradictions are woven into the text, I use the concepts of intertextuality and coherence. I demonstrate how, in order to read the text as coherent, readers draw on resources, some of which are in the text, but some of which have to be brought in from outside.

When we engage with written and spoken texts, we need to draw on a great deal more than our knowledge of the formal properties of language. The concept of intertextuality provides a view of the language user's relation to texts in which s/he is variously positioned as a social subject. We are all positioned by the discourses in which we participate, actively or otherwise, and we may shift position from one moment to the next. Indeed, it is not uncommon for the positions we enter into in our lives to be highly inconsistent. In terms of the intertextual view I present here, readers are involved in a 'textual dialogue' (Kristeva 1970: 68). In engaging with a text, we do not encounter a single, seamless object. A text is never a unified thing; it always contains external elements. These elements may not be recognised by readers; nevertheless they are needed in order to read a text *as though* it were a unified whole. In other words, they are essential for coherence to be possible at all. Reading a stretch of language as coherent requires the construction of intertextual connections as well as the establishment of linear, intratextual coherence. These *inter*textual connections draw in an indeterminate collection of 'voices' from outside. Through 'intertextual coherence', then, the very process of interpretation constructs the language user's subjectivity.

In my analysis I concentrate on discourse types and embedded prior texts as reader resources for constructing coherence. In what follows, I present some detail on two linguistic cues to these resources: reportage and verbal play. The full text of the article discussed here can be found in Talbot (1997), which contains fuller analysis and discussion, including detail of a third linguistic cue: naming practices.

Reportage in news genres can be highly complex. The news story contains quotations allegedly from statements uttered at the industrial tribunal; most of these are themselves quotations of the defendant's incriminating utterances. In fact, the voices from the tribunal itself are likely to be highly mediated. Only once is an individual tribunal official identified and supposedly quoted, and this is in order to rearticulate his alleged (and somewhat improbable) verdict: 'Tribunal chairman Brian Walton said Mr Alway was guilty of "galloping carnality".' The other prior texts selected for quotation are the defendant's so-called chat-up lines ('the old romantic told Marnie: "You make things happen in my trousers"') and selected statements from the two women pressing charges.

In most cases, the anonymous *Sun Reporter* credited in the by-line seems to have translated the language of the tribunal into a version of 'vernacular speech' favoured by *The Sun*. Without the actual transcripts of the tribunal's proceedings, of course, this is speculative, but there appears to be translation from one variety to another (from legal discourse to *The Sun*'s 'vernacular') in the lead paragraph:

A RANDY fish company boss who tried netting two young employees was branded a stinker by an industrial tribunal yesterday.

The reporting verb 'branded' is distinctive; it inevitably accompanies accusations and convictions in the traditional tabloid press. Even as it reports the judgement of the industrial tribunal, it signals the voice of *The Sun*. Of course, it is highly unlikely that the members of the tribunal actually called the defendant 'a stinker'; such name-calling is not a feature of legal discourse. It certainly is a feature of '*Sun* discourse', however. *The Sun* cultivates a demotic voice – claiming to speak for the people – and its idiom 'mimics a voice of popular, carnival disrespect and irreverent jesting and flippancy' (Conboy 2003: 47).

'Verbal play' is another very familiar characteristic of tabloid news coverage. Of course, the *stinker* insult was selected to continue the punning word play started in the headline ('£6,000 BILL PUTS RANDY FISH BOSS IN HIS PLAICE!'), doubtless inspired by the fact that the defendant was a seafood importer. The 'fish boss' feature mixes verbal play with information giving. It is bursting with alliteration, assonance and other forms of parallelism (for example, 'Mike Alway tried every way to go all the way'), dreadful puns on the theme of fish and occasional irony ('the old romantic'). Such 'poetic' devices are crammed into the attention-getting segments of the article (the headline and lead paragraph). This intense focus on playfulness combines with the framing of the news item as a page three story. This strongly cues an interpretation of the information content as non-serious, setting up a producer–audience relationship unlike that established in a 'straight' news story in the traditional tabloids or elsewhere. In this way, it undermines the legal discourse articulated by the tribunal. The coverage of the harassment case is set up as a source of entertainment. The verbal play contributes trivializing it, as does the dominating image of the nude pin-up.

The way this article appears to absorb feminism is intriguing. Firstly, in looking at the multi-voicedness of reader resources, I have pointed to a constellation of discourse types that I have called '*Sun* discourse'; this seems to be undermining both the legal discourse of the tribunal and the feminist discourse on gender that the tribunal is serving to articulate on this particular occasion. As I illustrated above, both are heavily mediated through '*Sun* discourse' so that the reader does not confront either of them head on. Secondly, it seems to be deflecting the blameworthy practice of sexual harassment on to an outsider, a scapegoat: the convicted employer is ridiculed as a randy, but ineffectual 'bearded, balding boss'. His physical shortcomings (indicated by 'balding' and possibly 'bearded' too) coupled with his middle-class status (as a 'boss') mean that he does not match up to an ideal of working-class masculinity thus

> providing male readers with an easy solution to the dilemma facing their masculinity: Mike Alway is clearly 'not one of us'. All of this means that male readers can condemn Alway's behaviour but without having to go through the uncomfortable business of actually changing their own ways.
>
> (Talbot 1997: 185)

This presumably places the working-class, male reader at a comfortable distance from the villain of the piece, despite the rather obvious parallels that can be drawn between sexual harassment and 'normal' male behaviour, such as ogling the pin-ups on page three.

In this section I have highlighted the dialogic quality of editorial mediation and intrusion using a single, detailed example of newspaper coverage. In the next, and final, section of Part One, I draw out issues of power and hegemony relating to dialogism in media discourse more generally.

Positioning, authority and erasure

In an engagement with debates over the trend towards personalisation and infotainment in current affairs coverage, Myra Macdonald points to the positive and negative potential of multi-vocality (see Chapter 2). Personalised case studies, or 'affecting and exemplary tales' (Macdonald 2003: 65), have been the staple of popular journalism since it began. She considers the use of case studies in two documentaries on *Panorama*, a British current affairs programme, on unemployed single mothers – a category of social welfare dependants demonised by the Conservative government in the early 1990s. In each case, as Macdonald notes, 'the emphasis was on *mothers* although policies or educational issues related to *families* and *parents*, caring was transformed, in line with dominant ideologies of both gender and the family, into a women-only role' (ibid.: 66). The use of case studies personalised the issues, allowing women to speak for themselves, so that, potentially, they could engage the viewer in a sympathetic and open-minded way. The first documentary was entitled 'Babies on benefit' (BBC1, 20 September 1993). It featured an unrepresentative sample, consisting entirely of young mothers selected from the same housing estate that was chosen by the Conservative government in their original attack, and it was used to feed existing prejudices about 'benefit scroungers'. The case studies were used to articulate a single perspective that was likely to be viewed highly negatively by the viewing audience:

By feeding already-stimulated prejudices, the case studies on this programme raised no new considerations for the audience to ponder: instead, viewers (predominantly consisting, for *Panorama*, of present or past taxpayers) were encouraged to set themselves against a group of exploitative 'others'.

(ibid.: 67)

By contrast, the second documentary, broadcast on 29 September 1997, offered a range of different perspectives in the context of a 'welfare-to-work' initiative by the newly elected Labour government. The women featured had very different life experiences. They differed widely in their views of the government initiative, so that the documentary offered a more representative sample of case studies that had the potential to open up the debate surrounding it. Macdonald's point is that the personalisation of case studies can be used productively and cannot simply be dismissed as 'dumbing down'.

Clearly, there is more to it than the simple presence of more than one voice. Evaluative framing of those voices and alignment to them are crucial too. Sometimes allowing people to 'speak for themselves' is an effective way of condemning them. Consider the following example:

1. **Muslims protest at Reid speech**
   By ONLINE REPORTER
   SEPTEMBER 20, 2006
2. A SPEECH on immigration by Home Secretary John Reid has been disrupted by a series of protests by Muslim radicals.
3. Abu Izzadeen – aka Trevor Brooks – shouted out for well over a minute as Reid spoke to a Muslim crowd.
4. 30-year-old Brooks accused the Home Secretary of being an 'enemy' of Islam, adding: 'How dare you come to a Muslim area!'
5. He added: 'State terrorism by the British police.
6. 'They are going to come in the morning to your house, kick your door down when you're in bed with your own wife, then drag you from your own bed.'
7. *Izzadeen – who is the leader of Islamist group Al Ghurabaa – has previously described the 7/7 London bombers as 'completely praiseworthy,' and openly admits wanting to die as a suicide bomber.*
8. He was led away by police and stewards, who ejected a second protestor a few minutes later.
9. By this time there were several Muslim men in the street outside conducting an impromptu press conference to news cameras.

10. When TV cameras turned back to Reid, he said, somewhat ironically: 'I was trying to make the point that we should never allow ourselves to be intimidated or shouted down.'

11. The Home Secretary appeared nervous up until this point, but seemed more at ease after the incident.

12. He continued: 'This is not a new experience for me or for those involved in politics.

13. 'There will always be people who will not be prepared to take part in a dialogue.

14. 'They are not confined to the Muslim community.'

. . .

(*The Sun Online*, 20 September 2006)

In the single sentence paragraphs in 4–7, the reporter uses direct quotation to condemn the speaker, since the views expressed are manifestly unacceptable to the target readership. In 4, the scare quotes and speech-act reporting verb 'accused' both contribute to distancing the reporter's voice from the usage of 'enemy' in this context; the longer quotation seems to be functioning to alienate the reader from its source, since it articulates a view about 'no-go areas' that would be considered totally outrageous for most readers. In 6, the speaker's 'own words' (real or invented) articulate what, in this context, reads like a hysterical exaggeration of police brutality that does not add credibility to his case. The directly quoted adjectival phrase in 7 places the speaker beyond the pale, in support of an atrocity that traumatised London. The reporting verb 'admits' in the next clause introduces an indirect speech act establishing it as a confessional one. The reporter's distanced disapproval from the words indirectly quoted is very clear. By contrast, alignment with the Home Secretary's voice is quite different. He is quoted without comment, overt or otherwise – with one exception. In 10, the reporter tags as ironic Reid's remark: 'I was trying to make the point that we should never allow ourselves to be intimidated or shouted down.' The reporter's view merges with Reid's in using the vocal protester in the audience as a case study of intolerance.[3]

Double-voicing and alignment in press reporting is one of the issues that Clare Walsh raises in her study of women in British politics (Walsh 2001). Critically exploring the masculinist arena of mediatised politics, she gives particular attention to the treatment of a senior female politician, Margaret Beckett. As deputy leader of the Labour party, Beckett became acting leader at the sudden death of John Smith in 1994. In the subsequent Labour leadership campaign, Walsh compares the editorial comment and profiles of candidates: Beckett, Tony Blair and John Prescott. The voices of the all-male editorial team in the *Daily Mirror* frequently merged with those of the two male candidates, with the effect of implicitly endorsing their views. A profile of Blair, for example, quotes him only once, but it articulates his views, and indeed his campaign catchphrases, throughout:

> The producers [of the profile] not only review his past commitment to 'strong community values' and a 'modern version of traditional socialism', but anticipate the future direction of his campaign. Thus we are told that, 'He will broaden this theme to cover the full range of policy as a leadership candidate – social action providing the framework for individual fulfilment'. The latter is recognisable as a campaign catchphrase, but the absence of quotation marks makes it clear that it is one with which the producers align themselves. The categorical modality used here occurs elsewhere, making it clear that the producers predict that Blair *will* become leader unopposed.
>
> (ibid.: 83)

Beckett is left to argue her own case, without endorsement. In her profile, there are frequent, explicitly marked quotations, introduced with 'neutral' reporting verbs and no evaluative framing:

> The profile of Beckett consists of a series of instances of secondary discourse, embedded in only occasional passages of primary discourse. There is no blending of the two. Thus we have the chaining of, 'She said . . . she stressed . . . she said . . . she said . . . She underlined her belief . . . she emphasized'. Although none of these statements is evaluated, either positively or negatively, *cumulatively* they have the effect of conveying the editorial team's distance from the case Beckett is making. Unlike her male colleagues, she is forced to plead her own case, with no help or hindrance for the editorial team.
>
> (ibid.: 84)

The profiles of the three candidates are all presumably based on press releases. However, in refashioning them, the journalists mark the intertextual connections very differently. In presenting Beckett's position as a candidate, dialogism is foregrounded throughout. In Blair's case, dialogism is suppressed; the writers articulate his position as monologic and authoritative.

Notes

1. Bakhtin postulates a range of different voice alignments within an utterance, as follows:

   Single-voiced: *Object-oriented*
                        (e.g., a 'straight' statement)
                        Objectivised
                        (e.g., 'straight' reported speech without comment or alteration)
   Double-voiced: *Single-directed*
                        (e.g., indirect quotation)
                        Hetero-directed
                        (e.g., parody)
                        Active
                        (e.g., self-deprecation)

2. An earlier essay offers a different set of speech roles: *Principal, Strategist, Animator, Figure* and, interestingly, *Audience* (1974: 540).

3. The contrast is bolstered by the photographs that accompanied the article. There is a single image of Reid. Dressed in suit and tie, he is expressionless and still, looking straight at the camera and not speaking. There are three photographs of a heckler dressed Muslim clothing; he is in motion, grimacing angrily and gesticulating.

Activity

Examine the double-voicing in a print or broadcast text (if you choose a broadcast text, you will need to transcribe it, unless a transcription is available online). Identify shifts in footing, evaluative framing and alignment and how these are achieved.

Further reading

Bakhtin, Mikhail (1986), 'The problem of speech genres', *Speech genres and other late essays*, Emerson, Caryl and Holquist, Michael (eds) trans. Vern McGee, Austin: Texas University Press (Extracts in Jaworski, Adam and Coupland, Nikolas (eds) (1999), *The discourse reader*, London: Routledge, pp. 121–40).

Clayman, Steven (1992), 'Footing in the achievement of neutrality: the case of news-interview discourse', in Drew, Paul and Heritage, John (eds) *Talk at work: interaction in institutional settings*, Cambridge: Cambridge University Press, pp. 163–98.

Goffman, Erving (1981), 'Footing', *Forms of talk*, Oxford: Blackwell, pp. 124–59.

Maybin, Janet (2001), 'Language, struggle and voice: the Bakhtin/Volosinov writings', in Weatherell, Margaret, Taylor, Stephanie and Yates, Simeon (eds), *Discourse theory and practice: a reader*, London: Sage.

Richardson, John (2007), 'Intertextuality', in Richardson John, *Analysing newspapers: an approach from critical discourse analysis*, Basingstoke: Palgrave Macmillan, pp. 100–6.

Talbot, Mary (1997), ' "Randy fish boss branded a stinker": coherence and the construction of masculinities in a British tabloid newspaper', in Johnson, Sally and Meinhof, Ulrike (eds), *Language and masculinity*, Oxford: Blackwell, pp. 173–87.

Walsh, Clare (2001), 'Women in the house: a case study of women labour MPs at Westminster', *Gender and discourse: language and power in politics, the church and organisations*, London: Longman, pp. 67–103.

Part Two

Representation and interaction

5 Simulated interaction

In Chapter 2, I discussed some shifts and reconfigurations that characterise the modern, media-saturated world. I dealt with issues around the 'stretching' of time and space as a consequence of technological developments in communication. Two other interrelated issues were the permeability of public and private social spheres and an increasing tendency towards informalisation in public discourses. I was exploring the way the nature of social interaction in modernity has been transformed. Developing these themes, this chapter looks more closely at attempts to close the gap between producers and audiences and the pervasiveness of 'chat' as a broadcast genre.

Three types of interaction

A useful starting point is a conceptual framework devised by a social theorist of the media. Exploring patterns of media action and interaction, John Thompson offers a three-way distinction between modes of communication (Thompson 1995). These are *face-to-face interaction, mediated interaction* and *mediated quasi-interaction.* Though he refers to all three as forms of interaction, his qualification for the third (as *quasi-*) indicates its dubious or, at least, marginal status as interaction. It is this third mode that is the subject of this chapter, but a preliminary exploration of this three-way distinction will be useful.

When two people interact face-to-face, their physical co-presence means that they will generally have a wide range of verbal and other cues available for understanding one another, among them prosodic features (such as pitch and loudness), facial expressions and gestures. The interaction is two-way. If the same two people communicate by phone, they will have fewer cues available. The interaction will still be reciprocal and they will still be able to draw on most of the subtle voice-quality cues to understanding that face-to-face talk provides, depending on the quality of the connection; however, no matter how good the phone line is, they will not be able to 'read' expressions or gestures. With mediated forms of engagement, their 'space–time constitution' will be less straightforward. In the case of a phone conversation, the interlocutors are distant physically but not temporally. If the caller leaves a message on an answering machine, however, that changes. They are still interacting with one another, but the distance between them has become temporal as well as spatial. The recorded message, like a letter, is a text that bridges the spatial-temporal distance between them.

Mediated quasi-interaction is different, in two crucial ways, as Table 5.1 indicates:

Table 5.1 Three types of interaction

	Face-to-face interaction	Mediated interaction	Mediated quasi-interaction
Space–time constitution	Context of co-presence; shared spatial-temporal reference system	Separation of contexts; extended availability in time and space	Separation of contexts; extended availability in time and space
Range of symbolic cues	Multiplicity of symbolic cues	Narrowing of the range of symbolic cues	Narrowing of the range of symbolic cues
Action orientation	Oriented towards specific others	Oriented towards specific others	Oriented towards an indefinite range of potential recipients
Dialogical/ Monological	Dialogical	Dialogical	Monological

Source: Thompson 1995: 85

In mediated quasi-interaction there is no specific addressee and the engagement has a one-way quality; it is not addressee-specific and it is not reciprocal. In our activities of reading, listening to the radio and watching television, we engage in mediated quasi-interaction:

> It creates a certain kind of social situation in which individuals are linked together in a process of communication and symbolic exchange. It is a structured situation in which some individuals are engaged primarily in producing symbolic forms for others who are not physically present, while others are involved primarily in receiving symbolic forms produced by others to whom they cannot respond, but with whom they can form bonds of friendship, affection or loyalty.
>
> (Thompson 1995: 84–5)

Given the non-reciprocal basis of this quasi-interaction, however, his observation about forming 'bonds' needs qualifying. Affection and loyalty can be one-sided, sadly, but I am not convinced that friendship can. What would 'one-way friendship' look like, I wonder? Is reciprocity not a defining characteristic? To be sure, the language circulating in mediated quasi-interaction is amenable to much of same description and analysis as face-to-face friendship-building talk. For instance, we could study attention to face in the use of hedging devices (mitigating potential face threat, avoiding been seen as boastful etc). Facial expression (smiling etc) could be fruitfully investigated, and gesture too. A speaker's use of such devices might well generate feelings of affection, and so on, in the recipient of their representation as a spectacle (a broadcast performance of friendship?). If the social engagement is mediated quasi-interaction, then the relationship must be 'mediated quasi-friendship'.

The typology represented in Table 5.1 is a useful characterisation of engagement with media. It is a valuable addition to cultural circuit and dialogism in building a picture of media and the circulation of discourse. The typology makes no claim to exhaustiveness or discreteness of categories. Computer-mediated communication clearly offers other possibilities, for instance, and, in actual situations, hybridity is highly likely. Different forms may be mixed. For example, a couple may be watching television chat show and chatting between themselves. Moreover, the typology overall is not without its problems. Moores (2005) points to the catch-all quality of mediated interaction for an account of communication technologies, for example. Also, the denominator of the second row (Range of symbolic cues) begs a raft of questions about the nature of spoken and written modes of language, multi-modal discourse etc (which this book does not have space to enter into).

Now I need to consider other contributions to understanding this 'mediated quasi-interaction'.

'Para-social interaction'

An article that first appeared in 1956, in the journal *Psychiatry*, offers an early insight into the nature of television as a medium. It attended to the simulation of co-presence of speakers and hearers, a phenomenon the authors called 'para-social interaction' (Horton and Wohl 1986). They refer to a 'simulacrum of conversational give and take' (ibid.: 189) that produces an illusion of co-presence. The effect is an impression of intimacy that is, however, entirely synthetic. The authors point to four means by which this illusion is carried off. Firstly, the main characteristic, as they say, is 'the attempt of the persona to duplicate the gestures, conversational style, and milieu of an informal face-to-face gathering' (ibid.: 191). The detail of how this is achieved is thin: general reference to hosts who 'maintain a flow of small talk' and to an early radio host's reflections on his delivery:

> Most talk on the radio in those days was formal and usually a little stiff. But I just rambled along, saying whatever came into my mind. I was introspective. I tried to pretend that I was chatting with a friend over a highball late in the evening, . . . Then – and later – I consciously tried to talk to the listener as an individual, to make each listener feel that he [sic] knew me and I knew him.'
>
> (Dave Garroway, quoted in Horton and Wohl 1986: 192)

In the case of television, the camera lens is engaged with as if it were an interlocutor. Secondly, they point to an informal camaraderie among the team in front of the camera, the cultivation of an informal intimacy in the use of first names, nicknames etc. Two further means that they point to involve mingling with a studio audience and 'subjective' camera work. Together these effects create the impression of 'sociability, easy affability, friendship, and close contact' (ibid.: 193). Such talk is 'hearably personal while being, at the same time, specifically impersonal . . . talk that crosses the boundaries between the "private" and the "public" in unique ways' (Hutchby 2006: 12).

Actually, the term 'para-social interaction' is inaccurate, as Moores points out (2005: 75). The *para-* prefix is in the wrong place; it would be more accurate to call it 'social para-interaction'. Following Thompson's typology of interaction modes, this 'non-reciprocal intimacy at a distance' (1995: 219) is clearly a form of mediated quasi-interaction.

Next, I turn to a key characteristic of media discourse, particularly broadcasting: its 'communicative ethos'.

Sociability

The social dimension of broadcasting is, according to Scannell, fundamental to its 'communicative ethos' (1996: 4). All broadcasting has a commitment to sociability because broadcasters are not in a position to control the communicative context. As I noted in Chapter 2, people tend to listen or watch in private. They do so on their own terms: 'if the programmes are not, really and truly, sociable in the ways they address viewers and listeners, then no one would care to watch or listen' (ibid.). The relationship between broadcasters and their audiences is 'an *unforced* relationship because it is unenforceable' (ibid.: 23) People are not, after all, obliged to switch on. This understanding of broadcast sociability is influenced by an early sociologist, Georg Simmel. It emphasises social interaction as an end in itself – talk for talk's sake. As such, it is very similar to the concept of 'phatic communication' associated with Malinowski and familiar to anthropologists and linguists. For CDA practitioners, there is also a clear connection with the interpersonal function: the function of language to establish and maintain social identities and relationships.

Work on broadcast sociability developed from archive research into BBC programming in the 1930s and 40s, including the pre-war light entertainment *Harry Hopeful* (1935–6), in wartime *Billy Welcome* (1941–2), 'an unholy mixture of propaganda and entertainment' (Scannell 1996: 39) and a long-running, post-war quiz show called *Have a go!* (1946–67). These early examples are fascinating for a British reader. However, twenty-first century equivalents are not hard to find, though big quiz shows with a studio audience were long ago transferred to television. A cookery contest current on TV at the time of writing will serve as an illustration. The following stretch of talk is from *Ready steady cook* (a US version is called *Ready set cook*). In it there is a friendly exchange of greetings between Ainsley Herriott, the host, Peter Birdman, one of the contestants and Lesley Walters, a chef, followed by some biographical detail about the contestant. Functioning interpersonally, it forms part of the run-up to the cookery contest itself:

AH: Ainsley Herriott (host)
PB: Peter Birdman (contestant)
LW: Lesley Walters (chef)

```
 1. AH:  How are you doing Pete?
 2. PB:  I'm fine
 3. AH:  Welcome to the show mate (.) come
 4.      and meet Lesley
 5. LW:  Hello Pete nice to meet you
 6. PB:  Hello yeah
 7. AH:  Well you are quite a versatile
 8.      chap when it comes to lang-
 9.      [moves P into camera shot] come
10.      here Pete move round (.) that's
11.      better Quite versatile with the
12.      old languages
13. PB:  Well you could say that yes (.)
14.      I speak one or two or three
15. AH:  One or two (.) six languages is it?
```

16. **PB:**   About that
17. **AH:**   And he's lived in four different
18.   countries Les (.)
19. **LW:**   Wow
20. **PB:**   yeh yeh
21. **AH:**   Have you a favourite among them?
22. **PB:**   Probably Italy
23. **LW:**   Yeh
              [
24. **AH:**   Yeh
25. **PB:**   Well my heart is Italian
26. **AH:**   Aw
27. **PB:**   I'm married to a lady who's half
28.   Italian and half Polish
29. **AH:**   Oh lovely
              [
30. **PB:**   so that's what gets the old
31.   strings going
32. **AH:**   Well tell us something in Italian
33. **PB:**   Te amo moltissimo Christina (xxxxxx)
                            [
34. **AH:**   Oh (xxxxxx)

This interaction is not, of course, part of the contest. It clearly establishes an identity for the contestant; it also establishes a relationship between him and the host before going on to the main business. The small sequence of sociable exchanges leads on to more obviously purposive exchanges about ingredients, procedures and so on. The paired greeting tokens (lines 1–6), interested-listener responses and gasps of appreciation (for instance, line 23) in the sequence are the sort of conversational objects that you would expect in friendly everyday talk between people. But unlike private interaction, this reciprocal dialogue is broadcast for consumption by absent viewers. They are 'doing' sociability on air, and in the process they are broadcasting that 'there is a pleasure to be found – a public, ... shareable, communicable enjoyment of good company' (Scannell 1996: 147).

The enjoyment of good company, being among friends, implies a relationship of equality. It is interesting to see equalising appeals in operation on programmes involving some form of expertise, such as *Ready steady cook*. The extracts below show the friendly, informal style of the host. The first illustrates his equalising self-presentation as a non-expert. In line 3, he asks the chef, Phil Vickery, for clarification about the use of dried apricots in a recipe involving filo pastry, thereby presenting himself as uninformed. Vickery responds with an explanation (lines 5–6) and a warning (line 7), both directed to Herriott:

```
PV:  Phil Vickery


1.  PV:   I'm going to wrap these herbs right inside
2.  AH:   Okay I noticed you put a couple of the
3.        dried apricots on top (.)
4.        always dried apricots or perhaps fresh?
5.  PV:   The thing about fresh is that they cause
6.        a lot of steam
7.        so be careful
8.  AH:   Okay
```

Ainsley Herriott is the host of the show and a professional chef. He is presumably not ignorant about the reason for using dried rather than fresh fruit in this method. His question is for the benefit of the audience, and with it he aligns himself with the audience/viewer (in ethnomethodological terms, he is 'doing "being ordinary"' (Sacks 1984)). Phil Vickery goes along with the pretence; in his description, each stage of the preparation process is directed to the show host. The food preparation and talk continue:

```
(Underlining: looking at camera)


 9.  PV:   So what I'm going to do here-
10.  AH:   Good tip there guys they cause a lot of
11.        steam and they loosen
12.        (.) the sort of the wrapping they're in
13.        (.) so buying dried
14.        apricots which are great actually and kids
15.        love to eat them it's good for us (.)
16.        nice and healthy
```

In addition to the equalising strategy the host/expert employs, his friendly informality is apparent in the viewer-address as 'guys', lexical choices ('kids', 'great'), the hedge ('sort of') and the appeal to shared circumstances, here of nutritional needs ('good for us'). A study from the USA examines the same phenomenon in *Martha Stewart living* (Davies 2003). Actually, with a contrary tendency, many TV 'experts' are at least as concerned with performing their expertise (such tendencies are addressed in Chapter 6 on 'Interpersonal Meaning in Broadcast Texts: Representing Social Identities and Relationships').

Recent hybrid genres – docu-soaps like *Hotel* in particular – have developed a kind of 'nosy sociability' (Corner 2000: 687). This notion of nosiness applies equally to 'Reality TV' shows like *Big brother*. Audience interest for this sort of fly-on-the-wall television is presumably inherently social, in Scannell's sense; it is hard to see what else it could be, at the time of viewing (though later it may serve the social function of providing something to talk about with friends and colleagues).

In *Radio, television and everyday life*, Scannell's interest is in entertainment programming, in which sociability is a primary function. But in his account it is intrinsic to broadcasting and unobtrusively suffuses broadcast talk, implicitly including the 'happy talk' between news anchors and presumably the fillers between scheduled elements. The latter are generally addressed directly to the audience and do not usually involve acts of on-air socialising, as such. For example, a music station prefaces a long advertising break on a weekday afternoon with this promise: 'More of the music we all love in a moment. To help you through your work day. *[jingle]*Virgin Radio'. This promise evokes (by means of a combination of presupposition and person deixis) the shared experience of music preferences and the reality of work. 'The music we all love' is the radio station's slogan, delivered hundreds of times a day, by a hundred different voices. The pronoun *we* functions in an inclusive way, as a person deictic (Scannell would call it an 'indexical term') that points to a group with shared musical tastes – the music station and the audience together. It is clearly functioning to construct a form of community identity.

Broadcast talk is institutional and available for shared access in the public domain. At the same time it is ordinary and domesticated, or strives to be:

> The world, in broadcasting, appears as ordinary, mundane, accessible, knowable, familiar, recognizable, intelligible, shareable and communicable for whole populations. It is talkable about by everyone. This world does not exist elsewhere. It is not a reflection, a mirror, of a reality outside and beyond. It is one fundamental, seen but unnoticed, constitutive component of contemporary reality for all.
>
> (Scannell 1992: 334)

Here we have a sense of broadcast media generating community, belonging, inclusion. It has the capacity to give people the company they need. Sociability holds the public domain of media together and draws the audience into its discourse. The concept was evoked in the context of defence of public service broadcasting against deregulation.

Scannell celebrates broadcasting 'as a public good, "a culture in common to whole populations" which needs to be defended against the fragmenting forces of deregulation' (Morley 2000: 119).

However, the reverse side of sociability is exclusion. The cultural inclusiveness of national broadcasting cannot include everyone:

> Scannell's celebration of broadcasting . . . simply fails to recognise that this public culture itself is already an ethnic culture and has a colour which is only common to some of the citizens of the nation which it supposedly reflects, and which it attempts to address.
>
> (Morley 2000: 119–20)

An issue Scannell ignores is the way sociability is enhanced by segregation into homogenous groups (Bonner 2003: 51). Sociability needs to, indeed must, erase difference; it depends on shared cultural background, implicit or otherwise. In the early radio broadcasts that Scannell discusses, the performances of community and belonging worked so well because the working-class participants, studio audience and absent audience had a great deal in common culturally (moreover, Morley points to an entirely unacknowledged white Englishness (2000: 119)). Scannell, indeed, does acknowledge that not all responses from listeners were positive; some dismissed *Have a go!* on what are (to me) clearly class grounds, as 'mawkishly sentimental . . . common and vulgar' (Scannell 1996: 56). Notwithstanding claims to inclusiveness, all programming relies on cultural specificity; the sociability that it broadcasts depends on taken-for-granted attitudes, ideas and values. This means that some people are included while others are not. You cannot have inclusion of some without exclusion of others. Even the lively sociability of *Ready steady cook* cannot reach everyone (for example, as a mother-in-law, I find Herriott's relentless banter at their expense highly irritating).

Scannell rejects the critical paradigm dominating media and cultural studies, objecting to what he perceives as reductiveness in its focus on the politics of representation. This rejection led to a broadside assault (the masculinist military metaphor seems entirely appropriate) on Birmingham Centre for Contemporary Cultural Studies, disseminated principally in Scannell (1989, 1992). He also, though less prominently, challenged the emergent CDA. Rather surprisingly, there have been few counter-challenges. Morley's is the most substantial critical engagement with Scannell's account of sociability (as far as I know):

> Sociability is simply not the indivisible Good which Scannell assumes it to be. . . . Sociability, by definition, can only ever be produced in some particular cultural (and linguistic) form and only those with

access to the relevant forms of cultural capital will feel interpellated
by and at home within the particular form of sociability offered by a
given programme.

(Morley 2000: 111)

Morley insists that power issues and political engagement are just as
important as understanding the role of national media in social cohesion;
he characterises them as 'vertical' and 'horizontal' dimensions of analysis
(ibid.: 110). Scannell is disinclined to accept the 'vertical'. In his history of
British broadcasting (Scannell and Cardiff 1991), power and politics
permeate the developments of broadcasting institutions and practices. He
is less willing to acknowledge their permeation of the programmes
themselves.

At the root of this disagreement, as Moores observes, is a theoretical
gulf between a consensus view of society and a critical one: 'The
perspective adopted by Morley puts an emphasis on cultural difference
(following his line of thought, it might perhaps be preferable to speak of
"sociabilities") and exclusion' (Moores 2005: 87). I would certainly go
along with Moores' concluding remark in *Media/theory*, that studies of the
media need some combination of these approaches, acknowledging that
'cooperation and social division are both contributing, simultaneously, to
the character of contemporary life' (ibid.: 178).

Synthetic personality and synthetic personalisation

Out of developments in the 'rhetoric of personality' in talk show performances on television has emerged the concept of 'synthetic personality'
(Tolson 1991). In broadcasting, personality is a performance. In Tolson's
early investigation of talk show discourse, a key example is a pastiche of the
broadcast genre that was called *The Dame Edna experience*. This programme,
screened in the 1980s, featured talk show host, Dame Edna Everage, who
was played by Barry Humphries, a male Australian comedian. The
character of the host was obviously synthetic, that is to say 'made up'. A
current example of a talk show format that is, in that respect, very similar is
The Kumars at no 42.[1] Sanjeev, the host, is performing 'himself' as a member
of a household in Wimbledon. The extended family has, as the BBC's *Guide
to comedy* website explains, 'hit upon a unique method of "Keeping up with
the Joneses": they have bulldozed their garden and erected a state-of-the-
art TV studio, wherein they host their very own chat show'. The *Guide to
comedy* website explains the format as follows:

The son, Sanjeev, pops the questions while his mother (Madhuri),
father (Ashwin) and mischievous granny (Sushila) sit and interrupt

from a nearby sofa. Each brings a distinctive personality to the mix: Sanjeev, unmarried and still living at home, is a trifle green about life; Madhuri is always plying food on to the guests and trying to get Sanjeev married off; Ashwin tells tedious tales and is obsessed with money; Sushila has a keen eye for male visitors and can be quite shocking with it. The guests include a number of prominent celebrities – Richard E. Grant, Michael Parkinson, Graham Norton, Art Malik, Warren Clarke, Minnie Driver, Melvyn Bragg, Leslie Phillips, June Whitfield, Jonathan Ross, Jerry Hall and Stephen Fry among them – all sportingly accepting the gentle ridiculing.

Here is an extract from a series broadcast in 2006. The three-generation family are awaiting the arrival of their first guest:

S: Sanjeev (played by Sanjeev Bhaskar)
M: Mum (Madhuri, played by Indira Joshi)
U: Ummi (Sushila, the grandmother, played by Meera Syal)
D: Dad (Ashwin, played by Vincent Ebrahim)
JC: Jamie Cullum (guest)

[Opening titles]
S: *[enters living room]* Alright mum? Big day tomorrow
     (.) birthday girl (.) Are you excited
M: Yes yes I I thought we-
S: Go and get us a drink could ye (.) parched
M: Something sweet and fizzy?
S: *[sits beside U]* Yeh with some fruit in it as well
     [mother leaves for the kitchen] (..) love you (.)
     mum (..) So what have you got her
U: Well don't say anything but I've got her two-toed socks (..) two pairs
[audience laughter]
S: Same as last year then
U: Yes (.) but this time they're not used *[audience laughter]*
S: Nice
U: What did you get her
S: Schwartzenegger boxed set (.) pen knife (.) Frisbee
[audience laughter]
U: Oy those were mine
S: Yeah but this way they stay in the family
     Anyway (.) it's the thought that counts innit? Dad?
D: *[from behind newspaper]* Yes Sanjeev?
S: What have you got mum for her birthday
D: Nothing

S: *[incredulous]* You forgot your own wife's birthday
U: hee hee hee
D: I didn't forget I never get her a birthday gift (.) never have (.)
        never will
U: *[hands to face]* Great big hee hee hee
D: I don't believe it (.) you don't have to buy
        someone a gift to show you care for them
U: Presents are nice (.) It's a gesture
D: I make affectionate gestures all the time (.) constructive criticism
        (.) lifts to the hospital (.) the list is endless (..) *[M appears with glass
        for S]* Oy where's mine *[M obediently retreats to kitchen]*
U: You haven't bought Madhuri a birthday present in forty years?
D: I certainly have not (. . .) anyway (.) your mother's fine with it
        [M returns with glass for D]
S: Mum (.) are you alright with him never ever having got you a
        present?
M: Well I was a bit upset the first fifteen years (. . .) but I got used to
        it
U: Madhuri stand up for yourself *[M starts to sit, then stands]*
        That confused little hobbit owes you forty years worth of
        presents and it's time to collect (.) How could you not buy her-
S: You haven't gave her a present in forty years in your own words
        and my mum you haven't got her a present my mum

Here we see stereotypes played out in a comedy routine centred on a
family's treatment of subservient and long-suffering Mum. Dad is
rescued from his son's and mother's indignation by the arrival of their
guest:

D: *[doorbell rings]* Shut up (..) that's Mr Cullum (.) let's be
        professional
        [All stand up, serious. JC enters, shakes hands with D]
JC: Hello (.) how you doing?
D: Very well (.) welcome to Number Forty Two Mr Cullum
JC: Thank you for having me (.) it's great to be here
D: This is my lovely family (..)
JC: Hello
S: It's her birthday tomorrow and he hasn't bought her a present (.)
        forty years and he's never bought her one present
U: Can you believe it never one present
D: Shut up (.) professionalism
S: Hello how do you do
        [

M: Hello how do you do

U: Oh you are so cute I could just-

S: Come on I'll show you my organ *[S enters stage set with exaggerated movements]* Thank you very much and welcome to <u>MY SHOW</u> *[sits at desk]* (.) now er my first guest has been called the (.) David Beckham of jazz *[show continues]*

(*The Kumars at No 42*, BBC1, Friday, 1 July 2006)

Sanjeev initially tries to draw the guest into their domestic dispute but then goes into role as show host.

As a concept, synthetic personality has grown out of the fruitful focus on sociability; consequently, it is mostly employed in discussion of entertainment formats (e.g., Bonner 2003). The *Kumars at no 42* provides a particularly clear illustration of the performance of synthetic personalities. Their joint performance as a fictitious family in a situation comedy setting is knowingly ironic, drawing on British Asian stereotypes of the spoiled son, the put-upon mother and so on. A different kind of synthetic personality can be seen in the drag queen host of *The Dame Edna experience* and, more recently, the gender-bending high camp of performers in other entertainment formats on British television (such as Lily Savage and Julian Clary)[2]. However, though far less prominently, Herriott's equalising strategies in *Ready steady cook* could be said to contribute to his performance of a synthetic personality: a 'celebrity chef'. Moreover, it is unclear to me why its use should be restricted to 'sociable' programming. After all, a performed persona is not necessarily 'friendly'. Jeremy Paxman's confrontational interview style is part of his act: his persona of 'public inquisitor' (Higgins 2007). Some critics, however, reject such an extended application of the concept (e.g., Bonner 2003: 77).

In Chapter 3, I outlined a CDA approach to producer–audience relations constructed in texts. This included a strategy known as synthetic personalisation, which involves the manipulation of interpersonal meanings and forms for instrumental purposes. Like the work in the broadcast sociability framework that I have covered in this chapter, it deals with minimisation of the distance between addresser and addressee by informalisation. Its key difference is in its aim, which stems from CDA's commitment to politically engaged analysis. In the section on sociability above, one of the examples I used was *Virgin Radio*'s slogan 'The music we all love', often used in transitions to advertising breaks. A CDA analysis would also pinpoint the slogan's contribution to constructing a community identity, but the focus on power relations would lead to a less benign view of its function. The community identity offered would be interpreted as part of a broader ploy to draw the listener into social relations of capitalism. The appeal to shared background knowledge would be seen to function ideologically, as an articulation of an 'ideological common sense'. The strategic attempts to minimise the distance between addresser and addressee would be viewed as exploitative.

In my view, the concept of 'synthetic personalisation' makes a valuable contribution to our understanding of modern media discourse. It adds to our understanding, for example, of the functioning of 'I'm really hoping that you're going to win tonight' and 'I'm hoping you'll have the winning combination' by the National Lottery presenter. I would suggest, however, that the term 'synthetic personality' is potentially confusing and unnecessary. It simply refers to a stage persona, generally a camped-up character, in light entertainment.

Simulated interaction on *Radio 1xtra*

Let me draw the chapter to a close with a more substantial illustration, using extracts from another music station, BBC's *Radio 1xtra* (all recorded in early 2006). The hosts on one show, 'Ace' and 'Invisible', engage in sociable exchanges with one another, including involved discussion about musicians and venues. According to a BBC press release, they are close friends who share a passion for music. Their face-to-face interaction is broadcast for consumption by absent listeners as entertainment. They also address the listener directly, with very frequent response-demanding utterances like the directives below (marked with →). The first is a plug for the next programme, the second for their own club appearance in Liverpool later that day:

> Yeah man
> → don't forget tonight (.)
> In case >>you didn't already know it<< it's all about Mobb Deep (.)
> In wiv Semtex (.) seven o'clock
> Hey
> → come and listen to Ace and Invisible (.) the troublemakers of radio

Other directives elicit mediated interaction (though the first does not really seem to be expecting a response):

> Ey we got millionaires listenin' to this programme.
> If you a millionaire
> → tex' me right now'

The hottest live black music
→ Register online right now
and every month you'll get an email about what's coming up

I: Myself and Ace went down to the (.) (listen) for their next album (.)
A: Yeah man (.) very impressed
I: Very impressive
>>Yeah ya can get on the message board an<< give your opinion
Are Mobb Deep still hot [website details]
You know what I mean
→ Have your say

A rapidly delivered signing off at the end of Ace and Invisible's slot contains two further examples. Ace also addresses the listener with expressive speech acts:

Well right man (.)
Back (.) Monday four till seven
→ >>>make sure you're here
→ Stay locked for Semtex<<< .hh wiv (.) Mobb Deep
>>We go in peace<<
Enjoy your weekend
[bar of signing-off music]
See you later

The double-act's delivery is animated and lively. From their accents, they are discernably black Londoners. The show is broadcast from London, but they offer a form of community identity that strives to be national. For example, a guest is talking about a forthcoming gig in Leicester (a city in the Midlands, therefore north of London):

Guest: . . . going down there
No I should say up there cos we're in the Midlands=
A: =No you should say Leicester cos we're in the whole of the UK (.)
We are where you are (.)
We're in your town right now

Deixis, use of inclusive *we* and direct address to listener as *you* contribute to the projection of community identity. The radio show *Ace & Invisible* is not attempting to cater for everyone's taste. It caters for people who want to hear garage and hip hop. It articulates a cultural identity that is specifically youthful, black and British – that is its remit, its purpose. They are doing sociability. They are in role in particular performance

personas (their synthetic personalities, perhaps). Part of their performance involves engaging in quasi-interaction with their listeners using
synthetic personalisation.

The identity of the hosts is also a specific kind of masculinity. A
performance of transgressive 'hardness' is sometimes evident ('Ace and
Invisible (.) the troublemakers of radio'). There is a casual sexism in some
of their throw-away remarks (for instance, 'All women want is your
money'). This performance and its offer of 'synthetic bruvahood' is
certainly amenable to a feminist CDA critical analysis. For such a
feminist critique to be effective, however, it would need to engage with
other performances as well, in media environments that are less regulated
than the BBC (Channel U, for example).

Notes

1. The BBC's *Guide to comedy* website names a range of adaptations including *The Ortegas* in USA (NBC 2003) and *Greeks on the roof* in Australia (Seven 2003).
2. It is hard to find equivalents in other cultural contexts for these TV performers. Their glamour as drag queens has similarities with the Las Vegas drag review 'superstar', Frank Marino, or the glamorous RuPaul and Harvey Fierstein. They may well not forgive me for pointing out that they are downmarket versions, however.

Activity

Tape a broadcast in an entertainment format. Identify the 'friendship-building' strategies employed in it and its implicit claims to inclusiveness. Who does it exclude? How? (To do this thoroughly, you will need to transcribe the text of the broadcast, though taking notes over repeated playbacks will give you a rough idea.)

Further reading

Morley, David (2000), 'Broadcasting and the national family', *Home territories: media, mobility and identity*, London: Routledge.
Scannell, Paddy (1996), 'Sociability', *Radio, television and modern life*, Oxford: Blackwell.
Thompson, John (1995), 'The rise of mediated interaction', *Media and modernity: a social theory of the media*, Cambridge: Polity.
Tolson, Andrew (1991), 'Televised chat and the synthetic personality', in Scannell, Paddy (ed.), *Broadcast talk*, London: Sage.
Toynbee, Jason (2006), 'The media's view of the audience', in Hesmondhalgh, David (ed.), *Media production*, Open University Press.

6 Interpersonal meaning in broadcast texts: representing social identities and relationships

Interaction as a performance for a viewing or listening audience has had no shortage of attention. Broadcast talk as a field of critical inquiry is reaching maturity, with several recent books in print. The body of work on broadcast talk is now quite substantial. Most of it is on verbal interaction between participants in specific genres of programming, such as news interviews and sports commentary. In the 1980s, early work in the field attended to news, especially interviews with an interest in the design of talk for overhearing audiences; other prominent work in the field examined the dynamics of phone-in talk (these are both topics of subsequent Chapters: Chapters 7 and 8 respectively). Tolson (2006) provides a useful overview of generic developments in media talk on radio and television.

This chapter focuses on broadcast text as spectacle. It deals with issues of participatory structure, power and control in enactments of social relationships offered as spectacle. In it I focus on factual programming, on TV texts depicting TV presenters and non-media people, both professionals of various kinds and 'ordinary' people. I have, of course, had to be highly selective, but the mediatised social identities and relationships that I address have relevance beyond the specific genres and programmes selected. Consumerist lifestyle television is the focus of the first two sections. In them, I look at TV presenters as tourists interacting with locals at holiday destinations, then at TV 'experts' and authority, the presenter-expert/novice relationship and sociability. The next section examines tensions in representations of patterns of interaction, social identities and relationships in a hybrid format: the documentary series, *Jamie's school dinners*. A further section attends to elite broadcasting genres and to the BBC's representation of a high-profile current affairs 'celebrity' in interview with politicians.

Travel broadens the mind?

. . . and promotes understanding across cultures? This is part of the founding myth of the Grand Tour as 'pleasurable instruction' (Batten

1978) but, according to critical studies of tourism, it is not the case. Such studies (e.g., Crick 1989) indicate tourists' superficial understanding of local cultures and insensitivity about local people, especially in 'exotic' holiday destinations. Voluntary Service Overseas and Tourism Concern, a campaign group, argue that travel-related broadcasting on British television perpetuates this situation, They express particular concern about coverage of developing countries as tourist destinations (Rice 2001).

Focusing on the two British television programmes criticised in the report, a recent study examines the interactions between the tourist-presenters and local people at the holiday destinations (Jaworski et al. 2003). The study looks at a full season's broadcasts of *Holiday* (BBC) and *Wish you were here?* (ITV), both screened at peak-viewing time in 2000–1 to an audience of seven to eight million each week. The authors were interested in discerning patterns of interaction between the tourist-presenters (who are seen as stand-ins, or proxies for the viewer and would-be tourist) and locals. Three distinct categories of role for the local people emerged:

- Expert/Guide, e.g. skiing instructor, distillery guide, park ranger, basket weaver, restaurateur, wine maker, golf pro, diamond dealer, naturalist, conservationist, biologist, instructor at a 'cowboy school'.
- Servant/Helper, e.g. waiter, cook/chef, receptionist, caddy, door-man, market seller, croupier, masseur, reflexologist, shop assistant, airboat driver.
- A third category, 'Other', accounted for a small number of local people depicted as part of heterogeneous groupings, e.g. tourist business owner/operator, strangers, people portrayed as part of the local landscape or scenery ('peoplescape').

(ibid.: 139)

In one of the segments studied, the presenter is detailing the delights of a luxury resort in the Maldives. A chef is preparing a meal exclusively for the tourist-presenter, Mary Nightingale. In this one-to-one relationship, the local person is in the role of a servant, helping a wealthy tourist to realise a culinary whim:

```
MN:     Mary Nightingale (presenter)
1. MN:  [v/o] the staff here really do go out of
2.      their way to indulge your every whim for
3.      example if you don't fancy eating in the
4.      dining-room (.) they'll set up a table by
5.      the water's edge (.) and if even that's
```

```
  6.      not remote enough for you (.) how about
  7.      this (.) your very own dinner cooked
  8.      especially for you on your own private
  9.      island
 10.      [to chef placing plate of food on her
 11.      table] thank you very much
 12.      Chef: you're welcome ma'am
```
(ibid.: 143–4)

The talk is mostly voice-over, concluding with the briefest of phatic exchanges between tourist and service provider. The adjacency pair – her expression of thanks (11) and his response (12) – is a highly formulaic part of the service encounter. With the respectful address term *ma'am*, the chef places Nightingale in the dominant position of a wealthy customer (ibid.: 144).

Longer formulaic exchanges in service encounters are quite common in the data. In several programmes these are in a local language. In the next extract, Joe McGann is depicted shopping at an open-air market with his daughter in St Malo, France (the first two lines are presumably voice-over):

```
JMc:   Joe McGann (presenter)
V:     Vendor
  1. JMc:  in the middle of the old quarter is a fish
  2.       market where we bought the ingredients for
  3.       our supper [approaching a fish stall]
  4.       bonjour madame
           good morning*
  5. V:    bonjour monsieur (.) messieurs dames
           good morning, sir
  6. JMc:  je voudrais un kilo de moules s'il vous
  7.       plait
           I'd like a kilo of mussels, please
             [
  8. V:      mais bien sûr (1.0) alors un kilo
  9.       [starts scooping mussels]
           of course, so, one kilo
 10. JMc:  et aussi quelque crevettes s'il vous plait
           and some prawns as well, please
                           [
 11. V:                    quelques crevettes
                           some prawns
```

```
12.  JMc:   aha
13.  V:     d'accord
            OK
14.  JMc:   merci madame
            thank you
15.         [turns to daughter] they look lovely don't
16.         they
```

* Authors' translation

(ibid.: 144)

The entire transaction is conducted in French, providing a 'flavour of the local language, which helps create a "linguascape" of the holiday destination' (ibid.: 145). The language is simple 'Tourist French', drawing on guide-book phrases, so that in effect it displays the relative ease with which such transactions can be conducted in a foreign language (note that in 5 the fishmonger evidently includes the camera crew in his polite greeting, although Jaworski et al. do not complicate the sample by translating it). Another study of travel-related programmes focuses specifically on the issue of local languages, examining the relationships established in programmes between protagonists, speakers of foreign languages and the viewing audience (Gieve and Norton 2005). Focusing on three travelogues, it identifies a tendency to erase linguistic difference altogether, that is, simply not to show interactions with 'others' who are not competent speakers of English. As David Dunn observes, television holiday coverage is more 'at ease with visual consumption of place and its facilities' than with interaction with the locals (Dunn 2005: 101).

Another broadcast features John Savident (who would be known to many viewers as a soap actor) in Fiji. In the following extract the local person, a masseuse, is present as silent servant, subservient to the hedonistic desires of the tourist:

```
JS:   John Savident (presenter)
1.  JS:   [raises head to look at the camera; as JS
2.         talks, camera pans out and JS is seen
3.         receiving back massage; the masseuse looks
4.         down throughout the clip]
5.         when I'm on holiday the hell with sports
6.         and activities I like to be relaxed and do
7.         nothing (.) well I am relaxed and I am
8.         doing nothing and I can think of no better
```

```
9.      place than here (.) in Fiji
10.     [lowers his head which is covered by a
11.     straw hat and looks down]
```

(Jaworski et al. 2003: 145)

The interaction represented between the masseuse and Savident is solely transactional. Not even eye contact is required from the masseuse as she mutely provides a paid service:

> the local is portrayed as an anonymous, distant, and subordinate "silent servant" – one of 'them', whereas the tourist, who is a celebrity on one of the British popular soap operas, is portrayed as a familiar, friendly and powerful tourist – one of 'us'.

(ibid.: 145)

The programmes imply little contact with local people, who form a small, relatively insignificant part of the tourist experience of local culture. Often portrayed as compliant and submissive, the locals are 'there to help, serve and inform' (ibid.: 159). Engagements with them are limited to brief formulaic encounters.

Another broadcast, featuring Judith Chalmers in Llafranc, on the Costa Brava in Spain, illustrates the 'personal touch' provided by small hotels in the region. A hotel receptionist appears in the expected servant/helper role in the segment, though, in this extract, she is briefly positioned as friend and expert/guide:

```
JC:  Judith Chalmers (presenter)
R:   Receptionist
 1. JC: [v/o] well-cleaned beaches are an obvious
 2.     attraction but what I wonder lies behind
 3.     the coast (.) who better to ask than my
 4.     friend at the hotel [cut to JC looking at
 5.     a map with the receptionist]
 6. R:  ten kilometres from here (.) this is the
 7.     village of (.) Pais that is me- medieval
 8.     town
 9. JC: good well you've given me some good advice
10.     many thanks indeed
11. R:  not at all
12. JC: bye
13. R:  bye bye
```

(ibid.: 147–8)

Here the brief, scripted interaction gives an impression of interpersonal involvement, but it is perfunctory, an empty claim to intimacy between tourist and local people.

Two further extracts from the same study feature a broadcasting couple, Chris and Ingrid Tarrant, at locations in Egypt. The first is in a museum in Cairo with a guide called Lavina. The local person is named and has a high status role as museum guide. She is, however, undermined by Chris Tarrant's flippant remarks and questions:

```
CT:  Chris Tarrant (presenter)
L:   Lavina (museum guide)
IT:  Ingrid Tarrant (presenter)
 1.  CT:  [v/o; panoramic view of Cairo] it's easy
 2.       to forget that this is home to a great
 3.       ancient civilisation much of it is
 4.       captured here at the Museum of Egyptian
 5.       Antiquities (.) the package includes the
 6.       services of a guide (.) we had Lavina
 7.       [cut to the Tarrants and their guide
 8.       standing in front of a slightly damaged
 9.       sculpture in the Museum]
10.       it's a bit rough this one isn't it (.)
11.       what's happened to him?
          [
11.  L:   yes [smiles hesitantly; starts the tour]
12.       all of th-=
13.  IT:  =Chri::s it's thousands of years old
            [
14.  CT:  well you know what I'm saying he's got
15.       sort of his eye::s closed [touches his own
16.       eye, grimaces, laughs] he looks like he's
17.       been in a pretty bad fight (.) [cut to
18.       another exhibit] so who are these two?
20.  L:   well uh this is Prince (Raha) with
21.       Princess Nafret his wife=
22.  CT:  =they look a bit like Richard and Judy
23.       [Lavina looks at CT; Lavina and IT laugh
24.       uneasily] but they do it's true::::=
25.  L:   [looking quizzically] =Richard and Judy=
26.  CT:  =they look like an early form of Richard
27.       and Judy
28.  L:   no
```

29. **CT:** yes you wouldn't understand that in Eqypt
30. **L:** no *[smiles]*
31. **CT:** trust me in England we know Richard and
32.   Judy

(ibid.: 151–2)

The museum guide is unable to perform her expert role as a professional. Her attempt to begin the tour (line 12) is disrupted by the Tarrants, who both interrupt her (lines 13 and 14). In line 18, Chris Tarrant questions her about an exhibit depicting a couple. Her informative response (lines 20 and 21) is curtailed as he interrupts again (line 22), comparing the figures to another couple familiar to a British audience as TV presenters. In his concern to find amusing things to say about the exhibits, his flippancy shifts the frame from serious to playful. In the process, he reverses roles in interaction with the guide, transforming her from expert (lines 20 and 21) to ignorant (line 25). He imposes a British popular culture meaning on to Egyptian ancient history (her expertise); this excludes her from the cultural reference. She is positioned as a 'stupid foreigner', even though the interaction takes place on her home ground, in the museum where she is employed. She maintains a limited role of polite host, despite being humiliated as a professional.

In the following week's broadcast, the same tourist couple present another Egyptian holiday package. This segment includes their encounter with a tour guide called Abdul, whom they seem to treat with a good deal more respect:

A: Abdul (museum guide)
1.   *[theme music from the film Raiders of the*
2.   *Lost Ark plays in the background]*
3. **IT:** *[looks at hieroglyphics]* I wonder what it
4.   all says?
5. **CT:** good question Mrs Tarrant a guide is a
6.   must (.) here's ours (1.0) *[to guide]* hi
7.   I'm Chris *[guide and CT shake hands]*
                    [
8. **A:**   (nice to meet you)
9. **CT:** Ingrid my wife
10. **IT:** *[shakes hands with the guide]* hi Abdul
11.   hello
12. **CT:** *[looks at the wall]* this is amazing isn't
13.   it?
14. **A:** this is one of the main magnificent tombs

15.   in the Valley of the Kings Ramses the
16.   Fourth (.) the colours are original dating
17.   to 1160 BC (.) we made it but it belongs
18.   to everyone all over the world

(ibid.: 153)

In this extract, there is an element of relational solidarity in the handshaking and exchange of first names (lines 6 to 11). As Jaworski et al. observe, the Tarrants are ignorant tourists in need of a guide; at least, I would add, Ingrid Tarrant is content to display her ignorance (lines 3 to 4), while her husband limits his display of knowledge and control to announcing the need for a guide and introducing him. Their host, in turn, is able to perform in his professional role of Egyptian museum guide (lines 14 to 18). He offers his expert knowledge as a member of an ancient nation and custodian of world heritage. The first-person plural in line 17 excludes his interlocutors; he uses it to position himself as a 'truly cosmopolitan, global citizen' (ibid.) sharing his nation's heritage. This is in striking contrast with the treatment of the museum guide called Lavina in the previous broadcast. Jaworski et al. do not speculate on the reason for it, but we can. Perhaps Chris Tarrant felt more comfortable allowing a man to take up the powerful position of expert; or perhaps he was criticised for his rudeness the previous week. The authority that Abdul manages to maintain in this encounter is interesting; however, unknown to him, the soundtrack undercuts it in the broadcast text of *Wish you were here?* The theme music from the film *Raiders of the Lost Ark* reframes the interaction, recontextualising it in popular culture.

Clearly, 'ordinary' people are not in control of the use of footage in which they appear. Pre-recording and tight editing leads to highly restricted subject positioning of participants who are not media professionals. They are at the mercy of editing, sound track additions etc and the potential that these processes have for recontextualisation.

Expertise, authority and 'taste' in lifestyle TV

As outlined in Chapter 5, the cultivation of ordinariness is at the heart of broadcast talk and media discourse's apparent seamlessness with domestic life. Broadcast sociability depends upon attempts to close the gap between producers and audiences, the pervasiveness of 'chat' as a broadcast genre and so on. There is a tension between these tendencies (involving equalising strategies, authenticity and sincerity) with their opposites (imposition of hierarchies based on expertise, performativity and playfulness). It is expertise I focus on here. Inequality is inherent in a relationship between an expert and their addressee, who is potentially positioned as ignorant, a novice. This can present something of a dilemma for the TV expert whose persona (or 'synthetic personality') is not authoritarian.

A study of British gardening programmes observes interesting shifts in displays of expertise in recent primetime lifestyle television (Taylor 2002). Didactic address directed at the viewer has been replaced, in shows like BBC's *Groundforce* and *Homefront in the garden*, with partnership with clients in a makeover. The traditional format of 'instructional close-up sequence of seed-sowing or pruning, accompanied by an authoritative voice-over is regarded as an outmoded means of engaging contemporary audience'; a more likely lifestyle format is to show the presenter 'in mid-shot partnership with his or her clients, assessing and interpreting their needs, or reframing their garden dreams to fit the transformative remit of a make-over design' (ibid.: 488). The makeover format involves less instruction and more spectacle, including elements of melodrama. Taylor observes the influence of the primetime slot in the presence of generic elements of the programming it has replaced:

> Lifestyle has largely replaced situation comedies and 'serious' high-status programmes in the primetime slot, but what programme-makers have chosen to retain from those previous genres, however, are some of the main ingredients required for the entertainment required from 8.00 to 9.00: drama, conflict, emotion and stereotypes.
>
> (ibid.: 489)

Other, more specialist gardening programmes have also shifted in the same direction. These now tend to consist of meetings between experts – gardener-presenter and gardener-guest – involving the representation of knowledge and expertise being shared and exchanged in friendly inter-action for the overhearing audience (ibid.: 490). Taylor's focus is 'ordinari-ness'. Even expert gardening programmes are 'ordinari-ised', that is, anchored in mundane, everyday activities (ibid.: 482). We can add that it avoids an explicit expert/novice relationship with the viewer, enables the presenter to maintain a voice of 'popular public service' (Ellis 2000: 32) and enhances the mediated quasi-interaction with the viewer.

It is also interesting to see how the presenter-expert/novice relation-ship with participants on programmes is represented. A recent study of a British property programme, *Property ladder*, observes that the presenter-expert, Sarah Beeny, is mostly present as voice-over (Smith 2005). When she does appear interacting with the house owners, she is friendly and supportive: 'Rather than being the authoritative expert, the host instead presents herself to the participants as being their friend, her knowledge and experience expressed as affability, helping them work out their problems' (Smith 2005: 9). Beeny's criticisms of the house renovators are addressed not to them but, over their heads, to the viewer. Citing Goffman's concept of frames (Goffman 1974), Smith accounts for the contrast in terms of friendship and credible expert frames. The use of voice-over has the added benefit of hindsight, giving an impression of wisdom and prescience to her displays of expertise (Smith 2005: 16).

Other lifestyle presenters, however, have no compunction about displaying their expert status in interaction with participants and at their expense. The presenter of *Hot property* makes frequent attacks on property owners' furnishing tastes, colour sense and other perceived stylistic shortcomings. In a segment featuring 'expert' Alice Beer and a property owner, Patrick, he is constructed as an undiscerning single male. As they enter his living room, the presenter sarcastically compliments him on the 'lovely colour' of the walls, mockingly asking him, 'Patrick what colour >is this< on the (.) colour chart'? The following jibe is a further simple example:

```
AB:  Alice Beer (presenter)
P:   Patrick
1.   AB and P standing on an      AB:  Spectacularly dodg::y
     imitation Oriental rug,           carpets inherited
     lower legs and footwear           [
     visible                      P:   hhh
                                  AB:  from some granny I
                                       suspect=
2.   edge of rug, clashing       P:   =it's a brand new carpet
     with mottled dark green           Alice it's lovely
     pattern on floor carpet
```

(adapted from Giles 2002: 616)

In this instance, Giles notes that 'an older female is blamed for the lapse in taste, although it might seem consistent with Patrick's apparent lack of discernment that he is happy to recycle hand-me downs from past generations' (ibid.), an assumption that he challenges in 2. Later in Patrick's segment of this property development programme, his attempts to position himself as accomplished handyman are completely ignored, while the presenter focuses on his interior decoration and furnishing 'lapses', aspects that are (from a property development perspective) irrelevant anyway.

In lifestyle programmes, what counts as expertise seems to have shifted. Lifestyle programming in general seems to be 'more about educating the audience in judgements of taste than disseminating skills and knowledge' (Giles 2002: 607). 'Lifestyle' here needs to be understood specifically in terms of consumer culture:

> within contemporary consumer culture it connotes individuality, self-expression and a stylistic self-consciousness. One's body, clothes, speech, leisure pastimes, eating and drinking preferences, home, car, choice of holidays etc. are to be regarded as indicators of the individuality of taste and sense of style of the owner/consumer.
>
> (Featherstone 1991; cited in Bonner 2003: 105–6)

Given the consumerism that lifestyle programming is premised on, the expert has been reconfigured as style advisor, whose role is to offer 'practical vocabularies of consumer transformation' (Taylor 2002: 485). In the specific case of lifestyle gardening shows, 'some of the lifestyle "experts" are less authoritative legislators conveying the hard facts of gardening, than friendly, well-researched consumers, interpreting the latest lifestyle shopping ideas for the would-be gardener' (ibid.: 487). Their status as specialists is diminished, since their knowledge is consumer advice rather than horticultural know-how. In the lifestyle format, experts become 'cultural intermediaries' who demonstrate desired consumption patterns (Bourdieu 1984; cited in Bonner 2005: 43).

Of course, in many genres the presenter's broadcasting persona is highly authoritarian. Some programming with a competitive format normalises a public style of talk characterised by bullying, exemplified by the adversarial hyper-masculine style of Simon Cowell (*American idol*), Donald Trump and Alan Sugar (US and British versions of *The apprentice*) and, arguably, Anne Robinson (*The weakest link*). Later in this chapter, I examine formal interviews in current affairs broadcasts in which this combative style is prevalent. In the next section, I turn to an individual TV expert making strategic use of his media access and, crucially, his TV persona.

'Transforming these school dinners is gonna be *tough*': Jamie's dinner ladies

> Jamie Oliver first came to prominence in *The Naked Chef*, marked by a cheeky persona and a can-do approach to cooking. His subsequent modulation into the more socially aware person . . . used both of these qualities to bring him closer to the apprentices and to contest the stereotypical image of the do-gooder.
>
> (Bonner 2006: 68)

Jamie Oliver is a 'celebrity chef', familiar from lifestyle TV. *Jamie's school dinners*, however, is something rather different. While it has lifestyle elements, it is a combination of docu-soap, celebrity biopic and make-over. More than that, as mentioned in Chapter 2, it is a kind of mediatised political activism: part of a campaign to improve the quality of food in British schools and, more broadly and even more ambitiously, impose constraints on the junk food industry and improve British eating habits. In this chapter on representations of patterns of interaction, social identities and relationships, the series is of particular interest because of a tension between two conflicting objectives: the maintenance of the celebrity's persona of likeable 'ordinariness' and the unfolding drama of epic transformation. At the centre of both are the dinner ladies, who are both his instruments and his greatest hurdle.

In the first two episodes, the epic transformation that he undertakes is the establishment of nutritious, freshly prepared food in a single secondary school in the London borough of Greenwich. Once he succeeds in that challenge (with many dramatic and conflictual engagements with both kitchen staff and children), he goes on to 'tackle' the whole Borough of Greenwich. The male voice-over (Timothy Spall, who has a South East English accent similar to Oliver's) asks: 'Can Jamie Oliver transform what 20,000 kids eat right across one London borough and change British school dinners?' This second challenge involves sixty schools in all and the voice-over tells us that 'Jamie will have to plan the borough takeover like a military campaign.' The third and ultimate aim is to take a blueprint for improving the standards of school meals directly to the Secretary of State for Education. The voice-over chimes in like a Greek chorus at regular intervals, making sure the viewer is aware of the enormity of the epic task at each stage. As an elaborate TV stunt it makes absorbing viewing and, as the biopic elements of the documentary make abundantly clear, this is a huge undertaking that has been conducted at considerable personal cost. From the docu-soap elements, it is also evident that the cost wasn't only Oliver's. This is dramatically represented in the interactions that have been selected for the finished programme, including those between the celebrity chef-expert and the dinner ladies (actually catering managers – 'head dinner ladies' – in London schools).

Before going on to examine some of these depictions, we need to consider the portrayal of Oliver himself. As I observed in Chapter 2, his social identity as a media celebrity is a resource on which his campaign depends. As such, his distinctive public persona as 'celebrity chef' needs to be foregrounded. Early sequences in the first episode outline the constraints of cooking to a small budget (an impossibly meagre thirty-seven pence per child) for a chef for whom money is no object. The comparison with a charismatic football star projects the TV chef's clear understanding of himself as celebrity:

> It's a bit like taking away (.) David Beckham's (.) Adidas football boots and giving him a pair of Jesus sandals really (..) he- (x) kick a few good balls but he's running around like a muppet and that's kind've what I'm doin'

Biopic elements (such as a book-cover photo shoot) contribute to this portrayal. At the same time, Oliver is 'constructed as ordinary, as "an Essex boy"' (Moseley 2001: 36), as in his first docu-soap cookery show, *The naked chef*. A media commentator describes him as 'effortlessly working class' (Ian McMillan on *Newsnight review*); though a silly remark, this implicitly acknowledges the performativity of a televised persona. Rachel Moseley's observations about his construction as ordinary and authentic in *The naked chef* apply equally to his later screen appearances. He is often shown with children, friends and family. He is shown being demonstrative and affectionate with both male and female colleagues. These scenes are 'unmediated by the presence of the director and are generally presented through a grainy, realist aesthetic which suggests the authenticity of home videos' (Moseley 2001: 38). Central to his authenticity is his enthusiasm and expressive intensity, including his swearing (for example, typical school meal provision is glossed as 'scrotum-burger shite'). In *Jamie's school dinners*, he also has a new persona of parent, conveyed in biopic sections but also articulated in his overall concern for the health of children nationally. His persona is interesting in terms of its articulation of a youthful masculinity. Moseley observes that, while he is presented as heterosexual, he is visually eroticised and in some ways constructed 'as a "girl" – he shops (even if he does complain) and "dances with the girls"; he cares, he cooks' (ibid.). This no doubt explains why writers for the men's magazine *Loaded* hate him so much.

In the view of another commentator, Tony Parsons, Oliver leaves this persona behind in *Jamie's school dinners*:

> He has got the nerve to step outside of his persona. If you want Simon Cowell on American Idol, he is the camp, bitchy record company executive. Alan Sugar in the Apprentice is the hard-arsed capitalist shouting at people. Jamie Oliver can't be the lovable Cockney wanker in this situation, because most of the time he is angry, irritated and frustrated, because he genuinely cares about the subject. That's why it's great TV [. . .] He allows a face to be shown which is not what he

has made his millions or his reputation on. It's quite moving. He is like a rebel chef, he genuinely cares.

(Newsnight review transcript)

However, my own view is that Oliver's anger, irritation and frustration contribute to his 'authenticity'. Clearly, the persona constructed from the film footage is inflected differently from in his cookery shows, but his heightened expressive focus, or intensity of feeling, remains the same and he continues to be represented as 'lovable'.

In stage one, Oliver enters the all-female space of Kidbrooke Comprehensive's school kitchen. His first morning is spent as a 'rookie dinner lady', as he learns about the daily routine. He reports his impression of the food, the kitchen manager and her staff to an off-camera (and unheard) interviewer:

> The food's obviously all shit isn' it I mean (.) it's not her fault she runs a tight ship don't get me wrong those girls are <u>great</u> (.) em er they're re- they're- (.) >what are they doing< (.) they're running a tight ship they're (.) cooking or reheating things (.) er <u>very</u> effectively (.) >good attention to detail< (.) but what they are reheating is <u>shite</u>

The voice-over chimes in: 'transforming these school dinners is gonna be <u>tough</u> (.) and he hasn't even met the <u>kids</u> yet'. In the first two episodes, much of the dramatic tension hangs on his developing relationship with the kitchen manager, Nora Sands, his dawning realisation of the practical difficulties in what he has taken on and the schoolchildren's repeated rejection of the fresh food prepared to his instructions.

As stage two ('the borough takeover') begins, the voice-over explains the first part of the next challenge facing Oliver: 'It's taken Jamie months to teach Nora how to successfully cook these dishes (.) he's got just three <u>days</u> to teach <u>sixty</u> others' (presumably, the more impossible the odds the better). The catering managers from sixty schools are sent on an intensive three-day chef training course coordinated by Greenwich Council, the army and Jamie Oliver at the Defence Food Services School, an army education centre at Aldershot. The third episode has opened with the voice-over's 'military campaign' simile; thirty minutes or so later, it starts to come to life. The programme gives no indication of army involvement whatsoever until seconds before the scene depicting the dinner ladies' arrival at Aldershot. A brief image of legs in camouflage marching and a short clip from footage of training-camp planning are intercut with a longer, domestic scene, depicting Oliver and his family the evening before the training camp. The switch is from very small children after bathtime to the following scene. The transition from the domestic scene to the dinner ladies' arrival at Aldershot is abrupt and rather startling:

```
S:   Sergeant
DL:  Dinner lady
 1. CU Soldier with            [bus engine]
    machine gun
 2. Greenwich bus         v/o: On Wednesday
    arriving                   morning
 3. zoom in on smiling faces   sixty dinner ladies
    of passengers              arrive at Aldershot
 4. Foreground: school sign
    side-on; LS armed guard,   at the school of army
    wire fencing               catering
 5. DL (Lesley) alighting      (.) they've given up
 6. walks towards soldiers     their half term
                               holiday for an
 7. CU S looking on            intensive three-day
                               course=
 8. CU throng of excited DLs S: [DLs chattering] =I hope
                               you're all ready to
                               march you're gonna march
                               over in your groups yeah?
 9. CU feet                    QUICK MARCH
                          DL:  [startled] oh
                               [DLs laughter throughout]
10. DLs in unruly line    S:   LEFT RIGHT LEFT RIGHT
11. DLs milling about          (xxx) co:me o:::n (.) ho:ld
                               your ho:rses
```

The women enter into masculine space and military discipline; the militarisation of roles and relationships positions them as dominated and disciplined. The producer has chosen to use the training school footage in this very particular way. Though keyed as humorous, it places them symbolically under male dominance and control.

After their first attempt to cook to the recipes that Oliver has prepared, there is a tasting inspection. In this second extract, Oliver is in role as teacher:

```
J:  Jamie Oliver
C:  Army Chef
 1. DLs working in tent    v/o: Jamie's campaign
```

(various shots)	will <u>hinge</u> on whether he can get the dinner ladies up to speed in the next two <u>days</u> (.) it's <u>cruci</u>al that they get his food tasting <u>right</u>
2. MCU **J**, **S** and 5 or so **DL**s gathered around canisters	**J:** well <u>that</u> looks nice (.) well pre<u>sented</u>?
3. Zoom CU **J**'s fork into canister	(..) who cooked this

His positively polite compliment (in 2) and show of interest (in 3) encourages one dinner lady to speak out. As a spokeswoman for the group, she begins to articulate the procedure they have gone through, thereby taking 'ownership' of it.[1] From the variable sound quality, I assume the dinner ladies were not wired up (though Oliver may have been) and the scene relies on a boom mike:

4. Tilt **J** lifting to mouth, looking at speaker	**DL1:** *[indistinct]* (it's a joint effort) [
	DLs: yeah yeah
5. **J** chewing, watched by **S**	**DL1:** *[indistinct]* we chopped all the (.) vegetables up
6. **DL1** gesturing	(.) yogurt

All is not well, however, and the camera takes in their reception of his face-threatening remarks:

7. **J** removing offending bit, watched by **S**	**DL2:** Oh I think he's got a bit of bone there
8. **J** scowling at sample in fingers	**J:** It's not <u>bone</u> (.)
9. CU **DL1** and **2**, attentive	it's <u>fat</u>
	DL1: *[surprised]* <u>is</u> it
10. CU **J**'s spoon in rice	**J:** Yeah

As Oliver moves on to the rice, he resorts to sarcasm. The advice in 12 is insincere; not advice at all, but criticism:

```
11. J  tasting rice
12. CU S                          Wants a bit of milk
                                  and bit of vanilla
                                  [
                          S:      yeah
                          J:      in there
                                  [
                          S:      a- abso<u>lute</u>ly
                          J:      (.) rice puddin'
13. DL1 and 2             S:      that's how you can
    half-smile, nodding           tur<u>n</u> it (.) into your rice
                                  pu<u>dd</u>in'
```

The sarcasm would be readily recognisable for the dinner ladies, even before Oliver draws out his implicature ('rice puddin'). As he speaks, the camera picks up the sergeant's amusement as he enthusiastically endorses Oliver. Then it turns back to the dinner ladies in 13, to register their response as the sergeant reiterates Oliver's insincere advice. After the two men's co-production of mockery, the continuing segment is intercut with commentary from Oliver on the dinner ladies' poor performance, with additional tasting images:

```
14. MCU J with           J:      [to interviewer
    clipboard, gesturing         off-camera]
                                 They're not concentrating
                                 on the detail (.) sticky
                                 rice instead of fluffy rice
                                 (.)
15. CU S tasting                 er and they haven't been t-
                                 I don't think anyone
16. J with inedible chunk        <u>tasted</u> what they were
    in teeth, grimacing          doin' they just sort've (.)
17. DL1 and 2 (annoyed?)         got <u>on</u> with it
18. MCU J with                   so me personally
    clipboard, gesturing         (.) th- this is m- my baby
                                 y'know I- I think they
                                 could do a lot better
```

After this critical assessment, it cuts straight to the dinner ladies' perspective. They are struggling with the unfamiliar army equipment:

```
19. DL3 (Lesley) with pan,     DL3:  [to interviewer
    in washing up area               off-camera]
                                     This is all designed for
                                     men not for women (this
                                     joke)
                               DL4:  (xxx)
20. Group washing pans         DL3:  We haven't got the-
                                     the strength for all this
                                     (.) It's really hard
21. Horseplay with water.      [laughter]
```

The narrative then switches to tasting with another group. The camouflage trousers that Oliver is wearing with his chef's coat visually align him with the army chefs. Again, all is not well. Oliver's initial assessment of a sample that he is tasting takes the following spectacular form:

```
22. MCU C and S grinning,
    J tasting, DLs watching
23. DLs watching               J:  Fuck me
24. J turning, ejecting food,      [spits]
    C and S still in shot
```

He utters a startled expletive, then performs projectile spitting involving a sudden, full body turn. The camera work also takes in the reactions of the dinner ladies (23) and the amusement of the two soldiers looking on (22 and 24). Oliver then begins a critical appraisal that has rather more ideational content. To the dinner ladies' dismay, he itemises the shortcomings of the food they have prepared:

```
25. CU food canister           the butternut squash (.) is
                               totally raw
26. Tilts up to dejected face  while the other stuff is
                               soft (.) or overcooked
27. Pans to J                  but erm there seems to be a
                               hell of a lot
28. Out to S, J and DLs        of oil in there girls
                          S:   yeah
```

'Girls' is the usual term of address for the groups of women, though all of them are older than Oliver. While it is doubtless intended to be friendly, it contributes to underlining the asymmetrical social relationship between them. As before, the sergeant joins in enthusiastically, endorsing

Oliver's assessment. This time he mitigates his criticism with humour (29–30) and follows it up with polite advice (32). The camerawork continues to register the women's reception of the men's face-threatening comments and the voice-over observes that they are not happy with the pressure Oliver is putting on them (35–7):

```
29. S's hands lifting canister       I could run me car on
    to camera                        that er for about er-
30. MCU DLs looking on               at least a year
31. CU DL laughing                   [laughter]
32. MCU DLs looking on               er if you get the
                                     opportunity to er get that
                                     back on it'd be
                                     worth your while givin'
33. J into shot, looking             it a touch longer=
    at canister
34. Back to DLs                  J:  ='alf an hour love
35. J tasting from              v/o: Jamie's way behind
    another canister
36. DL5 crouching over               schedule (.)
    canister, looking up at J        and his determination
37. J tasting                        to get their cooking up to
                                     scratch is taking its toll
                                     on morale
```

The two tasting scenes (2–13 and 22–37) are used to stand for Oliver's challenge; they illustrate the voice-over's pronouncements about what he is up against. In contrast with expressions of respect for the kitchen staff of Kidbrooke, here the dinner ladies are representing his problem and they are being disciplined. In selection of this particular footage, there has presumably been a decision to highlight their failure and Oliver's frustration for dramatic purposes. Oliver's irritation is played out in his interaction with them, with some colourful examples of his 'expressiveness'.

We do hear some comments from their perspective, however, as here (also 19–20 above):

```
38. DL5 and J                    J:    (well) how've you been
    handling large canisters           coping=
                                DL5:   =alright
                                 J:    really (.) you mean
                                       you're (shit)? (.) happy?
                                       not happy?
```

	DL5:	*[mumbles]* not happy
	J:	not happy
39. CU **DL5** looking	DL5:	no
at **J**		
40. Later. **DL3** seated in	DL3:	*[to interviewer*
tent, smoking		*off-camera]*
		bloody 'ell it's just non-
		stop

The tension and conflict of the episode is heightened by its multi-vocality. The voice-over has announced that he keeps them working for ten hours. In taking on the role of their teacher, he has given them unfamiliar ingredients to prepare (it is possible they have never eaten butternut squash, let alone cooked it) in an unfamiliar, difficult environment. And, moreover, as the voice-over has told us, 'they've given up their half term holiday for an intensive three-day course'. They certainly have cause for complaint.

Individual women emerge as characters in the documentary. While the most prominent of them is Nora Sands, another dinner lady, Lesley, has presumably demonstrated an ability to perform for the cameras (she is 'DL3' in 40 above). In the fourth and final episode, she features in a representation of the welling discontent of the dinner ladies and Oliver's ability to listen, in a scene that seems to reclaim his 'niceness'. The extension of the campaign to other schools in the Borough of Greenwich has led to a traumatic first day for Lesley at the primary school where she is catering manager:

L: **L**esley		
1. School sign: Wingfield	v/o:	This time it's not
Primary School		just the kids
		complaining (.)
2. MS through window, back		the dinner ladies find
view of Lesley on phone		cooking from scratch
		takes them <u>far</u> longer
3. CU side view of **L** on phone	L:	I feel (.) ex<u>haus</u>ted
(.) just after day one		
4. Back shot of **J** in car		and I made a real bad
passenger seat		(.)
5. Hands-free phone		(failure) today=
in dashboard	J:	=why
	L:	'cos I 'ave
6. Back shot of **J** in car	J:	but it's only day one
		babe

7. MCU side view of **L**	**L:** what I'm saying **J** (.) I'm not willing to kill myself to do it (.) I don't want this to ta- this is not my life right (.) this job (.) it might be other people's lives like Nora (.) er y'know what I mean it's not my life it's just a tiny little bit (.) of my life (.) . hh I work to t- to live I don't live to work
8. CU **J**'s face in car, reacting	then <u>you</u> come in with a face like thunder
9. MCU side view of **L**	and I j- y'know I just thought oh I can't believe this
10. CU **J**	**J:** why did I have a face like thunder
	L: cz y- (why) is that your normal face
	J: (.) yeah [slight smile]
	L: [laughter]
11. **L** turning to look at crew	[laughter]
	[Cut in audio here?]
12. MCU **J** seated	**J:** just (.) hang in there with us (.)
	L: ok
Pulls out to register driver's smiling face	**J:** er (.) and before you leave I'll cut my own arm off (.) er
	L: (you will) (.) what in front o' me [laughter]
	J: yeah (.) wiv an old blunt blade
13. MCU **L** seated	**L:** alright I wun't want you to do that (..) ok then (..) alright see you later (.) bye

Shots 3 to 9 are taken up with Lesley's complaint, with brief, supportive interjections from Oliver in 5 and 6. He is doing face-work through humour and self-deprecation. In 12, his undertaking to inflict punishment on himself functions as an indirect apology. The camera pulls out to take in the driver's amusement, signalling the intended humour in the absurd offer. The complexity of staging of this 'natural' and spontaneous phone conversation was by no means immediately apparent to me. It only became so as I examined it shot by shot, that is as a transcriber rather than a 'normal' viewer.

So what values, beliefs and norms do we have here? Well, the gender demarcation in cooking expertise is striking. The women are actually catering managers at the schools they work at. But men are the chefs; they know the business and they are in charge. This is highlighted by the symbolic space of the military training camp, thanks to the PR-conscious British Army being so willing to make their resources available.

The series – the whole campaign – also raises issues of class and taste. Oliver compares the training camp with the start of his own chef training: 'cooking properly (.) nothing- nothing posh at all it's kinda like week one of when I was at college when I was training to be a chef'. In other words, he presents it as a matter of professionalism rather than social class, or 'poshness'. His effort to educate the public on the health consequences of a regularly poor diet is a very positive use of the public platform available to him. One of the Kidbrooke girls, speaking on behalf of a hard core of resistance to dietary changes, epitomises the problem: 'we don't like being healthy'. However, he is not just promoting the reduction in intake of fat and salt and the introduction of fresh vegetables. In getting school kitchen staff to cook 'his food', he is imposing *his* food tastes, while presenting the issue as a purely dietary one (the jibe about rice pudding – a traditional and unfashionable English dessert – can only really be understood in this context). He places an outright ban on children's preferred foods, rather than working on their replacement with more nutritious versions (with the single exception of pizza). Butternut squash features so prominently in the series (the camera seems to pan across heaps of it in every episode) that it's hard to believe he isn't trying to convert the country *en masse* to its use. (I suppose, though, on a more positive note, the vegetable was once scarcely available and considered exotic in Britain and is now everywhere!)

The series foregrounds the celebrity chef's epic quest, including the tension and conflict with kitchen staff and schoolchildren. It offers a variant of the double-audience structure noted by Brunsdon (2003: 11). As in the 'reveal' climax in a more straightforward 'lifestyle makeover' show, the viewing audience needs to focus on reaction, for which an internal audience is needed – a function served by the dinner ladies and the children themselves. The series downplays much of the complex collaborative endeavour involved in its production over the course of the year. Jamie Oliver's voice is not mediated by the interviewer, who can be readily inferred but is neither seen nor heard throughout. There is some sense of the production community, but the producer's hand, in particular, is invisible.

Jeremy Paxman: 'Britain's number one interrogator'

The social identity of 'public inquisitor' (Higgins 2007: 19) refers to the discursive position bestowed upon a media figure who is empowered to engage in particular forms of aggressive, interrogatory dialogue. In Britain, this elite discursive role is at present particularly associated with one of the anchor-interviewers on BBC's *Newsnight*, Jeremy Paxman. As texts, broadcast interviews on *Newsnight* offer specific representations of elites with different institutional roles but similarly high status. In terms of interaction, these texts are interesting as spectacles of conflict and struggle. Paxman's on-air persona as an inquisitor figure was celebrated in a fifteen-minute Sunday supplement on *The Westminster hour* (BBC Radio 4, 18 June 2006). Entitled 'How to beat Jeremy Paxman', its presenter identifies him as 'Britain's number one interrogator'. The text consists of fourteen short interview extracts from a range of politicians with previous experience as Paxman's interviewees and twelve extracts of archive material from interviews, with framing and commentary by presenter, Steve Hewlett. The implied listener of the feature is invited to take the position of a hypothetical MP preparing to appear on *Newsnight*.

```
SH: Steve Hewlett
50. SH: so (.) imagine for a moment you're a
51.     politician waiting to go on (.) you've
52.     thought through the arguments (.) but are
53.     you ready for the whole body experience
```

This section of the book focuses on the way Paxman's persona and its highly valued discursive style are represented in the feature. I develop the programme's discussion of the characteristics of his interview style with further observations on some of the extracts used to illustrate it.

Giving a sense of insights into behind-the-scenes activities on *Newsnight*, it presents Paxman as an intimidating figure who dominates those around him in the arena of an on-air interview. A Liberal Democrat,

Lembit Opik, is credited with expertise in body language and offers the
following 'reading' of Paxman as an interviewer:

```
LO:   Lembit Opik
 94. LO:  as I watch (.) Jeremy Paxman I see
 95.      somebody .h who (.) not only (.) feels he
 96.      has the right to exert authority .h in
 97.      terms of body language in terms of facial
 98.      expression and in terms of tone of voice
 99.      (.) he's also keen on- on showing the
100.      person he's interviewing that he Jeremy
101.      Paxman has control of the studio
```

Several politicians offer accounts of feeling intimidated by Paxman
before the scheduled interview, by what they read as displays of control
in the studio. Take, for example, this observation by former Foreign
Secretary, Jack Straw, pointing to a lack of social engagement off air that
he presents as a deliberate strategy:

```
JS:   Jack Straw
 57. JS:  one of his techniques is if he is in the
 58.      studio with you >on the whole< not to look
 59.      at you erm so (.) or to look bored
```

Their accounts of feeling uncomfortable in his company before the
scheduled interview present him as strategic in his behaviour off air as
well as on air. Ignoring his interviewees is represented as 'one of his
techniques' in 57 above, for example, rather than preoccupation with the
job in hand, lack of social skills, or whatever.

In referring to the 'whole body experience' of the hypothetical interview in
line 53 above, the presenter is metaphorically representing it as a contact sport
such as boxing. Similarly, in the interviewees' meta-discursive comments on
their experiences on *Newsnight*, they explicitly represent the interviews as
combat. For example, according to one aggrieved former interviewee:

```
MH:   Michael Howard
108. MH:  it's a battle for control of the interview
109. SH:  is that how you see it
```

Howard characterises this as a 'battle' over control of topic, for which he
offers a disparaging explanation ('entertainment'), for which the booster
'of course' (line 116) claims commonsensical status:

```
110.MH:   it- it often is (.) erm you've got your
111.      agenda what you want to get across (.) erm
112.      the interviewer wants to test that
113.      perfectly reasonably (.) and wants to take
114.      yo:u to a certain destination and you
115.      might want to go to (.) quite another
116.      destination (.) because of course his
117.      technique is to treat it all as
118.      entertainment (.) and to (.) start off
119.      with a question that is designed to
120.      wrongfoot (.) [Newsnight music] and
121.      embarrass the person he's interviewing
```

Howard identifies an opening strategy of 'wrongfooting', to which he attributes a particular interpersonal function: to embarrass. The feature continues with a *Newsnight* extract illustrating this strategy. Like other interviewers, Paxman frequently employs an ambiguous double-voicing tactic in his questioning strategies. Distinctively, however, he sometimes uses the pose of merely animating the views 'authored' by others to insult his interviewees, while maintaining an allegedly neutral stance. Such questions can be highly aggravated and face-threatening, as in his second question in this next extract (lines 126–32):

```
JP:  Jeremy Paxman
DD:  David Davis
122.JP:  David Davis could the Conservatives win
123.     the next election with David Cameron as
124.     leader
125.DD:  (.) I reckon they could (.) yeah
126.JP:  In that case why should they (.) choose a
127.     man (.) described by your colleagues to us
128.     as (.) and these are direct quotes as a
129.     thug a bully an adventurer (.) disloyal
130.     (.) congenitally treacherous (.) and
131.     winner of the whips' office shit of the
132.     year championship
133.DD:  (.) how flattering
```

In Paxman's animation of the alleged words of Davis's Conservative colleagues, the ambiguity lies, of course, in his own alignment with them. From Davis's ironic response (line 133), it is apparent that he considers the pose of neutrality to be a transparently empty one. It forms part of an opening gambit of a type commonly employed by Paxman. Its recipient describes it as 'bowling a bouncer', using a cricket metaphor that is distinctively masculine and, in this context, English (lines 134–5 below). A 'bouncer' is an aggressive bowling move, designed to trick the batsman. The metaphor contributes to building the representation of Paxman interviews as gentlemanly sportsmanship. Davis follows it up with advice on how to respond (lines 139–40):

```
134.DD: Well he always sort've (.) bowls a bouncer
135.     right from the start. h and er that sets
136.     the tone (.) and the key thing is (.) not
137.     to get thrown by it (.) and to: >if
138.     necessary< take a bit of ti:me and the
139.     other key thing about him is don't get
140.     riled
```

A further aspect of this type of opening gambit that the feature highlights is Paxman's use of a lexis that is seemingly out of place in a political interview (for instance, line 131). In this context, his mildly transgressive use of taboo terms has shock value, no doubt, and also contributes to his performance of masculintity (de Klerk 1997).

Higgins (2007) explores the leakage of the discursive role of 'public inquisitor' into other media genres, in particular an elite quiz show. In 'How to beat Jeremy Paxman', the presenter introduces a further example of Paxman's aggressive opening gambit as a 'starter for ten', which would be familiar as a *University challenge* expression for most listeners. Describing Paxman's interpersonal style on the quiz show, Higgins observes that his 'curmudgeonly performance' while he is asking questions is 'framed within and set against an easy courtesy and bonhomie that might be associated with idealized notions of the debating society' (Higgins 2007: 14). The extracts under discussion illustrate this observation.

Dogged persistence is another characteristic of Paxman's interviewing style, with a tendency to repetition and interruption in grilling his interviewees. An extreme case is an interview with Michael Howard, who was a Conservative candidate in an earlier leadership election (the interview took place in 1997). In it, Paxman recycles the same question twelve times or more. Two of them appear in this extract (lines 312 and 317):

```
MH:  Michael Howard
310.MH: I was entitled to express my views? I was
311.    entitled to be consulted=
```

```
312.JP:  =Did you threaten to overrule him
                          [
313.MH:                   I- I was not entitled to
314.     instruct Derek Lewis and I did not
315.     instruct him and the truth of-
316.     the truth of the matter is that [fades]=
                          [
317.JP:  Did you threaten to overrule him
```

The commentary between extracts elevates the multiple repetition of this question to the status of a 'legend':

```
SH:   Steve Hewlett
318.SH:  =this interview has become one of
319.     television's golden moments (.) legend has
320.     it Paxman asks the same question fourteen
321.     times (.) in fact it was only twelve
322.     [interview fades back in]
```

The feature continues with another extract from the 'golden moment'. In lines 323 to 329, Paxman's delivery is very rapid while Howard's is ponderously slow:

```
323.MH:  . . . the House of Commons
324.JP:  I note you're not answering the question
325.     whether you threatened to overrule him
326.MH:  [extremely slow delivery] well the- the
327.     important aspect of this (.) which it's
328.     very clear to bear in mind
329.       (.)                    (i:s   this)-
          [
330.JP:  >>>I'm sorry I'm gonna be frightfully rude
331.     but-<<<
332.MH:  yes (you can)-
          [
332.JP:  >I'm so(h)rry<
[several seconds of indecipherable simultaneous talk]
```

In line 330, Paxman's formulaic apology functions as a negative politeness strategy, presumably softening the impending face threat of yet another repetition. Then, in line 332, another appears to be oriented to the breakdown in turn taking. Here Paxman is the dogged interviewer subjecting his interviewee to a gentlemanly grilling. It turns out, strangely, that the answer was no. The two extracts from the 'legendary' interview exemplify the confrontational interviewing style of the public inquisitor, with their high degree of simultaneous talk, dislocated turn taking and the interviewer's overt challenges in imposition of his agenda. (See Chapter 7 on 'Production communities and audience communities' for a different perspective on this interview.)

The Radio 4 feature is not, of course, for an audience of media discourse specialists. Unsurprisingly, then, it omits subtler elements of a combative interviewer style, such as uncooperative formulation (see Chapter 7 for an example), which would be more elaborate to present and lack impact. It largely focuses on sound bites, presenting selected high points from over twenty years. What it provides here, however, is more than simply a convenient source of extracts, with commentary from former interviewees. It offers a representation of a highly valued discursive style, how the BBC chooses to represent one of its own current affairs 'celebrities': as a heroic persona, a kind of discursive pugilist. A further *Westminster hour* supplement the following week provided a politicians' perspective on *Question time* (the BBC's television version of *Any questions?*). Significantly, I think, this follow-up did not single out the presenter in the title, which was 'How to beat *Any questions?*' (rather than 'How to beat a Dimbleby', for instance);[2] and the feature identifies fellow panellists and an undeferential studio audience as the panellists' adversaries.

The 'How to beat Jeremy Paxman' feature presents a combative interview style that shows some similarities to one observed by an Australian linguist, Joanne Winter. In her contrastive analysis of two political interviews she demonstrates that a political interviewer can operate very effectively without adopting adversarial patterns of inter-action typically viewed as masculine (Winter 1993). In fact, she argues that a non-combative approach is more effective ideationally, in terms of information delivery. However, it is Paxman whose celebrity the feature celebrates. Moreover, it presents his curmudgeonly persona as essential for democracy.

The representations of social identities and relationships covered in this chapter can be said to demonstrate hegemonic status. They depict constructions of identities and relationships that project the cultural values of consumerism, the individualism of 'celebrity' and the prestige of interactional norms perceived as masculine. While lifestyle program-ming presents foreigners as obliging, servile (and preferably English-speaking) and promotes domestic feminine expertise while reducing expertise to style advice, 'serious' news genres valorise the discursive fisticuffs of gentlemanly, sportsmanlike interviewers as essential for democracy. Above all, a discourse of celebrity pervades media discourse and informs our understanding of the social world beyond the print and broadcast media:

> mass media images and representations of famous people, stars and celebrities are vehicles for the creation of social meaning. A celebrity always represents more than him- or herself. So celebrity conveys, directly or indirectly, particular social values, such as the meaning of work and achievement, and definitions of sexual and gendered identity (Dyer 1986; Marshall 1997). In 'housing' the values, beliefs and norms of the day, celebrity coverage in the media . . . plays an essential role in organising our perception of the world. (Evans 2006: 2)

Notes

1. Following his engagements with children in schools, he has remarked on the importance of their involvement in the processes of food preparation, in terms of their 'ownership' of them.
2. The presenter of *Question time* is David Dimbleby; his brother, Jonathan Dimbleby, is presenter of *Any questions?*

Activities

Consider some contemporary media coverage of celebrities. What values, norms and beliefs does it 'house'?

Tape and transcribe a broadcast of one of the genres covered in this chapter and examine the roles and relationships represented in it (an online transcription is unlikely to be adequate for this purpose, though it could be used as a starting point).

Following on from the study above of masculinist discourse in current affairs broadcasting and its valorisation, one interesting next step would be to compare Paxman's interview style with that of a female interviewer in the same genre; for example, a 'celebrated' interview with Margaret Thatcher in 1990 conducted by Paxman's female counterpart on *Newsnight*, Kirsty Wark. Another interesting possibility would be to compare Paxman's distinctively British style with that of an American counterpart.

Further reading

Brunsdon, Charlotte (2003), 'The 8–9 slot on British television', *International journal of cultural studies*, 6(1): 5–23.

Clayman, Steven and Heritage, John (2002), *The news interview*, Cambridge: Cambridge University Press.

Evans, Jessica (2006), 'Celebrity: what's the media got to do with it?' in Evans, Jessica and Hesmondhalgh, David (eds), *Understanding media: inside celebrity* Maidenhead: Open University Press.

Giles, David (2002), 'Keeping the public in their place: audience participation in lifestyle television programming', *Discourse and society*, 13(5): 603–28.

Greatbatch, David (1986), 'Aspects of topical organisation in news interviews: the use of agenda-shifting procedures by news interviewees', *Media, culture and society*, 8: 441–55.

O'Keefe, Anne (2006), *Investigating media discourse*, London: Routledge.

Tolson, Andrew (2006), *Media talk: spoken discourse on TV and radio*, Edinburgh: Edinburgh University Press.

Winter, Joanne (1993), 'Gender and the political interview in an Australian context', *Journal of pragmatics*, 20: 117–39.

7 Production communities and audience communities

In the early hours of 1 January 1993, the morning after New Year celebrations in Hong Kong, the radio news reported a major incident, a crowd crush leading to twenty-one deaths. The reporters have been working without sleep:

CC: Charlie Charters
FM: Francis Moriarty
BC: Brian Curtis

```
 1. CC: Twenty have died after New Year
 2.     celebrations in Lan Kwai Fong went out of
 3.     control as crowds stampeded over fallen
 4.     party goers The government has promised
 5.     to hold an enquiry and police have sealed
 6.     off the area as they collect what evidence
 7.     remains of the nighttime tragedy Most of
 8.     the injured and dead were rushed to Queen
 9.     Mary Hospital and it's from there that
10.     Metro's Francis Moriarty joins us live
11.     with the latest details
12. FM: yes
        [long silence]
13. CC: Francis!
14. FM: I'm here
15. CC: Can you give us the latest details?
16. FM: The latest details?
17. CC: Yeah, the latest details on the injuries
18. FM: Um, I can only give you the figures that
19.     I've been given I don't know if you have
20.     anything further or more comprehensive
21.     than that
22. BC: Francis, we're live on the radio AM 1044
23.     in Hong Kong
```

```
24. FM:  Live, live on the radio, sorry, em [shift
25.      to 'radio narrator voice'] The latest
26.      figures that I have up HE::re are that,
27.      eh, there were eighty-six casualties [. . .]
         [report continues]
```

(adapted from Scollon 1998: 175)

Something is going badly wrong in this broadcast; the floor delegation in lines 9–13 breaks down. Reporter Francis Moriarty is responding to a private call, which has a different sequence, based on different expectations, rights and obligations. Inappropriately for a news broadcast, he is waiting for the caller to raise a topic, hence his long pause in 12. Charters, Moriarty and Curtis are members of a working community of media professionals who collaboratively deliver the radio news. Their job involves the assembly and performance of a complex media text for a distant audience.

This chapter shifts the focus of attention from media texts to the 'interactive frameworks of production . . . [and] reception' (Thompson 1995: 89) where communities of people engage in activities with one another. Here I want to present some of the complex of frontstage and backstage work in the creation of media texts for broadcast or publication. A preliminary definition of frontstage media activity is 'all that is visible for a distant audience', though this is problematised by contemporary trends in 'zoo media'. Then, in a final section on the overhearing audience itself, I turn to 'interactive frameworks of reception' (ibid.). My focus is not just 'audiences' in some generalised sense, but specific groups of viewers, listeners or readers, for example, an audience that is pottering around in a particular kitchen on a Friday evening when *Any questions?* is broadcast on Radio 4. It also attends to what Nick Couldry has called the 'extended' audience, a concept which 'requires us to examine the whole spectrum of talk, action and thought that draws on media, or is oriented towards media'. In this way, as he says, 'we can broaden our understanding of the relationship between media and media audiences as part of our understanding of contemporary media culture' (Couldry 2006: 196).

Frontstage in production-community interaction

All social activities can be said to have front and back regions (Goffman 1969). In a restaurant, for example, there are clear demarcations between the 'frontstage' of the public dining area and the kitchen where all the behind-the-scenes work of food preparation goes on. The production of a complex media text such as a news broadcast involves major backstage activity, including extensive newsgathering work: interviews over the phone, briefings from the chief editor and so on. Using an example from television of the 1950s, Goffman defines the media back region as:

> all places where the camera is not focused at the moment or all places out of range of 'live' microphones. Thus an announcer may hold the sponsor's product up at arm's length in front of the camera while he holds his nose with his other hand, his face being out of the picture, as a way of joking with his team-mates. (Goffman 1969: 121)

The Hong Kong reporter in the opening passage is initially unaware that he is on microphone and appears to be under the impression that he is participating in a backstage newsgathering activity. When he realises that he is in the media front region – in other words, on air – he rapidly switches to his professional frontstage voice of 'radio narrator' (line 25).

In media discourse, then, the broadcast or published text is what appears in the front region. Most media workers never appear there at all, yet all collaborate in the interactive framework of production of texts designed for a distant imagined audience. For media workers, the audience is largely an abstraction, perceived in terms of demographics, not as interlocutors (Bell 1991). Toynbee (2006) provides a valuable overview of perspectives on the media's perception of its audiences.

Media professionals interact among themselves in production teams in-studio and beyond. In the opening extract, a telephone call has been misrecognised as backstage activity, so that the reporter is unaware that a conventional frontstage procedure is in operation. According to Scollon, a news anchor's procedure for passing the conversational 'floor' to a colleague outside the broadcasting studio involves a delegation frame that has three stages: identification of location, identification of voice, identification of topic (Scollon 1998: 161). These are clearly visible, in that order, in lines 9 to 11 of the Hong Kong news broadcast above. In the British media, they do not always occur in the order he indicates, however. The following is an example from BBC Radio 4 of a delegation frame that is functioning properly:

VS: Vaughn Savage (newsreader)
WD: Wyre Davies (reporter)
 1. **VS:** The Israeli prime minister Ehud Olmert has
 2.   re<u>ject</u>ed an ultimatum by the three Palestinian
 3.   militant groups. h believed to be holding the
 4.   Israeli soldier. hh the militants who want the
 5.   Israelis to <u>free</u> detained Palestinian women

```
 6.        and young Palestinians. h said there would
 7.        be consequences if their ultimatum was ignored
 8.        .h the continuing stand-off is still affecting
 9.        many aspects of life in the Palestinian areas
10.        .h a third of the ministers in the Palestinian
11.        authority are still being detained as part of
12.        Israel's. h wide-ranging sanctions against Hamas
13.        following the abduction. hh so how is the
14.        Palestinian government functioning with so
15.        many enforced absentees. h Wyre Davies
16.        reports from the Palestinian parliament in
17.        Romala
```
[debating Arabic voices audible throughout the outside
broadcast sequence that follows]
```
18. WD:   Politics (.) in the Palestinian authority has
19.        never been easy (.) sessions of the legislative
20.        council in here in Romala have to be video
21.        linked to Gaza city because Israel expressly
22.        forbids most travel between the West Bank and
23.        Gaza [report continues]
```
(*PM* BBC Radio 4, 3 July 2006)

The newsreader identifies the topic in lines 13–15, the speaker in 15 and his location in 16–17.[1] Of this broadcasting delegation frame, Scollon observes that 'these social practices so seldom break down that we have very few instances of departures from expectation against which to test them' (Scollon 1998: 177). A radio sketch parodying news plays with this expectation. In the following extract, the first eruption of audience laughter (line 8) is triggered by a long silence (line 7) as the delegation frame breaks down for passing the floor from the news anchor, 'Nick' (Naylor) to the reporter, 'Ian' (Andy Parsons):

```
AP: Andy Parsons
N:  Nick
I:  Ian
 1. AP: Often reporters go to air (.) before anyone knows
 2.     (.) exactly what's happened
 3. N:  And we interrupt this show (.) to go straight
 4.     over to Heathrow (.) where we've just had news
 5.     of a crash er let's go over to our Heathrow
 6.     correspondent Ian Lang?. h Ian (.) what can you
 7.     tell us (.  .  .)
```

```
                          [
8.            [audience laughter] Ian
9.    I:      Hello?
```

As it continues, the reason for Ian's silence becomes clear. He hasn't a clue what Nick is talking about:

```
10.  N:   Er Ian we've just heard news (.) of a crash at
11.       Heathrow er what can you tell us
12.  I.   Ah right er (.) a crash you say. h have to say er
13.       details very sketchy here Nick? (.)er what I can
14.       tell you is you think there has been a crash (.)
15.       [laughter] and you are contacting me [prolonged
16.       laughter] what have you heard [audience laughter]
17.  N.   Er we've just heard that there's been a crash
18.       at Heathrow
19.  I.   Very possible? Very possible (.) Heathrow is an
20.       airport? [laughter] (..) lots of planes passing
21.       through it? (.)always a chance of a crash
22.  N.   So er what do you think the chances are that
23.       there has been a crash
24.  I.   Very early doors yet Nick? As far as I'm aware
25.       just the one report of a crash so far? (.) a:nd
26.       that has come from you Nick [prolonged laughter]
27.       I'm looking around everybody here (..) everybody
28.       goin' about their business as normal? They don't
29.       seem to be aware (.)that there has been a crash
30.       [laughter] actually they seem a little more
31.       agitated< now that I've mentioned the word (.)
32.       crash [laughter] [sketch continues]
```
                          (*Parsons and Naylor's Pull-out Sections*, BBC Radio 2)

In this sketch, the audience at Heathrow is at the mercy of frontstage workers who are making it up as they go along. The backstage news-gathering loop is clearly inadequate and seems to consist of just the news anchor and the outside reporter.

But the interactive framework of production does not solely involve media professionals. In news genres, they meet and interact with news-makers, mostly professionals from other occupational communities (politicians, 'celebrities'). The talk is designed for a distant audience and their frontstage interaction is tightly structured in clear genre formats. In current affairs interviews, for example, interviewers preface their questions with contextualising statements. Though addressed to the interviewee, this contextualisation is for the benefit of the imagined audience. There is an expectation that interviewee is familiar with the format, an assumption of 'complicity of practice' (Marr et al. 1999: 111) among members of different occupational communities. Several conversation analysts have produced detailed accounts of what happened when this convention broke down in an interview by Dan Rather of CBS with Vice-President George Bush Senior, widely perceived as a 'slugfest' (e.g. Hutchby 2006: 136–9).

There is a more complex frontstage interactive framework of production in operation in *Any questions?* It has four panellists and chair plus a studio audience and it is a public forum in which a single representative of government is very often set upon, discursively speaking, by the other participants. In common with other broadcast interviewers, the chair has the institutional role of talk manager. After an initial introductory stage, the programme follows this format: (1) the chair elicits a question from a pre-selected member of the studio audience; (2) the audience member gives their name then poses their question; (3) the chair expands or otherwise clarifies the question; (4) the chair nominates a first panel member to respond; (5) the panel member responds at some length, often 90 seconds or more; (6) the chair optionally follows up with a comment or supplementary question; and so on. Built into this format are the chair's frequent summaries or clarifications for the benefit of the overhearing audiences. The chair, usually Jonathan Dimbleby, follows up each question from the studio audience (known to him beforehand but not to the panellists) with a cooperative formulation. In this example, his formulation makes the question more explicit and adds contextual detail (lines 128–31):

125.   CALHOONE John Calhoone. What sanctions do we have over a country which is rich and dedicated both to the extinction of Israel and the acquisition of nuclear weapons?

    DIMBLEBY Iran clearly is your – is in your mind. Tessa Jowell, what can be done about Iran against the background of the Prime Minister's, what
130.   were described by many people as bellicose statements about Iran, if we don't do something we were being asked why not?

    (Transcript: *Any questions?* BBC Radio 4, 28 October 2005)

With panel members, however, he can be far less straightforwardly cooperative. In lines 138–9, he follows up Jowell's answer to the question with an inferentially elaborative probe. The inference that he draws out (from her comment in lines 134–5, in particular) pushes Jowell into an awkward position:

> JOWELL Well I think that the remarks by the President of Iran yesterday have caused, quite rightly, international outrage. They are at variance with membership of the United Nations and I think that – I certainly
> 135. welcome the intervention of Kofi Annan, this morning. And that very clearly the diplomatic steps that are urgently needed should be taken within the auspices of the United Nations.
>
> DIMBLEBY What does that mean – are you saying that Iran should be expelled from the United Nations, suspended from the United Nations? (ibid.)

Like Paxman in Chapter 6, he is functioning as an inquisitor, ostensibly on the audience's behalf. The discourse management role he performs is a powerful one; he reframes questions and formulates answers, while the panel members are under obligation to provide substantial responses. Panel members occasionally address questions and comments to each other, but the turn taking is mostly through the chair and under strict control, thereby open to potential abuse as, arguably, in the smoking ban discussion I looked at in Chapter 4. In this discussion, the sole government representative is Tessa Jowell, Secretary of State for Culture, Media and Sport. Here is a short extract from it again, in which Dimbleby is policing the topic as if Jowell is diverging from it:

> JOWELL . . . And let me say I think those of you who feel confused
> 375. about what the outcome of these negotiations this week actually is, I mean I think you can be forgiven for that. So I would like to focus on the – I'd like . . .
>
> DIMBLEBY I expect you'd like to focus on all sorts of other issues.
> JOWELL No, no, no . . .
> 380. DIMBLEBY Let's stick with this one.
>
> JOWELL No, I'm focusing on the second part of the excellent question, which is that . . .
>
> DIMBLEBY Compromise.
>
> 385. JOWELL . . . that where we did get to was a sensible compromise (ibid.)

In another passage later in the same topic discussion, he teases her in a display of his control of turn taking:

LAWS . . . I cannot understand and maybe I can invite her to explain to me, why it is that under this ban people who want to smoke, who positively want to smoke, will not be allowed to go into a room separately by

455.   themselves in a building where they're employed, to smoke. However, people who want protection from smoke in pubs that don't serve food will still have people being able to smoke on and pollute them. That doesn't make any sense at all to me. [CLAPPING]
       JOWELL Well let me . . .

460.   DIMBLEBY I think Tessa Jowell may want to answer the question.

       JOWELL She certainly does but we might have . . .

       DIMBLEBY No I think we will allow you to answer the question, then we may bring in your dear commentator.

       JOWELL Oh you're inviting me to . . .

465.   DIMBLEBY I certainly am.

       JOWELL I'm relishing the opportunity.

       (ibid.)

Jowell's frustration is evident in the comment she makes (line 494) as Dimbleby ends the topic segment with the customary invitation to the radio audience:

       DIMBLEBY Any Answers 08700 100 444. We'll go to our next.

494.   JOWELL I think I'll be phoning in myself.
       (ibid.)

Jowell has entered into the broadcasting working community of *Any questions?*, but she has limited control and is being given a hard time. The most powerful can choose the media arenas in which they appear. Prime Minister Tony Blair has been known to turn down the inquisitorial rigours of *Any questions?* or *Newsnight* and appear instead on *This morning*, a breakfast chat show (though he did choose Paxman as chair for a televised debate on the Iraq war). In Jowell's case, she seems to be struggling in a masculinist arena; there are frequent patronising comments from other panellists, especially Max Hastings (a right-wing media mogul with a knighthood), about her uncomfortable discursive position on the programme.

The chair and panellists wield institutional power of different kinds. Occasionally the chair attends explicitly to their respective rights and obligations in discursive control, as in the following discussion following a question about party leadership. The chair is Nick Clarke, standing in for Jonathan Dimbleby:

> SMITH . . . I mean Chris what's your view about whether or not you'd ever want to be?
>
> CLARKE I normally ask the questions.
>
> SMITH Oh sorry, sorry Nick.
>
> CLARKE But honestly it's fine. I bow to a chief whip, as who wouldn't. Chris Huhne.
>
> HUHNE . . .
>
> JOHNSON What's that to do with Menzies Campbell?
>
> HUHNE Well I think . . .
>
> CLARKE That's my job too.
>
> HUHNE I think [continues]
>
> (*Any questions?* transcript 22 September 2006)

As I argued in Chapter 5, face-to-face talk on-mike contributes to mediated quasi-interaction. Most frontstage work involves simultaneously engaging with immediate interlocutors and with the imagined audience. Combining the two successfully requires considerable skill, as there is potential conflict between the needs of face-to-face interaction and the needs of mediated quasi-interaction with viewers or listeners. There is an example of this kind of conflict in the holiday broadcast coverage in Chapter 6. This can be found in the extract on pages 104–5, where Chris Tarrant humiliates the Egyptian museum guide, Lavina. Tarrant seems to be more in tune with his imagined audience than with the museum guide he is actually talking to. On one level, as Jaworski et al. (2003) suggest, he seems to be being positively polite, aligning himself with British viewers; but this means he is being appallingly rude to his immediate interlocutor. It may be that he perceives Lavina's expertise and scholarly learning as a potential face threat for his non-specialist audience; the affront that it leads to may be unintentional. It contrasts with the careful 'image management' in programmes such as *Jamie's school dinners*. For example, in the extract containing Lesley's complaint on pages 118–19, the production team (Oliver's 'animators', in Goffman's sense) have employed resources for engineering of the front region; put more specifically, they have set up and edited footage to maintain Oliver's likeable persona. We can deduce backstage work in the artifice of the staged phone conversation that Lesley has with him. Such glimpses of backstage activities are the subject of the next section.

Backstage glimpses

Goffman's exploration of speech errors in broadcast talk includes attention to the inadvertent inclusion of backstage materials. The simple presence of a microphone, which may be on or off, introduces 'a frontstage, backstage problem of awesome proportions' (Goffman 1981: 267).). In July 2006, a live microphone at the G8 summit picked up conversation between George Bush and Tony Blair that caused some commotion, particularly because it caught Bush saying, 'See the irony is what they need to do is get Syria to get Hizbollah to stop doing this shit and it's over'. Some commentators engaged with Blair's attention to having the live mike switched off, as either indicating his wiliness or his wit; most focused on the utterance of a taboo word by the president and the censorship problems for networks in reporting it. One of Goffman's own examples – a children's programme presenter referring to his distant audience as 'the little bastards' when he thought he was no longer on air – illustrates the perils of making disparaging remarks about your target audience in the presence of a microphone. On occasion, broadcasters who unwittingly speak into an open microphone perform career-damaging gaffes, as British football 'pundit' Ron Atkinson did in 2004 (see Talbot 2007). Distinct from simple errors like these are issues of what Goffman calls 'subversion' of broadcasting conventions. Here, backstage material intrudes because the animator is resisting the author, taking issue with the given script, for example, 'snow flurries, or as it says here, slurries' (Goffman 1981: 297). For Goffman, such disregard, or subversion, of broadcasting conventions involves doing backstage work on air; it involves a kind of double-voicing that disrupts the broadcasting channel's impression of uni-vocality. Here is a more resistant example, where the announcer blurts out 'a behind-the-scenes comment to technicians present, using a "rough", informal voice, as if momentarily blind to – or uncaring about – its wide reception' (ibid.: 302–3):

> Newscaster: 'And rumor has it that the North Dakota lawmaker has been ill for quite some time and this illness was caused by his death. We tried to reach him but we were told at the Executive Mansion that he is away at present on a little vacation. . . . Who typed this goddamn thing?'

> (ibid.: 303)

The newscaster's frustrated outburst is backstage work, but it is performed in the front region. The vital backstage operations necessary for a smooth-running broadcast are occasionally exposed by such exasperated outbursts. Here is a recent example, in which BBC Radio 4's John Humphrys loses his script:

> It's eight o'<u>clock</u> (o::nd) I have <u>lost</u> the news <u>headlines</u> (and) the:y i:s a <u>panic</u> well you- >there is- clearly there's a panic because< I've lost the news headlines so <u>there</u> we <u>are</u> I've <u>found</u> them <u>now</u> *[continues]*
> (*Today* BBC Radio 4, repeated on *Pick of the Week*, Radio 4, 17 September 2006)

The appeal of out-take shows like *It'll be alright on the night* (and DVD extras along the same lines) is presumably in the sense of glimpsing behind the scenes, seeing the normally hidden workings of production communities in the broadcast media. A recent radio programme giving a sense of insight into behind-the-scenes activities on *Newsnight* is the 'How to beat Jeremy Paxman' feature that I looked at in Chapter 6. This *Westminster hour* supplement includes a politicians' perspective on what goes on behind the scenes. As noted in Chapter 6, these are powerful public figures who report feeling intimidated, on entering Paxman's domain, by his displays of control in the studio. Unsurprisingly, there is no account of Paxman as a team member in their recollections, or in the feature at all, which is representing him as a heroic individual not as a team worker. Such a perspective, however, can shed a different light on his curmudgeonly performances. Backstage operations shaped the 'legendary' Howard interview, in which he repeated a single question twelve times. Despite the impression of autonomy constructed by the 'How to beat' programme, the cause of his multiple repetitions was the producer's voice in his ear, not just heroic doggedness or a belligerent, masculine style. Delays with material for the next news item meant that he had to stall for time, treading water as best he could until technical problems with video footage had been resolved. My source for this detail (there are doubtless many others) was a different kind of behind-the-scenes documentary, *Twenty years of Newsnight*. This programme is about *Newsnight* and its history, as its title suggests, rather than singling out one of its presenters as an object of worship. Such glimpses offered are highly selective, to say the least; in this case, they serve to perpetuate 'the legend'.

Of course, long-term observation of a production community going about its everyday business offers far greater insights into backstage operations. Georgina Born is a media anthropologist who has conducted ethnographic research into BBC managers and programme makers at work. Her data includes observational notes, interview transcripts and official BBC documentation. An extract from her fieldwork diary, in Born (2002), contains a glimpse of backstage operations on *Newsnight* that makes interesting reading (the extract is also reproduced in Hesmond-halgh 2006: 80–2). She undertook her fieldwork with *Newsnight* staff in the weeks leading up to the 1997 general election. The diary extract is an account of preparation of one day's lead story. The chosen issue for the day is poverty in Britain, prompted by news of a Church of England poverty initiative. She describes the team's collaborative story develop-ment, from a morning meeting through to the final 'casting' of the feature to be broadcast live that evening. Here is a short extract:

> The first idea is to use representatives from the three parties. There is great reluctance; it will be mortally boring. . . . They plan the graphics: 'Serious stuff, with plenty of hard figures to bring edge and facticity', while the film will be 'fly-on-the-wall-ish'. They laugh a little at the crudity of having film of kids with rickets or TB. The angle is decided: 'The politicians on both sides have forgotten the poor' and the aim is to pin them down. . . .
>
> 6 p.m. Time is getting short. The program is on air at 10.30 p.m., and they still haven't found a poor person to appear. Now they're down to trying personal contacts and friends. (Born 2002: 65–6)

David Hesmondhalgh reports on his own mixed reaction to Born's account of the *Newsnight* team's collective activity:

> In some respects, there is clear evidence . . . of how television journalists working in the most prestigious areas of the media are completely cut off from the lives of working-class British people. Their frantic efforts to find one person from the poorest 30 per cent of the population to appear in the studio discussion of poverty is a sign of this. The discussion among the *Newsnight* team is in some respects

quite disturbing. The comment, 'They're so deprived they can't string two sentences together!' speaks volumes about how rarely working-class voices are heard on 'serious' current affairs programmes such as *Newsnight*. The process of 'casting' seems to conform to very un-adventurous ideas of what a discussion about poverty might involve. There is a strong sense of tokenism in the inclusion of one 'poor person' amidst the politicians and the representative of the Church poverty pressure group. (Hesmondhalgh 2006: 82)

Yet, as Hesmondhalgh goes on to note, they seem to be very much aware of their shortcomings in their attempts to represent people living in poverty:

> much of the humour in the *Newsnight* team's repartee seems to be directed back at themselves, for being so cut off. . . . The laughter at the 'crudity' of using film of 'kids with rickets' may be about the difficulty of representing poverty in a way that does not echo the conventions of the 'old' Reithian BBC. (ibid.: 82–3)

The production team use humour in dealing with this dilemma that they collectively face.

Born carried out her fieldwork on BBC current affairs programming from 1996 to 1998, during a period of major upheaval in the Corporation when marketing principles were impacting on its public service ethos. She notes that a new market-oriented audit culture sat uneasily alongside the 'still vital enunciations of the Reithian discourse of serving the public, universality, justifying the licence fee, and quality and integrity of output' (Born 2002: 81). Not only functioning as a mere 'Reithian icing on the new managerial cake', it has continued to circulate among BBC staff

> spoken informally with commitment and emotion by many indivi-duals at all levels of the institution, and often in the context of their angry denunciations of Birtist management – for destructive cuts and casualization, excessive bureaucracy, destroying the BBC's creative base, shifting the output in a crude commercial direction. (ibid.: 81–2)

and so on.

Here is a stark contrast indeed with the individualism of the textual representations examined in Chapter 6. We don't have Paxman the public inquisitor here; he is one of the team caught up in a situation. As news workers on BBC's flagship current affairs programme, their privi-leged position cuts them off from the population they are trying to represent. They seem to be responding as creative practitioners in the Corporation to tensions between public service principles and market capitalism. Born's only comment on her own diary extract is indirect, but ironic and astute: she follows the extract with some 'Reithian icing' from BBC audit documents entitled: 'Statement of promises to listeners and viewers'. One includes the claim that 'the BBC met its specific promise to: represent all groups in society accurately and avoid reinforcing prejudice in our programmes' (Born 2002: 67). This is easy for senior managers to say, perhaps; not so easy for production teams to achieve.

'Zoo' media

According to Goffman (1981), doing backstage work on air is a subversion of broadcasting conventions, since it involves a kind of double-voicing that disrupts the broadcasting channel's impression of uni-vocality. He assumes that backstage work is performed in the front region essentially by mistake, that it is unintentional exposure of the vital backstage operations necessary for a smooth-running broadcast. In some genres of contemporary broadcasting, however, there are regular breaches of professional broadcasting procedures. On some music radio, for instance, 'behind the scenes' chat with the studio crew is commonplace. In so-called zoo radio, backstage work revealing technical processes is frequently visible and interaction between the DJ and the rest of the production team in the studio is an integral element. It is not just a matter of indifference to the seams showing; they are viewed as a positive advantage. As Richardson and Meinhof point out, 'the "rawness" of the transmitted text – an indication that this is not to be taken too seriously' (1999: 55) – is precisely its appeal. It indicates authenticity, spontaneity and lack of pretension. Take the following example from BBC Radio 1 (the topic is eBay):

```
RJ:  Rachel Jones (producer)
CM:  Chris Moyles (DJ)
DV:  David Vitty ('Comedy Dave')
 1. RJ: actually I'll put the American tan one in
 2. CM: American tan
 3. RJ: with a shite sh-
 4. CM:                   Wha- What-
 5. DV:                         Hello
 6. CM:                              WO HO:::
 7. RJ: oh sorry >that was meant to be a< slight sheen
 8. CM: HAH HAH HAH HAH
 9. RJ: sorry
10. CM: 's (h) okay
```

```
11.  DV?: What denier would it be
          [
12.  RJ:  with a slight sheen       nothing (.)
13.       moving on
14.  DV:  with a slight sheen
15.  RJ:  sorry
16.  CM/DV:  [laughter]
17.  DV:  That's gonna bring the price down isn' it
```
                                    (*The Chris Moyles Show*, 30 August 2006)

Rachel Jones, the producer of the show, is also a vocal frontstage contributor. In line 3, she falls foul of a broadcasting occupational hazard: a speech error producing a taboo word (in this case, caused by anticipatory interference of an initial consonant (Boomer and Laver 1968; cited in Goffman 1981: 204)). The rest of the studio team respond to it with great hilarity. The producer's attempts to pass over it ('moving on' in line 13) are ignored. This needs to be understood in the context of regular complaints about the show's 'offensive' language, about which the producer will have been taken to task. Mistakes are not just tolerated, they are sometimes celebrated: *The Chris Moyles show* has a website archive with clips such as 'Dave messes up the tedious link'. A small sample of it follows:

```
1.  DV:  I'm thinking by your face that you haven't got the
2.       same track listing as mo:i=
3.  CM:     o:::h
           =[
4.  RJ:     d'you remember the conversation we had the
5.          other day on Friday (. . .) [music ends]
[. . .]
62.  CM:  Why are we playing Blur=
63.  DV:  =just play it
64.  CM:  AH HAH I'm waiting for it to load it takes like
65.       sixty seconds for it to load=
66.  DV:  =we can fill=
67.  CM:  =right
68.       Apologise to everybody for making a balls up of
69.       your track
[. . .]
75.  CM:  It's eighty-six percent loaded
76.  DV:  (xx)
          [
```

```
77. CM: trust me the second it's loaded I'm playin' it
78. DV: >>d'you want twenty-three seconds of Liverpool
79.     goals against Chelsea<<=
80. CM: =no n(h)o you're alright I couldn't handle that
81.     let's go [plays music]
```

The behind-the-scenes business of a music show becomes the topic. A long-running Australian radio programme (*The Stan Zemanek show*) has as one of its hallmarks an ongoing banter with the studio team that regularly reveals technical processes, along with insulting treatment of callers. Regular put-downs of the female producer are a feature of his banter with studio staff (Cook 2000: 70–1). Technical errors are always other people's fault and the studio staff, all female, are subordinated (ibid.: 69). Various DJs on BBC Radio 1 have adopted a variant of his style in recent years, Chris Moyles among them, though in the above example his target is male.

In the context of broadcasting, the term 'zoo' itself can be traced back to New York in the 1980s, to a radio show on Z–100 called *The morning zoo* that offered 'a wacky mix of music, conversation and comedy' (Popik 2006). A study of the launch of L!VE TV in London argues that an 'aesthetic of liveness' (Richardson and Meinhof 1999: 55) is a key component of 'zoo' media. The title of a British men's magazine – *Zoo weekly* – suggests that it has further connotations that are viewed positively by editors targeting a young male audience. It seems to signal an imagined 'transgressive' community (see the section on men's magazines in Chapter 3).

Television talk and talking with the television

Consider this fictional glimpse of a domestic scene with a television:

> Da thought he was great because he could sit in the same room as the television and never look at it. He only looked at The News, that was all. He read the paper or a book or he dozed . . . They always talked during The News; they talked about the news. Sometimes it wasn't really talk, not conversation, just comments.
> – Bloody eejit.
> – Yes.
> I was able to tell when my da was going to call someone a bloody eejit; his chair creaked. It was always a man and he was always saying something to an interviewer.
> – Who asked him?

The interviewer had asked him but I knew what my da meant.
Sometimes I got there before him.
– Bloody eejit.
– Good man, Patrick.
My ma didn't mind me saying Bloody when the News was on. (Doyle
1993; cited in Scollon 1998: 117–18)

Television here is part of everyday family life. Patrick is a small boy
learning about tastes and views from his father's engagements with the
spectacle of television, sensitive to his shifts in attention, to small
agitations of his chair and so on. In the process, he is picking up, among
other things, evaluation of TV genres and the context-dependency of
taboo-word acceptance.

Now consider two simple overheard events. In the first, a man is
absently humming a supermarket's jingle as he detaches one of their
shopping trolleys from its moorings. In the second, two women are
having a conversation in the changing room at my local gym. They are
gossiping at length about an absent other, who is evidently not keen on
either housework or personal hygiene. This is part of their outraged
exchange:

A: And she says she's a full-time job as a farmer and she hasn't got
    the time to clean
B: Eee!
A: And she sleeps in her clothes on the sofa to save time
B: Eee, well, she doesn't need to do that
A: Well I've never heard anything like it
B: Eee

It transpires, however, that the woman in question is not a smelly
neighbour (as I first assumed) but a 'guest' on *How clean is your house?*
My purpose in presenting these two scenes is to make the rather obvious
point that media discourse circulates not only in broadcasting studios,
press newsrooms and magazine editorial offices but also in our living
rooms and beyond.

Indeed, the media are 'stitched into the fabric of daily life', as Scannell
has put it, 'underpinning its routines, lubricating its conversations and
affirming its quotidian realities' (1984: 333). In making this point, he was
introducing two articles that pointed to the need for attention to actual
audiences and their daily use of media at a time when reception research
was already beginning to shift focus to the domestic viewing context. The
articles' observations are now commonsensical: about the importance of the
overall context of media consumption, its collective nature and the often

piecemeal and distracted way in which individual texts are consumed (Bausinger 1984: 349–50). Audience research has since been taken in interesting directions, exploring issues of dailiness and routine, the punctuation of daily lives with favourite radio programmes and so on (Hermes 1993, 1995; Scannell 1996; Moores 2005). However, in the process, media texts have tended to slip into the background or be forgotten altogether and along with them most traces of discourse and ideology.

In this context, the central place of discourse analysis is distinctive in some recent audience observation. A study of the 'mediated conversational floor' conducted by Helen Wood (2007) engages with TV viewers' participation in mediated quasi-interaction. Wood visited twelve women in their homes, where she watched talk shows with them. She recorded the talk from the television and the living room. In the mediated conversational floor in their homes, she distinguishes various levels of participation. The most basic is identifiable by the presence of second person pronouns, use of minimal responses and turn completion, all directed to a speaker on the television. For example, while watching a section of *Vanessa* on 'jealousy', Eve produces a response-demanding utterance, addressing the speaker as 'you':

		Studio	**Home**	
1.	Woman:	I just wanna say one		
2.		thing it takes two		
3.		to play tonsil tennis		
4.		it's not just the		
5.		woman's fault		
6.		he's doin it as well.	Eve:	Oh shut up
7.				you:::

(Wood 2007: 82)

Obviously, as Wood notes, she does not expect a response, but she makes the remark as if she does. Wood reports similar expressions of involvement from all the women in the study. All use minimal responses ('interested listener noises'), of which these are two examples:

		Studio	**Home**	
1.	Woman:	No matter <u>how</u> old they		
2.		are if the father lets		
3.		them down if the fa:ther		
4.		has a problem- children		
5.		make up their own		
6.		minds	Bette:	Mhm

		Studio	Home
1.	Caller:	erm right I've got	
2.		a problem with my	
3.		polystyrene coving	
4.		erm I've	Jenny: Ooo::h
5.		bought it and I haven't	[sarcastically]
6.		a clue <u>how</u> I'm going to	
7.		cut it to size	

(ibid.: 83)

Wood relates such use of minimal responses to Jennifer Coates' study of shared 'collaborative floor' in women's friendly conversation, arguing that the they signal: 'I am here, this is my floor too, and I am participating in the shared construction of talk' (Coates 1996: 143; cited in Wood 2007: 000). I must say, however, the sarcasm she hears in Jenny's voice suggests an element of hostile double-voicing too, using the caller's words against her will; the 'Ooo::h' in 4 suggests an unspecified 'rude' interpretation of 'I've got a problem with my polystyrene coving.' Wood presents the next extract to further illustrate collaborative aspects of the 'mediated floor':

		Studio	Home
1.	Woman:	What I'd like to say very	
2.		briefly is if the reward	
3.		for a ca::ring daughter	
4.		who sacrifices marriage	
5.		and career is to find	
6.		herself on the streets	
7.		that's	Alice: Homeless
8.		no encouragement for	
9.		anybody [. . .]	

(ibid.: 88)

In this example of joint turn construction, Alice chips in with the woman in the studio, as if helping her to get her point across by rewording 'on the streets' (line 6) as 'homeless' (line 7). That is Wood's analysis, at least; it may instead be offering sentence completion; following 'that's' with 'homeless'.

The viewers also signal active participation by engaging with adjacency pairs in the broadcast talk. They *always* respond to questions, for instance; sometimes in simple disagreement, but often with more sustained engagement in debate, as in this example:

```
                Studio                    Home
 1.  Kilroy:    Jonathan, ar::e the
 2.             police racist?
 3.             Jonathan: I think in some
 4.             cases the police are
 5.             very racist but like    Cathy: I: think so
 6.             in other cases it all           I don't think
 7.             sort of depends how             they're all racist
 8.             you sort of ta::lk to           but I think some
 9.             to the police I think if        of them are
10.             you talk to police with [. . .]
                                                        (ibid.: 86)
```

Wood points to the clear operation of 'double articulation' in this sample, as the addressees in the studio and home both respond to the question simultaneously. In my view, it also points to an audience double articulation (I will pick up this point later, in discussion of the presence of the researcher).

The viewers also participated in the mediated floor more actively, interrogating the broadcast talk. In a *Vanessa* segment on 'women bouncers', Bev is a bouncer and Maggie is her disapproving sister:

```
                Studio                    Home
 1.  Maggie:    You've gotta think of your
 2.             kids you're letting your
 3.             kids down you go home you
 4.             can go home and you can't
 5.             work ever again=
 6.  Bev:       =but you do a job to make
 7.             a better li::fe for your
 8.             kids
 9.  Maggie:    yeh but there's other    Jana:  So basically we
10.             ways of supporting you           shouldn't have
11.             kids than (x) come        female police women
12.             home injured               we shouldn't have
13.                                            female-
                                                        (ibid.: 92)
```

Jana engages critically with the broadcast discussion, using an unco-operative formulation to pull out an equal opportunities issue (lines 9–13). Her formulation here is clearly not functioning like the *Any questions?* chair's, for the benefit of studio and radio audiences, but it could be for the benefit of a small overhearing audience, that is, her companion in the living room. This is one of several extracts that Wood uses to argue that, over the duration of the broadcast, Jana challenges the talk show's representation of socio-political issues as personal, psychological ones (ibid.: 92). Elsewhere, viewers' disagreement with the discussants triggered substantial argumentative engagements with broadcasts and, as Wood notes, they were not constrained by the face needs of the participants. Here is one fairly simple example, with relatively short interjections into a phone-in discussion on *This morning* from a viewer who thinks she knows better:

		Studio	Home
1.	Caller:	Hello	
2.	Richard:	Hello now how long have	
3.		you been	Angela: you've told us
4.		trying to get pregnant?	now
5.	Caller:	erm about eighteen months	
6.		now erm	
7.	Richard:	Right go on	Angela: (xxx)
8.	Caller:	I don't have regular	
9.		periods so I erm	
10.		obviously don't know when	
11.		I'm about to ovulate-	
12.	Richard:	arrh	
13.	Caller:	erm I see my doctor	
14.		but he says to give it	
15.		two years before he's	
16.		willing to go any	
17.		fur- any further	Angela: t-. hh it should
		[	be a year hh
18.	Richard:	so-	
		[	
19.	Judy:	so- so another six	
20.		months basically	
21.	Richard:	so you and your partner	
22.		have had no specific	
23.		tests at all then	
24.		I mean he hasn't had his	
25.		sperm count checked or	
26.		anything like that	
27.	Caller:	no	
28.	Richard:	so you're just	

```
29.              trying=                    Angela: Blame him
30.  Caller:     =I mean my partner does            heh heh heh
31.              smoke and I don't know if
32.              that has anything to do
33.              with it but the main thing
34.              is that I am-
35.  Richard:    irregular
36.  Caller:     I have irregular periods
```
                                                        (ibid.: 95)

In the context of face-to-face interaction, Angela's comments would be barracking. At a point in the broadcast discussion when all three participants are talking at once (lines 17–19), she chips in as well with a challenge to the advice given by the caller's doctor (line 17). Later, her directive 'Blame him!' seems to be implied criticism of Richard's line of questioning (line 29). Wood also presents samples where viewers draw on personal experience at much greater length; also, an earlier article presenting the same research explores the women's narratives and autobiographies interwoven with media texts (Wood 2005).

Is this talking with the television all for researcher's benefit? Wood acknowledges that her presence as a researcher is highly likely to have prompted the viewers to talk, but she reasonably argues that their vocalisations might have been articulated as 'inner speech' (Voloshinov [1923] 1973) if they had been viewing alone. She could also argue that viewing in groups is commonplace in any case, so that her presence does not compromise the validity her findings. It is true that the researcher's expert status may very well have prompted displays of critical sophistication for her benefit, but she was simply present as a viewing companion. The mediated conversational floor that she describes has a double articulation, in that the speaking audience addresses both the studio and the home.

Audiences actively engage in media discourse in other ways as well. The media are 'reservoirs and reference points' (Spitulnik 1997: 162) of language use for their audiences. As noted in early sociolinguistics, the prestige of speakers in the media rubs off on the language they use (Gumperz 1972: 223). Slogans and catchphrases, for example, have a kind of currency in everyday talk. They can become resources in daily interaction. British examples include: 'Here's one I prepared earlier', 'Can I do you now, Sir?' 'I'm free!' 'You are the weakest link, g'bye', 'Yeah but, no but. . .', 'Ooh/Suits you, Sir', 'What about the vegetables?/They'll have the same as me!' The list is endless. The transition of such

catchphrases and routines into popular parlance is part of the programmes' attachment to their audiences, as Bonner has noted (2003:
5). Spitulnik provides an interesting example of a media routine recontextualised in everyday talk; it involves the mimicking of a production-community interactional framework in Zambian radio. Most
broadcasting in Zambia comes from its capital, Lusaka (radio predomi-
nates in Zambian broadcasting). However, ZNBC's Radio 2, an English-
language channel, regularly switches over to its studio in the regional
town of Kitwe. Since this leads to regular technical hitches, a routine
involving channel checking is an essential preliminary to the procedure
for passing the floor from Lusaka to Kitwe: 'Hello, hello? Kitwe can you
hear me? Hello, Kitwe?" etc. Spitulnik relates overhearing this being
evoked in a crowded supermarket in Lusaka:

> I noticed a woman trying to get the attention of a friend standing in the
> next aisle. She was whispering loudly in the friend's direction, 'Hello,
> hello? Hello?' The friend didn't respond, and the woman, a bit
> embarrassed over drawing attention to herself while still not able
> to attract the friend, laughed and shouted, 'Hello Kitwe?' This
> definitely got the attention of the friend, as well as several other
> customers, who were clearly amused by this clever allusion to the
> bungled ZNBC communication link.
>
> (Spitulnik 1997: 168)

Here the radio hand-over routine is used as a witty channel-checking
device in a face-to-face encounter. Shouting 'Hello Kitwe?' to gain a
friend's attention in the next aisle involves an inventive analogy between
the distance between broadcasting studio locations and between supermarket aisles. Spitulnik seems almost apologetic about this idiosyncratic
anecdotal example. But such unique, off-the-cuff recontextualisations
must be very common indeed.

Other audience research has focused on 'TV talk': not talking like the
radio, or talking with the television, but talking *about* television. Media
discourse is a resource in friendship building; it provides common
ground for work colleagues, for domestic hosts and their guests and
so on. In an ethnographic study, Marie Gillespie documents TV talk as 'a
ritualistic form of everyday interaction, whether in front of the TV set or
elsewhere', arguing that it is 'an important form of self-narration and a
major collective resource through which identities are negotiated' (Gillespie 1995: 205). In her fieldwork with Punjabi-British teenagers in
Southall, a London borough, she found that TV talk prompted discussions about issues of concern to them: dating, parental control, youth
styles, ethnic and national identity. Accounts sometimes supply glimpses

of family life with television, of the participation framework in Punjabi households in Southall:

> DILJIT (17): The moment he [Dad] sees Asians on the TV, not on *EastEnders*, he wants us to watch, he calls us down and we've GOT TO watch it and even if you're in the bath or something he'll start shouting 'There's something on about India and I don't understand it, come down!' (Gillespie 1995: 118)

A surprising finding in her initial questionnaire is the amount of news that they claim to watch. This is only partly because they are required to function as translators for adults. According to the teenagers' accounts, watching – and being able to talk about – the news takes on importance in their own transition to adulthood. They claim it aids them in acquiring and demonstrating adult qualities (ibid.: 112). On the other hand, their talk about television advertising offers insights into food preferences, with Coca Cola and McDonalds being pronounced as 'cool'. Being perceived as belonging to a wider culture that is non-compulsory, these branded products connote freedom. As Gillespie puts it, they are part of a 'common cultural property of global teenagerdom' (ibid.: 27). This offers some insight, perhaps, into the resistance of schoolchildren in Greenwich to Jamie Oliver's dietary interventions (noted in Chapter 6).

Audiences do far more with media discourse than simply watch, listen and read.

Note

1. Scollon finds an equivalent procedure in print journalism, where a sub-editor uses a by-line to pass the written 'floor' over to a reporter. In terms of the actual interaction among members of production teams, this conceptualisation is of limited usefulness. In assigning by-lines to stories, a sub-editor is performing one stage in the construction of a composite written text and may not be interacting with the reporters who composed them at all.

Activities

Listen to some music radio. How prominent is the backstage production team? What contribution does the team make to the overall 'feel' of the broadcast?

Make your own field notes of people's use of catchphrases and inter-actional routines. Are there particular contexts in which they occur? How are they recontextualised?

Further reading

Crewe, Ben (2003), *Representing men: cultural production and producers in the men's magazine market*, Oxford: Berg.

Gillespie, Marie (ed.) (2006), *Media Audiences*, Open University Press.

Hesmondhalgh, David (ed.) (2006), *Media production*, Open University Press.

Hutchby, Ian (2006), 'News interviews: journalists and politicians on the air', *Media talk: conversation analysis and the study of broadcasting*, Open University Press.

Richardson, Kay and Meinhof, Ulrike (1999), 'Liveness as synchronicity and liveness as aesthetic', *Worlds in common? Television discourse in a changing Europe*, London: Routledge, pp. 50–64.

Scollon, Ron (1998), 'Acts of reading and watching: observation as social interaction', *Mediated discourse as social interaction: a study of news discourse*, London: Longman.

Spitulnik, Debra (1997), 'The social circulation of media discourse and the mediation of communities', *Journal of linguistic anthropology*, 6(2): 161–87.

Tolson, Andrew (2006), 'Youth talk', *Media talk: spoken discourse on TV and radio*, Edinburgh: Edinburgh University Press.

8 Interactivity

As we enter an era of interactive media technology, the interface between media texts and audience is transforming, including new ways of accessing content and new possibilities for social engagement in a virtual environment, be it radio, television, the (still) largely written mode of the Internet, or a combination of all three. The late Roger Silverstone reflected that

> our [twentieth] century has seen the telephone, film, radio, television become both objects of mass consumption and essential tools for the conduct of everyday life. We are now confronted with the spectre of a further intensification of media culture, through the global growth of the Internet and the promise (some might say the threat) of an interactive world in which nothing and no one cannot be accessed, instantly.
>
> (Silverstone 1999: 4)

A convenient example of this, for me, is a university website providing contact details for staff. It is now common to be contacted by students worldwide, not just those at the same university. This generates a sense of being a globally available 'amenity', a phenomenon that can be experienced as an imposition or a pleasure in equal measure. But the Internet also offers such amenities as interactive maps, downloadable music resources on demand and so on. The notion of 'interactivity' raises interesting issues of definition (see, for example, Christensen 2003, Downes and McMillan 2000, Jensen 1999, Schultz 2000). Here, I am understanding it not primarily it in terms of enhanced content and access, but as social interaction. This final chapter turns to interactivity between members of audience communities and members of production communities: the reality and the rhetoric.

Backstage engagements

In the media back region, there have been print- and telephone-mediated interactions between production teams and audience members for many

years, in recent years, email and text messaging too. I begin this section
with an aspect of backstage interaction: *The Sun* newspaper's use of phone
voting and the phone-in in its self-presentation as champion of the
people (Conboy 2003: 51). In March 2000, they set up an 'interactive
democratic hotline' (ibid.: 52) inciting rage over asylum seekers:

YOU TELL US
We want to know what you think about the way refugees are treated
in Britain. Call us on this number, we'll ring back.

(The Sun, 13 March 2000)

As asylum seekers were represented negatively throughout the same
issue (as 'grasping nomads', for example), the newspaper seemed to be
working on a consensus. Two days later, they reported the outcome. The
readers' responses were represented as one voice, a consensus reiterated
in the headline:

Time to kick the scroungers out
Angry *Sun* readers jammed our phone lines yesterday demanding:
'Kick the scroungers out.'

(The Sun, 15 March 2000)

The Home Secretary, Jack Straw, felt obliged to respond to this
campaign, an indication of the government's perception of the influence
of the newspaper.[1] The same issue ran a phone voting feature. The
feature established as shared knowledge that there was a refugee crisis
and Jack Straw should be doing something about it:

STRAW ANSWERS OUR TEN QUESTIONS
YOU THE JURY
IS Jack Straw doing enough to solve the refugee crisis?
If you think yes phone . . .
If you think no phone . . .

(The Sun, 15 March 2000)

'An amazing 98 per cent of votes' (*The Sun*, 17 March 2000) critical of
Straw was the entirely unsurprising outcome of this flamboyant act of
'phone democracy' (Conboy 2003: 52). In fact, in its representation, the
participation that readers were offered was as much juridical as democratic. Readers were explicitly assigned the subject position of jury
members (and the newspaper implicitly set itself up as judge). But a
key point here is that the newspaper was engaging in a rhetoric of
dialogue (Conboy 2006: 20–2). In the guise of giving a voice to the
people, the newspaper was very clearly setting up a predetermined

position on asylum for readers to occupy. It is likely that, in voting, *Sun* readers were also positioned as consumers, taking part in a commercial transaction with interactive services supporting their participation. This is certainly the case with voting on 'reality' shows in the *Big brother* format (Nightingale and Dwyer 2006).

Channels for complaints about the press and broadcasting offer other opportunities for backstage interaction. I shall consider an example that I think is interesting in the light of earlier observations (in Chapter 6) about the contemporary broadcasting genre of lifestyle TV. *Gardeners' question time* is a long-running specialist programme on BBC Radio 4 with a dedicated audience. When the presenter solicited comments from its listeners on BBC TV's coverage of the Chelsea Flower Show in 2005, they received the biggest response ever on a single subject, only two per cent of which was favourable. Extracts from a few of the letters received were read out on a mailbag edition of the radio programme:

> I get <u>so</u> cross with seeing presenters standing in <u>front</u> of the plants instead of letting me see the plants
>
> you have to wade through the endless fake mate-iness the joshing between thee- er the gardeners which makes me want to <u>throw</u> things at the television screen
>
> the inarticulate Irishman clowning around with an effeminate character who had little to say about plants makes for very diluted gardening viewing and therefore not worth watching
>
> (*Gardeners' question time*, BBC Radio 4, 1 March 2006)

They are clearly articulating dislike of the introduction of a lifestyle TV format (in the third example, apparently effeminacy is also considered offensive). Other letters report being put off by 'the behaviour of the male presenters', 'embarrassed' and 'appalled by the presentation of the so-called personalities and the flimsy coverage of the plants'. Clearly, the lifestyle TV makeover of coverage of this popular annual event in the gardening calendar is, to put it mildly, not well received by the Radio 4 *Gardeners' question time* audience. They share the view that the interpersonal focus of infotainment (and, I suppose, contemporary notions of celebrity/personality more generally) should not take precedence over ideational content: here, plants and planting schemes. The executive producer's defence was that it was scheduled for the 8.00 p.m. slot and was 'not a specialist horticultural show for a niche audience' (like *Gardeners' question time*). The following year's coverage of the Chelsea Flower Show in 2006 indicated that the irate audience had exerted some influence, at least, on programme content.

When the *Gardeners' question time* listeners had their letters read out, their voices were animated in the front region, thereby giving them several seconds – if not fifteen minutes – of fame. Technological differences aside, this is not a new phenomenon; there have been dedicated letters pages in publications since the early seventeenth century. In early magazines, some readers were also regular contributors, and not just of letters (see, for example, Ballaster et al. 1991, Beetham 1996). The next sections explore audience participation in the contemporary media front region.

Frontstage: fifteen minutes of fame

In discussing the textual construction of community in men's magazines earlier (in Chapter 3), I pointed to the high degree of audience involvement, with features centred on email and other correspondence, the submission of photos and so on. These participatory elements make a significant contribution to the construction of masculine community. The letters pages of magazines and newspapers provide raw material for the rhetoric of dialogue. *The Sun*'s is headed: 'The page where you tell Britain what you think'. *The Daily Star*'s announces, even more explicitly: 'It's the bit you write'.

In some audience-participation genres in broadcasting, there is a live audience in the front region, in other words in the studio. Such shows have received considerable critical attention – for example, talk shows as institutional talk (Gregori Signes 2000; Tolson 2001) and as a forum for democratic debate (Livingstone and Lunt 1994; Hair 2003). In phone-ins on 'open-line' programming, the broadcast conversational floor is opened up to members of the viewing or listening audience. For the radio listener, this produces 'an impression, however misleading, created by those phoning in of innumerable *other* listeners who approximate to the community at large' (Crisell 1994: 195). In mid-2006, a new talk radio station went on air serving East Central Scotland. Touting it as 'radio for the twenty <u>first</u> century' and 'the most fantastic gift' for Scotland since free libraries, the host, 'Scottie McClue' (the radio persona of Colin Lamont), promotes it as follows:

> It's public access radio and it's interactive of course Now you might not be used to this .h you might not have <u>heard</u> of this before .h and of course it's a wonderful wonderful invention It's a marvellous gift .h to Scotland and I for one (.) am so proud .h that Scotland has got its own talk radio station at long long last .h cos let's not kid ourselves .h

there's nobody talks better than we do The Scots are wonderful talkers
.h you .h me .h and all the rest of the people coming on here

(*Scottie McClue*, Talk 107, 21 September 2006)

Here, he seems to be establishing trust, building up a new audience base
for his late-night slot on this new twenty-four-hour talk radio station. He
makes much of Scottishness and shared identity. Strangely, he goes on to
explain the concept of the phone-in to the people of Edinburgh, Fife and
the Lothians. This (surely unnecessary) measure may be because he has a
degree of infamy as a highly confrontational talk radio host and feels that
he needs to put them at ease:

If you're not used to phoning in then get into the habit of it .h There's
nothing to fear >I know a lot of you are saying at home that< 'I'd love
to talk to Scott McClue but (xxxxx)' It's no a difficult thing .h If you've
ever spoken to someone on the telephone .h then that's (.) all that's to it

(ibid.)

Well, no it isn't, actually. The callers' participation is severely limited.
For a start, they are competing with other callers. Calling an open-line
radio station is not at all like making a private phone call. Indeed, with
something of a contradiction of his own reassurances, he goes on to
emphasise its competitiveness:

we <u>do</u> want to <u>hear</u> your opinion .h so the most important thing is that
you get into the habit of it now .h Like winning the lottery .h if you
don't buy a ticket you won't win .h If you don't pick up the phone and
phone me .h then you won't get on the wireless .h and you won't get to
hear the sound of your own voice .h And you <u>know</u> you <u>want</u> to
because <u>every</u> <u>single</u> Scottish person has got something to say

(ibid.)

He is implicitly offering a moment of fame on air as a prize, a commodity.
In some kinds of phone-in, they are also competing for other scarce
commodities, as in a promotion on *Galaxy* radio of their sponsor (a mobile
phone company): 'cos I want you guys to get interactive and win some
fantastic prizes (.) some amazing holiday breaks this weekend' (24
September 2006). 'Getting interactive' here involves competing with
other callers for a chance of a few seconds' airtime. In such telephone
interactions, the opening sequence: 'Hello/ohmigod!' is not at all unusual.

In the case of television shopping channels such as QVC, making a
purchase is a necessary precondition for the most valued commodity:
speaking with the host on air (Bucholtz 1999, 2000). As Mary Bucholtz
argues, the virtual community offered by the show is a key attraction, and

it is created in no small measure through interactivity between the studio host and the viewing audience at home. Here is an example of the host bridging the physical distance through topic choice (shared experience of extreme winter weather conditions):

```
H:   Host
C:   Caller
,    fall-rise intonation
.    falling intonation
 1. H:   Did you all get much snow there in West Virginia?
 2. C:   Oh we've got um (pause) we got about three foot
 3.      of snow and um-
                [
 4. H:           Whoo
 5. C:   we've got drifts up to sixteen feet. So
                                            [
 6. H:                                      Wow.
 7. C:   It- We're snowed in for a couple of days.
 8.      [laughter]
         [
 9. H:   That's- so are we I tell you.
              [
11. C:              I'm sticking by the TV. [laughter]
12. H:   I was- I was glad to come in today. I was bouncing
13.      off the walls a little earlier so- [laughter]
14. C:   Yeah We went out and tried to- to take a walk
15.      earlier but we didn't get too far. [laughter]
16. H:   I can imagine with three feet of snow goodness.
                                         [
17. C:                                   Yeah.
18. H:   Well (.) g- try to stay warm and thanks for
19.      stopping by.
20. C:   Thank you
21. H:   You have a good night Dorothy.
22. C:   You too.
```

(Bucholtz 2000: 201–2)

The neighbourly farewell in lines 18–19 contributes to building an illusion of domestic hospitality and physical co-presence, an impression that is created through language. The characterisation of the call as 'stopping by' represents it as a friendly visit by a neighbour. The next extract provides a further example (lines 7–8):

```
1.  C:  You all are great I tell you,
2.  H   [low volume] Well thank you.
3.      What's your husband's name?
4.  C:  Uh (.) Michael
5.  H:  [mock shout] Hi Michael how you doing?
6.  C:  [laughter] He says hi.
7.  H:  [laughter] Okay. Well I'm glad both of you
8.      stopped by to say hello.
```

(ibid.: 206)

The device for manufacturing intimacy starting in line 3 has been made possible by the caller indirectly mentioning her husband ('we') earlier in the call. The phatic greeting with the caller's husband, with his response relayed by the caller herself, contributes further to the interactively generated impression of community. Shared identity is indexed by use of a second-person plural pronoun 'you all' that is distinctively southern United States (in the opening lines of both extracts).

From the broadcasters' perspective, the caller's primary function in consumer programming is to supply a satisfied customer's testimonial, endorsing claims made by sales people. In the following extract, Varna from Tyne and Wear (a county in north-east England) is waiting to talk about the apparent merits of silicon flexi-bake kitchenware:

```
AD:  Anne Dawson (presenter)
V:   Varna (caller)
MH:  Malcolm Harradine ('expert')
 1.  AD: While you bring the erm the dishes out Malcolm
 2.      we're gonna go to the er phone lines because Varna
 3.      from Tyne and Wear is waiting to have a chat with
 4.      us this afternoon good afternoon Varna
 5.  V:  Hello
            [
 6.  MH: Hello Varna
 7.  AD: Hello there now I understand you've gone for these
 8.      before
 9.  V:  Yes I have
10.  AD: What do you think of them
11.  V:  Ah they're absolutely excellent I mean you don't
                                         [
12.  MH:                          Fantastic
13.  V:  have to grease them (.) or anything I mean so you
14.      know I (.) found them absolutely excellent
```

15. **AD:** Oh that's <u>brill</u>iant What about cleaning them up
16.   after you've done your cooking Varna (.)
17. **V:** erm (.) th- well all you've got to do is just wipe
18.   them around
19. **MH:** heh
20. **V:** or you can just like put them into like a bowl of
21.   water but I mean (.) see like if you're making a
22.   lasagne you've got no bits or anything
          [
23. **AD:**   Yeah   yeah
24. **MH:** Mhmm
25. **AD:** (.) That is- Again it just makes the cleaning up so
26.   much easier
             [
27. **V:**   yeah
28. **AD:** cos I don't know about you Varna but sometimes what
29.   I cook is er dictated by how much mess I'll have
30.   afterwards Heh heh
                [
31. **V:**   heh heh
                [
32. **MH:**   heh heh
33. **AD:** after what you're going to eat you know like fish-

Like Bucholtz's callers and hosts, the parallel accounts contribute to creating a sense of community, through shared domestic experience. Here we have broadcast sociability in the service of product promotion. This caller, however, also has her own agenda; she is a consumer making demands. Judging by the host's response in line 41 and expert's in lines 42–5, they find her demand provocative:

34. **V:** Can I just ask Malcolm something
                      [
35. **AD:**   Yes <u>please</u> do
36. **MH:** Yes (.) certainly
37. **V:** Hiya
38. **MH:** Hi
39. **V:** Er yeah was just to ask you if you had any of the
40.   fairy cake moulds (.)
41. **AD:** Ooooh
42. **MH:** Yes (.) We have done those in the past I've er
43.   <u>act</u>ually go a meeting with the buyers er Varna er

```
44.      after the show so I'll ask the question That's put
45.      them on the (xx) hasn't it heheh
46. AD:  yeah well
47. MH:  yeah but they are very popular I know
                                          [
48. V:                                    yeah
49. AD:  The little moulds the flexi-moulds you can do your
50.      Yorkshire puddings in
                          [
51. MH:              that's it
52. V:   yeah
53. AD:  and do your cakes and muffins and all sorts in
54.      there Well Malcolm I have on good authority he is
55.      going to be talking to the buyer after the show and
56.      he'll put it to them and hopefully we'll get them
57.      back for you Varna as soon as we can
```

The caller plays her part with great aplomb. She has asserted herself as a testimonial-giving consumer with demands to make of the guest expert and 'the buyer'. She goes on to reward host and expert with a further testimonial and report of product promotion, containing some lively 'local colour' in a voice she animates (62–3):

```
58. V:   It was just to erm tell you as well that erm I'm
59.      actually disabled and (.) erm I'm actually in a
60.      cookery class and I er took my flexi-bake into er
61.      my cookery class and they said [more localised
62.      accent] 'you cannae put tha' into the oven it'll
63.      melt'
64. AD:  heh heh
         [
65. MH:  heh heh
66. V:   And I said 'it won't' heheh but I mean I'm er
67.      trying to get them to get the flexi-bake as well
68. AD:  Oh that's fantastic Varna
                        [
69. MH:              fantastic fantastic
70. AD:  What a great story thank you very very much my love
71.      for calling in
             [
72. V:       thank you
73. AD:  and good luck
```

```
                [
74. V:          bye
                [
75. MH: Thanks Varna
76. AD: and we'll try get those moulds in er as soon as we
77.     can That was Varna calling us from Tyne and Wear
```
                                                    (QVC, 2005)

Within the (very) narrow context of consumer television and specific
product promotion, Varna from Tyne and Wear has some small power to
set the agenda.

Asymmetries

Mediated interactions have built-in advantages for producers and are
highly asymmetrical. In the case of radio phone-ins, the radio station
and host clearly have the technological advantage over callers (Kress
1986: 415–6). Hosts on talk programming call the shots as talk
managers. I have already mentioned queuing. Callers do not have
direct access to the host but have to compete with other callers for the
attention of switchboard operators, who function as gatekeepers. If
successful, a caller may still be put on hold, or cut off altogether,
whenever the host feels so inclined. For example, a talk show host,
George Galloway, decides to set a caller straight and puts him on hold
with: 'I'll let you back in in a minute' (*Talk sport*, 1 October 2006). He
goes on to present, at great length, an account of trade unions in the
1970s, before letting the caller back in again. To me, as a listener, this
intervention seemed to be justified (and the account refreshingly
accurate). The host's entitlement stemmed from his status as a politician with knowledge of the political world and trade-union history
that far exceeded the caller's. But the point here is that the intervention
is a luxury that would be hard to achieve in face-to-face talk.

As a controversy-courting MP with his own radio phone-in, Galloway
is exceptional, but he exploits the technological edge that he has over
callers no more than other hosts do. To date, I have not heard him cut off
a caller, in contrast to what happens in this exposure of empowering
technology in use:

```
M:   Michael (caller)
SZ:  Stan Zamenek
1.  M:   Oh Stan I was wondering
2.  SZ:  yes
```

```
3.  M:  How do you cut off people
4.  SZ: Very easily [music sting]
```

(Cook 2000: 68)

The 'music sting' in line 4 presumably accompanies the act of cutting off
the caller. The topicalisation of normally hidden processes is typical of
zoo radio. It is a feature of the Australian *Stan Zamenek show*, from which
this example is taken. A show host always has the institutional power to
terminate a call. The careful pre-closing sequences normal in a private
call (Schegloff and Sacks 1973) may be drastically reduced, even in
highly affiliative, non-confrontational phone-in conversations. In a particularly abrupt termination of a rambling conversation on air, Scottie
McClue concluded with 'I'll have to dash' (Talk 107, 10 October 2006).
The double articulation here is very clear: this colloquial conversational
closing is affiliative for listeners, but hardly for the caller. A little later on
the same evening, he terminated a long call involving rambling inanities
with an abrupt: 'I haven't time to talk to you all night'.

Another issue relating to asymmetry on air is abuse of callers; again
Scottie McClue is interesting in this regard. His appeal to cultural
sameness on Scottish radio (last section) contrasts sharply with the
relationship he sought with the audience on a previous radio station,
catering for north-west England. There he used Scottishness differently,
to mark his difference from listeners, in cultivation of an abrasive
confrontational persona. In this context, his signature tune ('Hoots
Mon', a 1958 charts hit from a Scottish band called Lord Rockingham's
XI) underlines his difference:

```
SM:  'Scottie McClue'
W   Wally (caller)
 1.  SM: [signature tune in background] >You're listening
 2.      to Scottie McClue's Mega Phone-in Back to the
 3.      telephone because< we're stowed out through the
 4.      board n' stappit through with calls Now that is
 5.      Scottish for saying that we are extremely busy so
 6.      I don't want any idiots I don't want any plonkers
 7.      .h I don't want any fools [background laughter]
 8.      That covers most of you I think [music fades] and
 9.      WALLY
10.  W:  yeah
11.  SM: That's an appropriate name to pop up next isn't it
```

(Scottie McClue's Mega Phone-in, Century 105, 1998)

'Idiot', 'plonker', 'fool' and 'wally' are all terms for somebody very silly. His aim here is to insult both the listening audience and the caller; it is clearly not affiliative. Though his Scottish accent is far less marked than in the broadcast to fellow Scots on Talk 107, in lines 3–4 he deliberately selects expressions that require his own authoritative 'translation'. This is not to say that for his new Scottish audience he is now smoothing the abrasiveness of his established persona. He still performs a character who does not suffer fools gladly, as in the abusive banter in the next extract. The caller has not made a very good job of arguing that women would not be interested in male pole dancers:

```
C:  Cristabel (caller)
 1. SM:  >You know what I think< (.) .h I think that you're
 2.      a half-witted idiot (.)    That's what I think
                                  [
 3. C:                       Well I know better
 4. SM:  I think you're a half-witted idiot And I've never
 5.      heard so much rubbish talked in all my life (.)
 6. C:   But you (xxx)-
           [
 7. SM:     And if you're gonna come on here and talk to me
 8.      you're goin' to have to do a bit better than that
 9.      chummy
10. C:   But (.) you know nothing about me?
11. SM:  No (.) you've told me enough about you I know that
12.      you're >as daft as a brush<
13. C:   No:: I know you're as mad as a barrel of monkeys
14. SM:  I may be as mad as a barrel of monkeys but you're
15.      definitely as daft as a brush (.) I tell you
                                         [
16. C:                               [laughter]
17. SM:  So there you go:: [dispute continues]
```
                    (*Scottie McClue*, Talk 107, 10 October 2006)

This exchange of insults is good humoured, but with it McClue maintains his position of authority in argumentation, as observed in male phone-in hosts on Australian talk radio (Cook 2000; Flew 2004). Scornful meta-discursive comments on the inarticulacy of callers are a feature of confrontational talk radio. Another aggressive British host, James Stannage, for instance, once berated a caller by repeatedly shouting at him: 'stop saying "basically"!'

On many phone-ins, callers set the agenda at the outset and the host may have no idea what it is going be. However, this apparent advantage does not put the caller in control, as Ian Hutchby has observed:

> Although it may seem that the caller, in setting the agenda for the call, is in a position of control over what might count as an acceptable or relevant contribution to their topic, in fact it is the host who tends to end up in that position.
>
> (1996: 41)

Hutchby's study of how this happens suggests that phone-in argument sequences have a built-in generic feature that means it makes a big difference whether you speak first or second. Setting the agenda, for callers, means always speaking first. The interaction is asymmetrical from the start. In CA terms, it puts the host in a favoured second position that a confrontational phone-in host has the option of using to their advantage,

> this means that the host can find it relatively easy to go on the offensive in disputes, whereas the caller finds him or herself in a defensive position with regard to the agenda they began by introducing . . . going second actually means having the *first* opportunity for opposition.
>
> (ibid.: 47–8)

Opposition may take the form of challenges to the validity of the caller's point ('So?' 'What's that got to do with it?' and so on). Another, slightly more elaborate form of validity challenge is the 'You say "X" device', where a caller's entire stance may be undermined by challenges to small details ('You say ninety-six percent Have you done your own market research on this?' (ibid.: 66)). In openings, the host can, if they wish, hide behind a privileged position as challenger without ever establishing their own view on the issue under discussion; even better, in closings, they are able to put their own point of view without ever allowing the caller to respond (ibid.: 94–5). The host can always have the power of the last word, which in the front region is always the broadcast word.

I have to say, however, that as a listener I am sometimes glad of the host's intervention. In this extract from *Any answers?*, the caller is commenting on the Iraqi occupation:

MT: Marjorie Totchin (caller)
JD: Jonathan Dimbleby
  1. **MT:** . . . they needed a strong governor (.) but they
  2.   removed him .h we had a world war leader in USA-
  3. **JD:** When you say >>they needed a strong governor<<
  4.   you mean they nee- they nee- they nee- er they nee-

```
                                   [
 6.  MT:                                      er Saddam Hussein
 7.  JD:  They needed Saddam Hussein
 8.  MT:  They did
 9.  JD:  That's a pretty (.) er er rum view isn' it? that er
10.       er those people >>needed Saddam Hussein?<<
            [
11.  MT:  Well not if you look back into history .hh
          [continues]
```

(Any Answers, BBC Radio 4, 14 October 2006)

Here Dimbleby formulates the caller's controversial claim (lines 3–7) then follows up with a validity challenge (line 9). He is not a confrontational host, however; his uncharacteristic disfluency (line 4) and hesitant care in choice of lexis (line 9) seem to serve a hedging function, softening the antagonism of his formulation and challenge.

There is an interesting study of political talk radio that involves interviews with participants in radio phone-ins and offers insights into the experience from the callers' perspective (Ross 2004). Here are two examples of callers expressing discontent over their phone-in encounters with politicians:

> I think he [Jack Straw] treated me with total contempt, and not only me but also other people that he spoke to. If it was something that he found to be not to his taste, he was very dismissive. In effect he called me an idiot, which basically sums up, I think, the arrogance of the current Labour Cabinet. I think David Dimbleby [sic] tried very, very hard to allow that [to ask a follow-up question] to happen but I think the nature of the question and the way I phrased it wasn't exactly to [Straw's] taste . . . (Vincent)
> I think one needs to practise doing this obviously. Some people interrupt quite a lot. Some questioners interrupt quite a lot and I'm not really into interrupting people but I think perhaps one has to a little bit, you know, steer them back on to target. (Rosemary)

(ibid.: 795)

Callers are isolated; they are in domestic space, rather than in the studio with the politician and programme host. Citing Thornborrow (2002) on the dynamics of three-way phone-in talk, Karen Ross observes that this isolation puts them at a disadvantage on the conversational floor (2004: 795). Callers report their impressions that politicians and media professionals are in cahoots; they acknowledge, in effect, that they are engaging as outsiders with an extended production community of media and other professionals. Ross also notes the production team's selection of 'ordinary' people with individualised concerns and emotional appeal. Their grounds for such selection of callers is that 'strong views make "good radio"'; in effect, however, their preference for 'ordinary' people screens out political activists (ibid.: 789–90).

The participation of audience members is strictly on broadcasters' terms (the same, of course, can be said about print journalism). There are conditions for being on air at all. On the radio, practitioners sometimes exercise a preference for female callers: for phone-ins involving competitions, their licensed expressiveness is considered more suitable than the more subdued responses of successful male contestants. Calls containing whooping excitement and enthusiasm are often recorded and edited to improve their impact and may end up in promotional material (Richard Berry, personal communication). Female callers attract female listeners, who in turn attract advertisers. 'Girly' excitability makes for good radio all round, it seems. The self-perpetuation is clear here, in terms of gendered behaviour. Broadcasters have specific requirements of their phoning audience. This involves a particular construction of audience that callers obligingly project back at them. The gendered identities of female callers are commodified, as they win a few seconds of airtime by articulating broadcasters' conception of feminine.

Similarly, potential candidates for 'reality TV' programmes face fierce competition for access and in the process they are squeezed into stylised, formulaic presentations of self. Alison Hearn observes the influence of the 'reality TV' genre on projections of identity by aspiring contestants, seeing in their performances 'pre-set, freeze-dried presentations of self, molded by prior knowledge of the dictates of the reality television genre and deployed strategically to garner attention, and potentially, profit' (Hearn 2006: 134). What is distinctive about the 'reality TV' format is the labour performed by the audience:

> What is new about reality television production is the way in which viewers themselves are summoned to get inside the mechanics of the industry and offer their bodies and labour up to the image-making machinery for free. Much like donning Mickey Mouse ears at Disneyland, becoming a part of the immersive television experience involves adopting a 'persona' consonant with its dictates: the jock, the vixen, the asshole, the gay guy, the rich bitch, the grizzled vet, the buddy. Reality television entices viewers to go on its various 'rides' and calls this 'real'. (ibid.)

So it seems that the asymmetrical framework for such audience participation requires synthetic personalities all round – the price of entry into the mediated community for the audience (the same can be said for audience entry into the mediated community of zoo radio (Tolson 2006: 129)).

New technology

New technologies – cable, satellite and especially the Internet – have facilitated a convergence of media forms. This has created the potential for greatly enhanced audience participation. I conclude with some attention to the extent to which this potential is being realised.

Will Brooker writes of 'overflow' of one media form into another: a 'tendency for media producers to construct a lifestyle experience around a core text, using the Internet to extend audience engagement and encourage a two-way interaction' (2002: 323). These days there can be few broadcast shows, printed newspapers or magazines without a dedicated website offering a range of features. For example, *Newsnight* now has heightened interactivity in the content-access sense. With the necessary technology at their disposal, viewers can watch a broadcast at any time during the week. The *Newsnight* website also currently offers highlights in the form of a downloadable podcast and advanced notice of the evening's content in a daily newsletter by subscription. The newsletter also facilitates responses from its recipients with an invitation that is also the channel itself, such as a link entitled 'Click here to comment'. Another enhancement is 'Talk about *Newsnight*: a blog and forum', which is advertised on the homepage with a topical comment that has been posted on it by a viewer. In addition, distinct from this forum, viewers have email access to the production team. In a blog item discussing email, the *Newsnight* editor claims that the team is influenced but not bullied by it (Baron 2006a). A small study of *New York Times* journalists' responsiveness to email correspondence indicates that the quantity received is 'manageable' but occasional spamming is highly irritating; however, as as one respondent commented: 'Since the *NYT* has a million daily readers, I would dread the day when all started emailing me!' (Schultz 2000: 213).

It is common for live broadcasters to invite comments and occasionally read out emailed questions to guests as topics are discussed. From the production team's perspective, websites with a comment facility are much like phone-ins and have a telegenic or radiogenic function: 'to verify that the station has an audience and that this audience is capable of understanding and responding' (Crisell 1994: 189). The participation rate in such comment facilities tends to be very low. The total number of posts is similar to the number of successful callers given airtime. For example, the comment section of the *Newsnight* website on 13 October

2006 had just ten postings. This is not untypical of the response rate. In the same week, the lowest was six and the highest was thirty (largely a slanging match between two contributors). Over a period of one month, I checked the postings on a daily basis: the all-time high was 155 (the topic was Madonna's adoption of a one-year old from Malawi). Of course, the reading audience is very much larger; the editor claims around 50,000 blog readers (Baron 2006b), presumably on the basis of information about numbers signing up for the newsletter.

In a recent observational study of the production team on *BBC breakfast news*, Claire Wardle professes surprise at her own conclusion – that the production team take emails and text messages seriously, to the extent that they influence the morning's coverage. The producer maintained that they 'helped him to get a sense of what is interesting to the audience "outside the bubble of Television centre"'(Wardle 2006: 13). (This consciousness of being out of touch with the audience echoes Georgina Born's study of *Newsnight*, referred to in Chapter 7.) However, participation is very small: approximately 300 messages per day to a programme with a viewing audience of around one million. The Internet-facilitated interactivity is functioning like the more traditional channels (letter, phone call), except that the connection, and any response, is very much more rapid.

Invitations to 'make the news' have been a feature of some local radio stations and their websites for some time. Listeners are encouraged to text in items as 'breaking news'. In other words, they are establishing the audience as potential news gatherers. At the time of writing, the solicitation of user-generated content is proliferating. In late October 2006, the website for *Saturday live* (BBC Radio 4) began to invite members of the audience to be a 'Guerrilla Reporter': 'This is where YOU become the reporter' and 'snatch the microphone from us'. In early November, *Newsnight* launched 'Oh my *Newsnight!*' a website feature eliciting video footage from viewers. Within a couple of weeks, however, the editor's newsletter was querying the lack of uptake (Baron 2006b). The newsletter query generated a healthy crop of responses that evening (twenty in all). The following post provides the gist of many of them rather well:

> BBC, you are the news organization, we are the audience. Don't expect us to do your job for you. Few of us have the time or skill to submit professional results. That's why YouTube exists, for people to display their enormous collection of amateur junk to a disinterested [sic] world. You (usually rightly) criticize what little you get and you won't pay for it no matter how good it is anyway. So you keep cooking it up and dishing

it out and we'll tell you how good or bad we think it tastes and smells. It's either that or make the site a one way street again (Mark)

The appropriacy or otherwise of user-generated content on BBC's flagship news programme continues to simmer as a 'controversy' in the *Newsnight* forum, with frequent allusion to Paxman's curmudgeonly dismissal of the whole idea.

A study of a Dutch radio programme provides insights into the experience of radio as a two-way street. It looked at the experience of live interactive web presence for both presenters and listeners on a show called *BuZz* (van Selm et al. 2004). The radio programme catered for a young audience, some of whom were keen Internet users. Its website features included a downloadable archive, a 'visitors' book' inviting comments on the site, and two on-air features: live images from a webcam in the studio and a live chatbox that was readable on the spot by the host. Questions and comments from the chatbox were fed into the ongoing radio talk as it was broadcast. These were sometimes elicited by the host. The study focused on the two on-air elements; it was based on interviews with studio staff and focus group discussions with listeners. For the listeners, the chatbox was better than a phone-in and the chance to influence programme content was appreciated, as these two comments illustrate:

You start with a radio programme and it depends on the listeners as to where things go, in what direction; that is interactivity.
It's like me asking a question in the chat room and I immediately hear it being asked in the program! That's really interactive

(van Selm et al. 2004: 274)

However, some listeners expressed disappointment at the hosts' lack of uptake and enthusiasm. From the staff perspective, the chatbox channel was also preferable to the more traditional phone-in, in so far as it was less costly to staff and operate. But they reported finding the listeners' comments distracting and intrusive: a disconcerting divergence from routine (ibid.: 275).

'Interactivity' came into early prominence with 'reality' TV. As well as being offered 'empowerment' as voters, viewers are encouraged to pass judgement on televised participants. The outcomes of such audience participation may then be deliberately channelled back into the ongoing producer-controlled broadcast text. See, for example, an account of the complex interactivity of a show called *The Salon* (Holmes 2004). As Su Holmes remarks, it 'foregrounds what may become the increasing difficulty of constructing an opposition between textual analysis and audience research, given that comments from "real" viewers are central to the textual fabric of the series itself (ibid.: 217).

So, interesting things are happening and the way that media discourse circulates is becoming more and more complex. The dialogism between media producers and their audiences has never been greater. The boundaries between production and consumption are in some ways becoming blurred, so that the definition of 'audience' becomes difficult (Livingstone 2006: 44). Internet-enriched media consumption is no longer fixed in a domestic environment, yet media suffuse and permeate daily life and many of us are increasingly becoming 'multi-taskers'. There are probably significant generational differences in perception of media-related activity, especially with television and online media. For Charlotte Brunsdon, young people are 'more "television-minded", in that television is much more readily accommodated into other activities (eating breakfast, doing homework, making phone calls), and is thus both more ordinary, and less important' (Brunsdon 2003: 14). As online media converge with television and radio, we are no doubt becoming more 'Internet-minded' too.

However, as audiences gain greater control of access, producers' anxieties about losing control increase. 'Interactivity' and 'enhancement' need to be understood in this broader context of reduction in broadcasters' capacity to control the terms of audience engagement (Nightingale and Dwyer 2006: 31). Picking up Brooker's water metaphor again, they are careful irrigators, tapping into audience involvement in order to channel it for their own ends. As Holmes observes in relation to *The Salon*'s web forums:

> This is 'overflow' which, in keeping with Brooker's metaphor, is deliberately channelled to 'trickle back' into the hands of the producers. The forum and email links are precisely set up so that the products (or 'labour') of interactivity can be exploited in the service of an ongoing narrative for televisual consumption.
>
> (Holmes 2004: 221)

Within the industry's own, finance-focused discourse, we read of the 'leveraging' of consumer generated content and its potential for product enhancement and marketing purposes (for example, NATPE website and newsletters).

I finish now with some brief attention to claims about media as democratic space. The Internet offers huge potential for 'small media' that contribute to 'horizontal' communication. Media spaces that are not state controlled may be sites of public democratic and potential emancipatory space; 'small genres' such as email, can, like leafleting, text messaging and so on, function 'as participatory, public phenomena, controlled neither by big states nor big corporations' (Sreberny-Mohammadi and Mohammadi 1994). In the 'big genres' that have been the subject of this book, however, online polls such as those set up by newspapers are 'pseudo participation' (Schultz 2000: 209). While they use the language of participation, they do not engage with it as social practice.

In Britain (as elsewhere), political parties are slow to pick up on the possibilities of genuine interactivity offered by new technologies. Participation by parliamentary political parties is patchy. Reporting an interview with Stephen Coleman, a social scientist researching e-democracy, a journalist observes that

> parties ... will become effective internet users only once they recognise that voters want to talk to them and not just receive officially approved messages.
> 'The internet is the greatest listening mechanism ever invented. The party that finds a way of entering into genuine discussion with voters will be the one that starts to get real benefits from all of this.'
> (Richards 2005: 17)

Receiving 'officially approved messages' in podcasts is no different from receiving them in other formats. There are a few politicians experimenting with use of the Internet as a two-way street. The official website of Jacqui Smith MP, for example, recently enticed her young constituents to air their views with a chance of winning a coveted commodity: 'Are you 13–18 years old? Tell me what you think – for a chance to win an MP3 Player' (website, posted 22 September 2006).

But if big states are not claiming control, big corporations are. There is increasing corporate control of the Internet, both in terms of content and management and in terms of technology (that is, software and bandwidth) (Dahlberg 2005: 95). With the mobile phone industry as the technological and economic driver of developments, audiences of the future will be firmly placed in a subject position as consumer.

Note

1. In October 2006, I was alert to the possible emergence of another tabloid campaign of this kind, in anticipation of the entry of Bulgaria and Romania as two more member states in the European Union. It is an indication of the Government responsiveness to the traditional tabloids' self-appointed role as 'champion of the people', however, that there was no need for such a campaign. The new Home Secretary, John Reid, pre-empted it by imposing severe restrictions on entry to citizens of the new members states, presumably to avoid the predicament experienced by his predecessor, Jack Straw. This to a backdrop of headlines such as 'Thousands of Romanians and

Bulgarians get green light to invade Britain' (*Daily Express* 27 September 2006) and 'On the day the 30m citizens of Bulgaria and Romania were given the right to come to Britain, this was the queue for visas in Bucharest' (*Daily Mail* 27 September 2006) (the latter, unusually lengthy headline accompanied a photograph of a large crowd of people).

Activities

Look at the participatory elements in a newspaper and examine the rhetoric of dialogue surrounding them.

Tape a phone-in programme from radio or television. Examine the asymmetrical distribution of contributions from the host and the callers, including the host's discourse strategies as talk manager. To do this, you will need to transcribe extracts from the taped material.

Choose a website linked to radio, television or publishing and monitor the audience participation on it over a period of time.

Further reading

Herring, Susan (2003), 'Gender and power in on-line communication', in Holmes, Janet and Meyerhoff, Miriam (eds), *The handbook of language and gender*, Oxford: Blackwell, pp. 202–28.

Holmes, Su (2004), '"But this time *you* choose!" approaching the "interactive" audience in reality TV', *International journal of cultural studies*, 7(2): 213–31.

Hutchby, Ian (1996), *Confrontation talk: argument, asymmetry and power on talk radio*, Mahwah, NJ: Lawrence Erlbaum.

Kress, Gunther (2003), *Literacy in the new media age*, London: Routledge.

Livingstone, Sonia and Lunt, P. (1994), *Talk on television: audience participation and public debate*, London: Routledge.

Myers, Greg (2001), '"I'm out of it; you guys argue": making an issue of it on *The Jerry Springer show*', in Tolson, Andrew (ed.), *Television talk shows: discourse, performance, spectacle*, Mahwah, NJ: Lawrence Erlbaum.

Nightingale, Virginia and Dwyer, Tim (2006), 'The audience politics of "enhanced" television formats', *International journal of media and cultural politics*, 2(1): 25–42.

Schultz, Tanjev (2000), 'Mass media and the concept of interactivity: an exploratory study of online forums and reader email', *Media, culture and society*, 22(2): 205–21.

Sociolinguistcs and Computer Mediated Communication. Special issue of *Journal of sociolinguistics*, 10(4).

Thornborrow, Joanne (2002), 'Questions and control: managing talk in a radio phone-in', *Power talk: language and interaction in institutional discourse*, London: Longman.

Glossary

Address, term of

Form used to refer to or name someone. This includes names, titles, endearments and insults.

Adjacency pair

A sequence of talk consisting of two parts, each produced by a different speaker. Examples are question and answer, offer and acceptance/ rejection, greeting and greeting. The first-pair-part sets up an expectation of the second-pair part, so that if it does not occur its absence is noticeable.

Animator

Someone who utters words on another's behalf: 'the talking machine' (Goffman 1981: 167). It is one of three 'speaker' roles in Goffman's essay on 'footing', the other two being **Author** and **Principal**.

Author

The person who selects the actual wording of an utterance. It is one of three 'speaker' roles in an influential essay on 'footing' (Goffman 1981), the other two being **Animator** and **Principal**.

Booster

A device (often an adverb or adverbial phrase) used to intensify the force of an utterance, for example, 'That's an *incredibly* difficult decision for anyone to make.'

Coherence

For a text to 'work' fully for a listener or reader, it needs not only appropriate lexical and grammatical links between sentences (cohesion) but also the concepts, propositions or events to be related to each other and to be consistent with the overall subject of the text. This semantic and propositional organisation is called coherence. In effect, a coherent text is one that 'makes sense'. See Gough and Talbot (1996).

Deictics/deixis

Deixis means pointing or indicating. Deictics are items used to 'point' to the context surrounding an utterance. Common deictic words are personal pronouns ('I', 'you', 'she' etc), demonstratives ('this', 'that', 'these', 'those') and time and place adverbials ('now' and 'then', 'here' and 'there').

Delegation frame

A relatively fixed pattern for passing the conversational floor from one member to another within an institutional participation framework (see Scollon 1998: 161).

Didactic address

A mode of address that is overtly asymmetrical and teacher-like. The relationship set up between participants is that of instructor and student.

Directive

An utterance designed to get someone else to do something. Commands in imperative form (for example, 'Get out of here!') are the most direct form, but requests, suggestions and many hints are also directives.

Equalising strategy

A discursive strategy designed to minimise or conceal the asymmetry of a social relationship.

Ethnomethodology

Not to be confused with *ethnography* or *ethnographic methodology*, this refers to a specific body of research that explicitly sets out to 'describe methods persons use in doing social life' (Sacks 1984: 21). It is particularly associated with sociologist Harold Garfinkel (1967). From it has grown the field of language study known as conversation analysis (e.g., Hutchby and Wooffitt 1998).

Expressive

Function of language focusing on speaker-state: conveying feelings, opinions, exclamations, likes and dislikes.

Face

Public self-image; what someone loses when they are embarrassed or humiliated. It has two aspects:
1. Negative face: the need to be left alone, to be independent and not imposed upon;
2. Positive face: the need to be liked, to be part of a social group.

Face-threatening act

An attack on a person's **face**. Face-threatening acts include criticisms, demands and other impositions; also insults, snubbing and so on. See **negative politeness, positive politeness**.

Formulation

A rewording of someone else's previous utterance. This may be done in a cooperative way, as in a broadcast interviewer's summary or clarification for the benefit of an overhearing audience. It may, however, be un-cooperative, as in the 'inferentially elaborative probes' often used by broadcast interviewers with provocative intentions. See Hutchby (2006), Thornborrow (2002).

Frame

Frames are, according to Goffman, the 'basic frameworks of under-standing available in our society for making sense out of events' (1974: 10). As such they have the potential to be manipulated in order to engage in activities such as play. See **key**.

Hedging device

Used to soften or weaken of the force of an utterance. Some hedges are: 'sort of', 'I think', 'a bit', 'as it were', 'kind of', 'isn't it?' They are mitigating devices and may be used to avoid appearing overbearingly dogmatic, or to soften criticism.

Hegemony

Control by consent; more fully, the attempt by dominant groups in society to win the consent of subordinate groups and to achieve a 'compromise equilibrium' in ruling over them (Gramsci 1971). This winning of consent is achieved when arrangements that suit a dominant group's own interests have come to be perceived as simply 'common sense'. For a clear account, see Storey (2001).

Ideational function

One of the three language meta-functions in systemic functional linguistics, this refers to the function of language to communicate ideas, to language as representation. The other two meta-functions are **interpersonal** and textual.

Implicature

An implied meaning generated by an indirect **speech act**. If someone shouts: 'That TV's loud!' there is a probable implicature that they would like it to be turned down (or off); if this is the case, it is functionally a **directive**.

Interpersonal

One of the three language meta-functions in systemic functional linguistics, this refers to the function of language to establish and maintain social identities and relationships.

Key

Keying, a term coined by Goffman (1974), refers to the way in which speakers can exploit a **frame** in order to communicate play activities, jokes, irony, half-seriousness, ambivalence and so on. In bilingual communities a speaker may, for example, adopt the language not typically associated with their group, in order to distance themselves from what they are saying. The same effect can be achieved, of course, in a monolingual context by strategic use of speech genres, styles etc. stereotypically associated with other groups.

Metaphor

The attribution of a quality to something to which it is not literally applicable – for instance, 'an icy stare'. 'The essence of metaphor is understanding and experiencing one kind of thing in terms of another' (Lakoff and Johnson 1980: 5). For CDA, metaphors are important because they are ideologically loaded and can be powerful rhetorical devices, particularly when their metaphorical nature is not immediately obvious. Representations of refugees in the news provide clear examples. Refugees are individuals who have been forced, each in unique circumstances, to leave their homes and livelihoods and seek asylum in a foreign country. They are sometimes subjected to crude dysphemism ('bad naming') involving use of metaphor ('dross', 'vermin', 'human sewage'). More frequent, however, are less crudely obvious metaphorical expressions that nevertheless dehumanise their subject. For example, if the arrival of a group of people in the host country is reported in the news as a 'wave' or 'flood', their arrival is likened to the movement of a large body of water. They are being presented not as individuals but as a potentially dangerous mass or force. The metaphor generates a way of talking and writing about people as if they were not people at all; they can 'erode', require 'floodgates' etc.

Minimal response

These 'interested listener noises' or 'vocal nods' typically signal support for the speaker and listener's active participation in a conversation, although this is dependent on how they are said and where they are placed linguistically. Cooperatively realised by such items as 'mm', 'yeah', 'right', they provide evidence of how a conversation is jointly produced.

Modality

Degree of speaker-commitment to what they say, conveyed by various means including modal auxiliary verbs (for example, 'may', 'must'), related adverbs (for example, 'possibly', 'probably') and **hedges**. There are two main kinds of modality, relating to truth and obligation:

1. Truth-modality. This relates to the degree of certainty about a
    statement, to the speaker's commitment to it as true. It therefore
    relates to **expressive** value. Consider the difference between 'I think
    that may be mine' and 'That's mine'. If someone speaks with the
    modality of categorical certainty they make an authoritative state-
    ment.
2. Obligation-modality. This relates to a person's commitment to a
    statement as necessary, as in 'All coursework submitted must be
    type-written and double-spaced'.

Negative politeness

Respect behaviour; the signalling of deference or of consideration for
others' independence. Negative politeness strategies are employed to
avoid potential threats to negative **face**. A person wanting to borrow a
pen from a stranger, for instance, might minimise the imposition involved
in the request by **hedging** and prefacing it with an apology; 'Sorry to
bother you but could I just borrow your pen a moment?'

Nominalisation

A process represented in a noun or noun phrase – for example, 'the
bombing of villages'. When processes are represented in this way (rather
than in verbs, as in 'X bombed villages') they are mystified. In particular,
it can be difficult to work out the agency involved: who or what is
responsible for the process.

Phatic

The phatic function of language is concerned with maintaining social
contact. 'Small talk' is almost entirely phatic in function. The term was
introduced by the anthropologist Malinowski (1923). It is also associated
with an early inventory of language functions (Jakobson 1960).

Positive politeness

Friendly behaviour; signalling closeness, similarity. Positive politeness
strategies are employed to avoid potential threats to positive **face**.
Someone requesting help from a fellow passenger, for example, might
soften the imposition by using an affectionate term of address: 'Help me
with these bags, would you, love?'

Presupposition

'Preconstructed' background knowledge. A 'classic' example from philosophy is that the statement 'The King of France is bald' presupposes that *there is a King of France*. Presuppositions have 'constancy under negation', so that 'The King of France isn't bald' would still presuppose that *there is a King of France*. For another example, take a handwritten notice on a coffee vending machine which read, 'This coffee isn't free!' and deserved the graffiti response: 'It isn't even coffee!' In these examples the presuppositions are 'triggered' by 'the' and 'this' respectively.

Other triggers are iteratives like 'again': 'They saw the flying saucer again' presupposes that *they saw a flying saucer before*, and factive verbs like 'regret': 'Laura regrets drinking Sean's home brew' presupposes that *Laura drank Sean's home brew*. For a detailed account, see Levinson (1983).

Principal

The person whose position or views are being expressed by an utterance. It is one of three 'speaker' roles in an influential essay on 'footing' (Goffman 1981), the other two being **Author** and **Animator**.

Speech act

An action performed in saying something. Speech act theory has attempted to classify them into constatives (for example, asserting, claiming, reporting), directives (for example, demanding, ordering, suggesting), commissives (for example, promising, offering, threatening) and expressives (for example, thanking, congratulating, blaming). For a recent account, see Cutting (2002) or, for more detail and critical commentary, Mey (1993).

Bibliography

Abercrombie, Nick and Longhurst, Brian (1998), *Audiences: a sociological theory of performance and imagination*, London: Sage.

Airey, Dawn (2005), *The Golden Age of Television: Myth or Reality?* Hugh Wheldon Lecture, BBC2, 22 March 2005.

Aitchison, Jean and Lewis, Diana (eds) (2003), *New media language*, London: Routledge.

Allan, Stuart, Atkinson, Karen and Montgomery, Martin (1995), 'Time and the politics of nostalgia: an analysis of the Conservative party election broadcast "The Journey"', *Time and Society*, 4 (3): 365–95.

Anderson, Benedict (1983), *Imagined communities: reflections on the origin and spread of nationalism*, London: Verso.

Atkinson, Maxwell and Heritage, John (eds), *Structures of social action: studies in conversation analysis*, Cambridge: Cambridge University Press.

Atton, Chris (2004), *An alternative internet: radical media, politics and creativity*, Edinburgh: Edinburgh University Press.

Bakhtin, Mikhail (1973), *Problems in Dostoevsky's Poetics*, trans. Caryl Emerson, New York: Ardis.

Bakhtin, Mikhail (1981), *The Dialogic Imagination*, ed. Michael Holquist trans. Caryl Emerson and Michael Holquist, Austin/London: University of Texas Press.

Bakhtin, Mikhail (1986), 'The problem of speech genres', *Speech genres and other late essays*, ed. Caryl Emerson and Michael Holquist, trans. Vern McGee trans, Austin: Texas University Press.

Ballaster, R., Beetham, Margaret, Fraser, Elizabeth and Hebron, Sanda (1991), *Women's worlds: ideology, femininity and the woman's magazine*, London: Macmillan.

Baron, Peter (2006a), ' "600,000 killed": Is that a story?' *Talk about Newsnight: a blog and forum*, 13 October.

Baron, Peter (2006b), 'Appear on Newsnight; or not' *Talk about Newsnight: a blog and forum*, 24 November.

Barthes, Roland (1967), *Elements of semiology*, London: Jonathan Cape.

Barthes, Roland (1973), *Mythologies*, London: Paladin.

Batten, C. L. (1978), *Pleasurable instruction*, Berkeley: University of California Press.

Bausinger, Hermann (1984), 'Media, technology and daily life,' trans. Liliane Jaddou and Jon Williams, *Media, culture and society*, 6(4): 343–51.

Baym, Nancy (2000), *Tune in, log on: soaps, fandom and online community*, London: Sage.

Beetham, Margaret (1996), *A magazine of her own? domesticity and desire in the woman's magazine 1800–1914*, London: Routledge.

Bell, Allan (1991), *The language of news media*, Oxford: Blackwell.

Bell, Allan (1997), 'The discourse structure of news stories', in Bell, Allan and Garrett, Paul (eds), *Approaches to media discourse*, Oxford: Blackwell, pp. 64–104.

Bell, Allan (2002), 'Dateline, deadline: journalism, language, and the reshaping of time and place in the millennial world'. *Georgetown University round table on languages and linguistics 2000*, pp. 46–66.

Bell, Allan (2003), 'Poles apart: globalisation and the development of news discourse in the twentieth century', in Aitchison, Jean and Lewis, Diana (eds) pp. 7–17.

Benwell, Bethan (2002), '"Have a go if you think you're hard enough": male gossip and language play in the letters pages of men's lifestyle magazines', *Journal of popular culture* 35(1).

Benwell, Bethan (2004), 'Ironic discourse: evasive masculinity in men's lifestyle magazines', *Men and masculinities*, 7(1): 3–21.

Benwell, Bethan (2005), '"Lucky this is anonymous": ethnographies of reception in men's magazines: a "textual culture" approach', *Discourse and society*, 16(2): 147–72.

Bonner, Frances (2003), *Ordinary television*, London: Sage.

Bonner, Frances (2005), 'Whose lifestyle is it anyway?' in Bell, David and Hollows, Joanne (eds), *Ordinary lifestyles: popular media, consumption and taste*, Maidenhead: Open University Press.

Bonner, Frances (2006), 'The celebrity in the text', in Evans, Jessica and Hesmondhalgh, David (eds) *Understanding media inside celebrity*, Maidenhead: Open University Press.

Boomer, Donald and Laver, John (1968), 'Slips of the tongue', *British journal of disorders of communication*, 3: 2–11.

Boorstin, Daniel (1963), *The image, or what happened to the American dream*, Harmondsworth: Penguin.

Booth, Wayne (1961), *Rhetoric of fiction*, Chicago: University of Chicago Press.

Born, Georgina (2002), 'Reflexivity and ambivalence: culture, creativity and government in the BBC', *Cultural values*, 6(1/2): 65–90.

Bourdieu, Pierre (1984), *Distinction: a social critique of the judgement of taste*, London: Routledge.

Brooker, Will (2002), 'Overflow and audience', in Brooker, Will and Jermyn, Deborah (eds) *The audience studies reader*, London: Routledge, pp. 322–33.

Brown, Gillian and Levinson, Stephen (1987), *Universals in language use: politeness phenomena*, Cambridge: Cambridge University Press.

Brown, Gillian and Yule, George (1983), *Discourse analysis*, Oxford: Blackwell.

Brunsdon, Charlotte (1982), '*Crossroads*: notes on soap opera', *Screen*, 22(4).

Brunsdon, Charlotte (2003), 'The 8–9 slot on British television', *International journal of cultural studies*, 6(1): 5–23.

Bucholtz, Mary (1999), 'Purchasing power: the gender and class imaginary on the shopping channel', in Bucholtz, Mary, Liang, Alison and Sutton, Laurel (eds), *Reinventing identities: the gendered self in discourse*, Oxford: Oxford University Press, pp. 348–68.

Bucholtz, Mary (2000), ' "Thanks for stopping by": gender and virtual intimacy in American shop-by-television discourse', in Andrews, Maggie and Talbot, Mary (eds), *'All the world and her husband': women in twentieth-century consumer culture*, London: Cassell, pp. 192–209.

Cameron, Deborah (1997), 'Performing gender identity: young men's talk and the construction of heterosexual masculinity', in Johnson, Sally and Meinhof, Ulrike (eds), pp. 47–64.

Chouliaraki, Lilie and Fairclough, Norman (1999), *Discourse in late modernity: rethinking critical discourse analysis*, Edinburgh: Edinburgh University Press.

Christensen, Lars Holmgaard (2003), 'The "impact" of interactivity on television consumption – stay tuned, visit our website, press the red button . . .', Centre for Society, Technology and Media Research Paper, Dublin City University http://www.stem.dcu.ie/

Christie, Christine (2000), *Gender and language: towards a feminist pragmatics*, Edinburgh: Edinburgh University Press.

Clark, Romy and Ivanič, Roz (1997), *The politics of writing*, London: Routledge.

Clayman, Steven (1992), 'Footing in the achievement of neutrality: the case of news-interview discourse', in Drew, Paul and Heritage, John (eds) *Talk at work: interaction in institutional settings*, Cambridge: Cambridge University Press, pp. 163–98.

Clayman, Steven (2002), 'Tribune of the people: maintaining the legitimacy of aggressive journalism', *Media, culture and society*, 24: 197–216.

Conboy, Martin (2003), 'Parochializing the global: language and the British tabloid press', in Aitchison, Jean and Lewis, Diana (eds) pp. 45–54.

Conboy, Martin (2006), *Tabloid Britain: constructing a community through language*, London: Routledge.

Cook, Jackie (2000), 'Dangerously radioactive: the plural vocalities of radio talk', in Lee, Alison and Poynton, Cate (eds), *Culture and text: discourse and methodology in social research and cultural studies*, St Leonards, New South Wales: Allen & Unwin.

Corner, John (2000), 'What can we say about "documentary"?' *Media, culture and society*, 22: 681–88.

Couldry, Nick (2006) 'The extended audience: scanning the horizon', in Hesmondhalgh, David (ed.), *Media production*, Maidenhead: Open University Press. pp. 184–222.

Crick, Malcolm (1989), 'Representations of international tourism in the social sciences: sun, sex, sights, saving, and servility', *Annual review of anthropology*, 18: 307–44.

Crisell, Andrew (1994), *Understanding radio* (2nd edn), London: Routledge.

Crisell, Andrew (2004) (ed.), *More than a music box: radio cultures and communities in a multi-media world* New York/Oxford: Berghahn Books.

Cruz, Jon and Lewis, Justin (1994), 'Reflections on the encoding/decoding model, an interview with Stuart Hall', in Cruz, Jon and Lewis, Justin (eds), *Viewing, reading, listening: Audiences and cultural reception* Westfield Press.

Curry T. (1991), 'Fraternal bonding in the locker room', *Sociology of sport journal*, 8: 119–35.

Cutting, Joan (2002), *Pragmatics and discourse: a student coursebook*, London: Routledge.

Dahlberg, Lincoln (2005), 'The Internet as public sphere or culture industry? From pessimism to hope and back', *International journal of media and cultural politics*, 1: 1 pp. 93–6.

Davies, Catherine Evans (2003), 'Language and American "good taste"', in Aitchison, Jean and Lewis, Diana (eds), pp. 146–55.

de Klerk, Vivienne (1997), 'The role of expletives in the construction of masculinity', in Johnson, Sally and Meinhof, Ulrike (eds), *Language and masculinity*, Oxford: Blackwell.

Downes, Edward and McMillan, Sally (2000), 'Defining interactivity: a qualitative identification of key dimensions', *New media and society*, 2(2): 157–79.

Doyle, Roddy (1993), *Paddy Clarke ha ha ha*, New York: Viking.

Dunn, David (2005), 'Venice observed: the traveller, the tourist, the post-tourist and British television', in Jaworski, Adam and Pritchard, Annette (eds) *Discourse, communication and tourism*, Clevedon: Channel View.

Dyer, Richard (1986), *Heavenly bodies: film stars and society*, London: BFI Publishing.

Eco, Umberto (1976), *A theory of semiotics*, Bloomington: Indiana University Press.

Eco, Umberto (1979), *The role of the reader: explorations in the semiotics of texts*, London: Hutchinson.

Ellis, John (2000), 'Scheduling: the last creative act in television?' *Media, culture and society*, 22(1): 25–38.

Evans, Jessica (2006), 'Celebrity: what's the media got to do with it?' in Evans, Jessica and Hesmondhalgh, David (eds), *Understanding media: inside celebrity*, Maidenhead: Open University Press.

Evans, Jessica and Hesmondhalgh, David (eds) (2006), *Understanding media: inside celebrity*, Maidenhead: Open University Press.

Fairclough, Norman (1992a), *Discourse and social change*, Cambridge: Polity.

Fairclough, Norman (ed.) (1992b), *Critical language awareness*, London: Longman.

Fairclough, Norman (1994), 'Critical discourse analysis and the marketisation of public discourse: the universities', *Discourse and society*, 4(2): 133–68.

Fairclough, Norman (1995a), *Media discourse*, London: Arnold.

Fairclough, Norman (1995b), *Critical discourse analysis*, London: Longman.

Fairclough, Norman (2001), *Language and power* (2nd edn), London: Longman.

Fairclough, Norman and Wodak, Ruth (1997), 'Critical discourse analysis', in Van Dijk, Teun (ed.), *Discourse as social interaction*, London: Sage, pp. 258–84.

Fiske, John (1987), *Television culture*, New York: Routledge.

Flew, Terry (2004), 'A medium for mateship: commercial talk radio in Australia', in Crisell, Andrew (ed.), pp. 229–46.

Foucault, Michel (2002), *Archaeology of knowledge*, trans. A. Sheridan, London: Routledge.

Fowler, Roger, Kress, Gunther, Hodge, Robert and Trew, Paul (1979), *Language and control*, London: Routledge.

Frazer, Elizabeth [1986] (1992), 'Teenage girls reading *Jackie*', in Scannell, Paddy, Schlesinger, Philip and Sparks, Colin (eds), pp. 182–200.

Frow, John (1990), 'Intertextuality and ontology', in Worton, Michael and Still, Judith (eds), *Intertextuality, theories and practices*, Manchester: Manchester University Press, pp. 45–5.

Garfinkel, Harold (1967), *Studies in ethnomethodology*, Cambridge: Polity.

Gieve, Simon and Norton, Julie (2005), 'Dealing with linguistic difference in media representations of encounters with others', Language in the media: representations, identities, ideologies, University of Leeds, 12–14 September 2005.

Giles, David (2002), 'Keeping the public in their place: audience participation in lifestyle television programming', *Discourse and society*, 13(5): 603–28.

Gillespie, Marie (1995), *Television, ethnicity and cultural change*, London: Routledge.

Glasgow University Media Group (1976), *Bad news*, London: Routledge.

Glasgow University Media Group (1980), *More bad news*, London: Routledge.

Goffman, Erving (1969), *The presentation of self in everyday life*, Harmondsworth: Penguin.

Goffman, Erving (1974), *Frame analysis: an essay on the organisation of experience*, Harmondsworth: Penguin.

Goffman, Erving (1981), *Forms of talk*, Oxford: Blackwell.

Gough, Brendan (2001), ' "Biting your tongue": negotiating masculinities in contemporary Britain', *Journal of gender studies*, 10(2): 169–85.

Gough, Val and Talbot, Mary (1996), ' "Guilt over games boys play": coherence as a focus for examining the constitution of heterosexual subjectivity on a problem page', in Caldas-Coulthard, Carmen Rosa and Coulthard, Malcolm (eds), *Texts and practices: readings in critical discourse analysis*, London: Routledge pp. 214–30.

Graddol, David and Boyd-Barrett, Oliver (eds) (1994), *Media texts: authors and readers*, Clarendon: Multilingual Matters.

Gregori Signes, Carmen (2000), *A genre based approach to daytime talk on television*, Valencia: Universitat de Valencia.

Guendouzi, Jackie (2001), ' "You'll think we're always bitching": the function of cooperativity and competition in women's gossip', *Discourse and society*, 3(1): 29–51.

Gumperz, John (1972), 'The speech community', in Giglioli, Pier Paolo (ed.), *Language and social context*, Harmondsworth: Penguin, pp. 219–31.

Gurevitch M. and Blumler J. (1990), 'Political communication systems and democratic values', in Lichtenberg (ed.), *Democracy and the mass media*, Cambridge: Cambridge University Press.

Habermas, Jürgen (1989), *The structural transformation of the public sphere*, trans. T. Burger, Cambridge: Polity.

Hair, Carolyn (2003), 'The conversationalisation of television talk: a critical discourse analysis of the daytime talk show and the docu-soap', Southampton Institute: Unpublished PhD thesis.

Hall, Stuart (1980), 'Encoding/decoding', in Hall, Stuart, Hobson, Dorothy, Howe, Andrew and Willis, Paul (eds), *Culture, media, language*, London: Routledge, pp. 128–38.

Hall, Stuart, Hobson, Dorothy, Howe, Andrew and Willis, Paul (eds) (1980), *Culture, media, language*, London: Routledge.

Hall, Stuart (1997), 'Introduction', in Hall, Stuart (ed.), *Representation: cultural representations and signifying practices*, London: Sage, pp. 1–11.

Halliday, Michael (1978), *Language as social semiotic*, London: Arnold.

Halliday, Michael (1985), *An introduction to functional grammar*, London: Arnold.

Hearn, Alison (2006), ' "John, a 20-year-old Boston native with a great sense of humour": on the spectacularization of the "self" and the incorporation of identity in the age of reality television', *International journal of media and cultural politics*, 2(2): 131–47.

Heath, Stephen and Skirrow, G. (1977), 'Television: a world in action', *Screen*, 18(2).

Hermes, Joke (1993), 'Media, meaning and everyday life', *Cultural studies*, 7: 493–506.

Hermes, Joke (1995), *Reading women's magazines: an analysis of everyday media use*, Cambridge: Polity.

Hesmondhalgh, David (2006), 'Media organisations and media texts: production, autonomy and power', in Hesmondhalgh, David (ed.), *Media production*, Maidenhead: Open University Press. pp. 49–90.

Hesmondhalgh, David (ed.) (2006), *Media production*, Maidenhead: Open University Press.

Higgins, Michael (2007), 'The "public inquisitor" as media celebrity', *Cultural politics*, 3(3).

Hodge, Robert and Kress, Gunther (1988), *Social semiotics*, Cambridge: Polity.

Hollway, Wendy (1984), 'Gender difference and the production of subjectivity', in Henriques, Julian, Hollway, Wendy, Urwin, Cathy, Venn, C. and Walkerdine, Valerie (eds), *Changing the subject: psychology, social regulation and subjectivity*, London: Methuen, pp. 227–63.

Holmes, Su (2004), ' "But this time *you* choose!" approaching the "interactive" audience in reality TV', *International journal of cultural studies*, 7(2): 213–31.

Horton, Donald and Wohl, Richard [1956] (1986), 'Mass communication and para-social interaction: observations on intimacy at a distance', in Gumpert, G. and Cathcart, R. (eds), *Inter/media: interpersonal communication in a media world*, New York: Oxford University Press.

Hutchby, Ian (1996), *Confrontation talk: argument, asymmetry and power on talk radio*, Mahwah, NJ: Lawrence Erlbaum.

Hutchby, Ian and Wooffitt, R. (1998), *Conversation analysis: an introduction*, Cambridge: Polity.

Hutchby, Ian (2006), *Media talk: conversation analysis and the study of broadcasting*, Maidenhead: Open University Press.

Hyland, Ken (2005), *Metadiscourse* London: Continuum.

Jackson, Peter, Stevenson, Nick and Brooks, Kate (2001), *Making sense of men's magazines*, Cambridge: Polity.

Jakobson, Roman (1960), 'Closing statement: linguistics and poetics', in Sebeok, T. A. (ed.), *Style and language*, Cambridge, MA: MIT Press.

Jaworski, Adam, Ylänne-McEwan, Virpi, Thurlow, Crispin and Lawson, S. (2003), 'Social roles and negotiation of status in host-tourist interaction: a view from British television holiday programmes', *Journal of sociolinguistics*, 7/2: 135–63.

Jensen, J. (1999), 'Interactivity – tracking a new concept in media and communication studies', in Mayer P. (ed.), *Computer media and communication: a reader*, Oxford: Oxford University Press.

Johnson, Sally and Meinhof, Ulrike (eds) (1997), *Language and masculinity*, London: Routledge.

Kress, Gunther (1986), 'Language in the media: the construction of the domains of public and private', *Media, Culture and Society*, 8: 395–419.

Kress, Gunther (1990), 'Critical discourse analysis', *Annual review of applied linguistics*, 11: 84–99.

Kress, Gunther and van Leeuwen, Theo (2001), *Multimodal discourse: the modes and media of contemporary communication* London: Arnold.

Kristeva, Julia (1970), *Le Texte du roman*, The Hague: Mouton.

Kuiper, K. (1991), 'Sporting formulae in New Zealand English: two models of male solidarity', in Cheshire, Jenny (ed.), *English around the world: sociolinguistic perspectives*, Cambridge: Cambridge University Press.

Labov, William (1972), *Sociolinguistic patterns*, Philadelphia: University of Pennsylvania Press.

Lakoff, George and Johnson, Mark (1980), *Metaphors we live by*, Chicago: University of Chicago Press.

Leech, Geoffrey (1966), *English in Advertising*, London: Longman.

Leech, Geoffrey and Short, Mick (1981), *Style in fiction*, London: Longman.

Levinson, Stephen (1983), *Pragmatics*, Cambridge: Cambridge University Press.

Lewis, Justin (1991), *The ideological octopus: an exploration of television and its audience*, London/New York: Routledge.

Livingstone, Sonia and Lunt, P. (1994), *Talk on television: audience participation and public debate*, London: Routledge.

Livingstone, Sonia (2006), 'Media audiences, interpreters and users', in Gillespie, Marie (ed.), *Media audiences*, Maidenhead: Open University Press, pp. 9–50.

Macdonald, Myra (2003), *Exploring media discourse*, London: Arnold.

Macleod, Donald (2006), 'School dinners have had their chips', *The Guardian* (Friday, 16 May).

Malinowski, B. (1923), 'The problem of meaning in primitive languages', in Ogden C. K. and Richards I. A. (eds), *The meaning of meaning*, Routledge & Kegan Paul.

McRobbie, Angela (1978), *Jackie: an ideology of adolescent femininity*, CCCS Stencilled Occasional Paper SP No. 53.

Marr, Liz, Francis, Dave and Randall, Dave (1999), '"The soccer game" as journalistic work: managing the production of stories about a football club', in Jalbert, Paul (ed.), *Media studies: ethnomethodological approaches*, Lanham, MD/ Oxford: University Press of America, pp. 111–33.

Marshall, P. David (1997), *Celebrity and power: fame in contemporary society*, Minneapolis: University of Minneapolis Press.

Meinhof, Ulrike (1994), 'Doubletalk in news broadcasts: a cross-cultural comparison of pictures and texts in television news', in Graddol, David and Boyd-Barrett, Oliver (eds), pp. 212–23.

Meinhof, Ulrike and Smith, Jonathan (1995a), 'The media and their audience: intertextuality as paradigm', in Meinhof, Ulrike and Smith, Jonathan (eds) *Intertextuality and the media: from genre to everyday life*, Manchester: Manchester University Press, pp. 1–17.

Meinhof, Ulrike and Smith, Jonathan (1995b), '*Spitting image:* TV genre and intertextuality', in Meinhof, Ulrike and Smith, Jonathan (eds) *Intertextuality and the media: from genre to everyday life*, Manchester: Manchester University Press, pp. 43–60.

Meinhof, Ulrike and Smith, Jonathan (eds) (1995), *Intertextuality and the media: from genre to everyday life*, Manchester: Manchester University Press.

Meinhof, Ulrike and van Leeuwen, Theo (1995), 'Viewers' worlds: image, music, text and *The rock 'n' roll years*', in Meinhof, Ulrike and Smith, Jonathan (eds) *Intertextuality and the media: from genre to everyday life*, Manchester: Manchester University Press, pp. 62–75.

Mey, Jacob (1993), *Pragmatics: an introduction*, Oxford: Blackwell.

Meyrowitz, Joshua (1985), *No sense of place: the impact of electronic media on social behavior*, New York: Oxford University Press.

Montgomery, Martin (1986), 'D-J talk', in Coupland, Nikolas (ed.), *Styles of discourse*, London: Croom Helm, pp. 85–104.

Moores, Shaun (1992), 'Texts, readers and contexts of reading', in Scannell, Paddy, Schlesinger, Philip and Sparks, Colin (eds), pp. 137–57.

Moores, Shaun (2005), *Media/theory: Thinking about media and communications*, London: Routledge.

Morley, David (1980), *The Nationwide audience*, London: British Film Institute.

Morley, David (1981), 'The Nationwide audience: a critical postscript', *Screen education*, 39: 3–14.

Morley, David (1986), *Family television*, London: Comedia.

Morley, David (2000), *Home territories: media, mobility and identity*, London: Routledge.

Mort, Frank (1988), 'Boy's own? Masculinity, style and popular culture', in Chapman, R. and Rutherford, J. (eds), *Male order: Unwrapping masculinity*, London: Lawrence & Wishart.

Moseley, Rachel (2001), ' "Real lads do cook . . . but some things are still hard to talk about": the gendering of 8–9', in Brunsdon, C., Johnson, C., Moseley, R. and Wheatley, H. 'Factual entertainment on British television: The Midlands TV research group's "8–9 Project",' *European journal of cultural studies*, 4(1): 29–62.

Myers, Greg (1994), *Words in ads*, London: Arnold.

Newman, Janet (2005), 'Going public: people, policy and politics', Inaugural professorial lecture, Open University, May 18th 2005.

Nightingale, Virginia (1996), *Studying audiences: the shock of the real*, London: Routledge.

Nightingale, Virginia and Dwyer, Tim (2006) 'The audience politics of "enhanced" television formats', *International journal of media and cultural politics*, 2(1): 25–42.

Nixon, Sean (1997), 'Exhibiting masculinity', in Hall, Stuart (ed.) *Representation: cultural representations and signifying practices*, London: Sage, pp. 1–11.

Orrey, Jeanette (2005) *The dinner lady*, London: Bantam Press.

Osgerby, Bill (2004), *Youth media*, London: Routledge.

Parkin, F (1972), *Class inequality and political order*, London: Paladin.

Pearce, Michael (2001), ' "Getting behind the image": personality politics in a Labour party' election broadcast, *Language and Literature*, 10(3): 211–28.

Pearce, Michael (2005), 'Informalization in UK party election broadcasts 1966–97', *Language and literature*, 14(1): 65–90.

Pennycook, Alaistair (2001), *Critical applied linguistics: A critical introduction*, Mahwah, NJ: Lawrence Erlbaum.

Popik, Barry (2006), www.barrypopik.com/index.php/new_york_city/.

Radway, Janice (1984), *Reading the romance: Patriarchy and popular literature*, Chapel Hill: University of North Carolina Press.

Rice, A. (2001), *Tourism on television: A programme for change*, London: Tourism Concern and Voluntary Service Overseas.

Richards, Huw (2005), 'Voters who double-click don't want double talk, just real interaction with their politicians', *Times Higher Education Supplement*, 1 April 2005 pp. 16–17.

Richardson, Kay and Corner, John [1986] (1992), 'Reading reception: mediation and transparency in viewers' reception of a TV programme', in Scannell, Paddy, Schlesinger, Philip and Sparks, Colin (eds), pp. 158–81.

Richardson, Kay and Meinhof, Ulrike (1999), *Worlds in common? Television discourse in a changing Europe*, London: Routledge.

Ross, Karen (2004), 'Political talk radio and democratic participation: caller perspectives on *Election call* ', *Media, culture and society*, 26(6): 785–801.

Sacks, Harvey (1984a), 'On doing "being ordinary",' in Atkinson, Maxwell and Heritage, John (eds), pp. 413–29.

Sacks, Harvey (1984b), 'Notes on methodology', in Atkinson, Maxwell and Heritage, John (eds), pp. 21–7.

Saussure, Ferdinand de [1916] (1960), *Course in general linguistics*, London: Peter Owen.

Scannell, Paddy (1984), 'Editorial', *Media, culture and society*, 6(4): 333–5.

Scannell, Paddy (1989), 'Public service broadcasting and modern public life,' *Media, culture and society*, 11(2): 135–66.

Scannell, Paddy (1992), 'Public service broadcasting and modern life', in Scannell, Paddy, Schlesinger, Philip and Sparks, Colin (eds), pp. 317–48.

Scannell, Paddy (1996), *Radio, television and modern life*, Oxford: Blackwell.

Scannell, Paddy (ed.) (1991), *Broadcast talk*, London: Sage.

Scannell, Paddy and Cardiff, D. (1991), *A social history of British broadcasting: serving the nation 1923–1939*, Oxford: Blackwell.

Scannell, Paddy, Schlesinger, Philip and Sparks, Colin (eds) (1992), *Culture and power: A Media, culture & society reader*, London: Sage.

Schegloff, Emanuel and Sacks, Harvey (1973), 'Opening up closings', in Turner R (ed.), *Ethnomethodology*, Harmondsworth: Penguin pp. 233–64.

Schrøder, Kim, Drotner, Kirsten, Kline, Stephen and Murray, Catherine (2003), *Researching audiences*, London: Arnold.

Schultz, Tanjev (2000), 'Mass media and the concept of interactivity: an exploratory study of online forums and reader email', *Media, culture and society*, 22(2): 205–221.

Scollon, Ron (1998), *Mediated discourse as social interaction: A study of news discourse*, London: Longman.

Silverstone, Roger (1999), *Why study the media?* London: Sage.

Smith, Angela (2005), 'Lifestyle television programmes and the construction of the expert host', 3rd Language, Communication, Culture International Conference, University of Évora, Portugal, 23–5 November.

Spitulnik, Debra (1997), 'The social circulation of media discourse and the mediation of communities', *Journal of linguistic anthropology*, 6(2): 161–87.

Spitulnik, Debra (2000), 'Media', *Journal of linguistic anthropology*, 9(1–2): 148–51.

Spitulnik, Debra (2002), 'Alternative small media and communicative spaces', in Hyden, Goran, Leslie, Michael and Ogundimu, Folu (eds), *Media and democracy in Africa*, New Brunswick, NJ: Transaction, pp. 177–205.

Sreberny-Mohammadi, Annabelle and Mohammadi, Ali (1994), *Small media, big revolution: communication, culture and the Iranian revolution*, Minneapolis: University of Minnesota Press.

Stephens, John (1992), *Language and ideology in children's fiction*, London: Longman.

Storey, John (2001), *Cultural theory and popular culture* (3rd edn), London: Prentice Hall.

Storey, John (2003), *Cultural studies and the study of popular culture* (3rd edn), Edinburgh: Edinburgh University Press.

Talbot, Mary (1986), 'Reading Jackie', *Society of strip illustrators newsletter*.

Talbot, Mary (1992), 'The construction of gender in a teenage magazine', in Fairclough, Norman (ed.), *Critical language awareness*, London: Longman, pp. 174–99.

Talbot, Mary (1995a), 'Synthetic sisterhood: false friends in a teenage magazine', in Hall, Kira and Bucholtz, Mary (eds), *Gender articulated: language and the socially constructed self*, New York/London: Routledge, pp. 143–65.

Talbot, Mary (1995b), *Fictions at work: language and social practice in fiction*, London: Longman.

Talbot, Mary (1997), ' "Randy fish boss branded a stinker": coherence and the construction of masculinities in a British tabloid newspaper', in Johnson, Sally and Meinhof, Ulrike (eds), *Language and masculinity*, London: Routledge, pp. 173–87.

Talbot, Mary (2000), '"It's good to talk"?: The undermining of feminism in a *British Telecom* advertisement', *Journal of sociolinguistics*, 4(1): 108–19.

Talbot, Mary (2007), 'Political correctness and freedom of speech', in Hellinger, Marlis and Pauwels, Anne (eds), *Language and communication: Diversity and change* (Vol. 9 *Handbook of applied linguistics*), Berlin: Mouton de Gruyter.

Talbot, Mary, Atkinson, Karen and Atkinson, David (eds) (2003), *Language and power in the modern world*, Edinburgh: Edinburgh University Press.

Taylor, Lisa (2002), 'From ways of life to lifestyle: the "ordinari-ization" of British gardening lifestyle television', *European journal of communication*, 17(4): 479–93.

Thompson, John (1995), *The media and modernity: a social theory of the media*, Cambridge: Polity.

Thornborrow, Joanne (2002), *Power talk: language and interaction in institutional discourse*, London: Longman.

Tolson, A. (1991), 'Televised chat and the synthetic personality', in Scannell, P. (ed.), *Broadcast talk*, London: Sage.

Tolson, A. (ed.) (2001), *Television talk shows: discourse, performance, spectacle*, Mahwah, NJ/London: Lawrence Erlbaum.

Tolson, A. (2006) *Media talk: spoken discourse on TV and radio*, Edinburgh: Edinburgh University Press.

Toynbee, Jason (2006), 'The media's view of the audience', in Hesmondhalgh, David (ed.), *Media production*, Open University Press.

Tulloch, John (2000), *Watching television audiences: cultural theories and methods*, London: Arnold.

Ursell, Gillian (2006), 'Working in the media', in Hesmondhalgh, David (ed.), pp. 133–72.

van Selm, Martine, Jankowski, Nicholas and Kleijn, Bibi (2004), 'Dutch web radio as a medium of audience interaction', in Crisell, Andrew (ed.), *More than a music box: radio cultures and communities in a multi-media world*, New York/Oxford: Berghahn Books, p. 265.

Voloshinov, Valentin [1923] (1973), *Marxism and the philosophy of language*, trans. L. Matejka and I.R. Titunik, New York: Seminar Press.

Walsh, Clare (2001), *Gender and discourse: language and power in politics, the church and organisations*, London: Longman.

Wardle, Claire (2006), '"Text us and let us know how you feel": exploring the theoretical implications of interactive comment in television news', 2nd CRESC conference: Media Change and Social Theory, University of Oxford: 6–8 September 2006.

White, Cynthia (1970), *Women's magazines, 1694–1968*, London: Michael Joseph.

Winter, Joanne (1993), 'Gender and the political interview in an Australian context', *Journal of pragmatics*, 20: 117–39.

Wood, Helen (2005), 'Texting the subject: women, television and modern subjectivity', *The communication review*, 8: 115–35.

Wood, Helen (2007), 'The mediated conversational floor: an interactive approach to audience reception analysis', *Media, culture and society* 29(1).

Index